ORIGIN STORIES

ORIGIN STORIES

Fans, Scholars, and the Superhero Comics That Shaped Their Identities

Edited by
Michael Kobre and Peter Nagy

University Press of Mississippi / Jackson

The University Press of Mississippi is the scholarly publishing agency of the Mississippi Institutions of Higher Learning: Alcorn State University, Delta State University, Jackson State University, Mississippi State University, Mississippi University for Women, Mississippi Valley State University, University of Mississippi, and University of Southern Mississippi.

www.upress.state.ms.us

The University Press of Mississippi is a member of the Association of University Presses.

Select passages from "Horsey-Come-Lately: No Asian American Superhero Comics Until Little Monkey" are drawn from Sheng-mei Ma's chapter 13 in *Cultural Bifocals on Chinese TV Series and Diaspora Fiction* (Routledge 2025).

Parts of Anna F. Peppard's chapter are reworked from previous web-based essays and writeups, including: "Nightcrawler Is a Sex-Positive Superhero. Here's How—And Why It Matters"; "Blue Becomings: Revisiting *Excalibur* #4"; and "The Multiverse According to ComicsXF!" All of this content has been substantially rewritten.

Manufactured in the United States of America
∞

Publisher: University Press of Mississippi, Jackson, USA
Authorised GPSR Safety Representative: Easy Access System Europe – Mustamäe tee 50, 10621 Tallinn, Estonia, gpsr.requests@easproject.com

Library of Congress Cataloging Number: 2026951600

Hardback ISBN 978-1-4968-6492-5
Trade paperback ISBN 978-1-4968-6493-2
Epub single ISBN 978-1-4968-6494-9
Epub institutional ISBN 978-1-4968-6495-6
PDF single ISBN 978-1-4968-6496-3
PDF institutional ISBN 978-1-4968-6497-0

British Library Cataloging-in-Publication Data available

CONTENTS

ORIGIN STORIES

INTRODUCTION

UNSTABLE MOLECULES

Michael Kobre and Peter Nagy

In *Fantastic Four* #6, published in June 1962, Jack Kirby and Stan Lee introduced the concept of "unstable molecules," when Reed Richards, Mr. Fantastic, stretched his elasticized body out of a window of the team's headquarters in the Baxter Building and then across the street in order to prop his elbows on the windowsill of a room in a nearby hospital and visit a sick boy who's written a letter to the Fantastic Four. "The reason my costume stretches to any length," Reed explains as he chats with the boy in the hospital bed, "is that it's woven from chemical fibers containing unstable molecules that shift in structure when I affect the change" ("Captives of the Deadly Duo!" 134). As Kirby and Lee would declare a year later in "Questions and Answers About The Fantastic Four" in *Fantastic Four Annual* #1, unstable molecules "were one of Reed's greatest discoveries" (46). They kept the Human Torch's costume and street clothes from burning up when he ignited his flaming body, and the fabrics woven from them would disappear too when Susan Storm vanished as the Invisible Girl. Over time other characters, like Ant-Man in *Tales to Astonish* #35, would also make their costumes out of unstable molecules.

But aside from being a foundational scientific principle of the Marvel Universe, unstable molecules are also only another example of the almost accidental poetry generated by superhero comics. In James Sturm and Guy Davis's 2003 graphic novel *Unstable Molecules*, which is presented as a biography of four characters from the late 1950s who—in this universe at least—were the models for Kirby and Lee's characters, Reed's discovery is a metaphor for the "tenuous and mercurial" relationships of the dysfunctional family at the core of the narrative. In Ramzi Fawaz's groundbreaking 2016 study of queer history and superhero comics, *The New Mutants*, Fawaz suggests that the concept of unstable molecules "mimicked the malleable plastics and synthetics of postwar material science [and] revealed that the interaction between the physical self and the material world could produce nonnormative or 'queer' effects" (66–67).

In a way, in fact, the entire superhero genre is formed out of unstable molecules. Not only do its protagonists inhabit bodies that are constantly transforming—warped into new shapes by magic words, secret formulas, Red Kryptonite, obscure and often painful surgical procedures, and a whole spectrum of radioactive beams—but the vast body of narratives that make up the genre are subject to constant transformations too as familiar characters are continually revised and retconned over decades by generation after generation of new creators and as these narratives are consumed, in turn, by new audiences. Is any popular genre as volatile and unstable, as sensitive to changing cultural contexts and forms of production, as superhero narratives? Consider, for instance, Superman, who was, at one moment in time, a working-class Depression-era hero and later a hypermasculine jingoist icon, and then became, under Mort Weisinger's editorial direction in the 1950s and early '60s, a spectacle of bizarre and endless transformation. Beneath the veneer of a stolid paterfamilias presiding over a family-like structure of friends and other super beings—including Supergirl, Superdog, Supercat, Superhorse, and the entire population of the bottle city of Kandor—Superman was also a trippy, Red Kryptonite changeling who was continually, in the words of Grant Morrison in *Supergods*, "letting the freakishness, the alien-ness, all hang out" (69).

Superheroes, over almost a century of endless adventures and transformations, are intrinsically protean forms that can evoke and embody all kinds of desires, fantasies, and anxieties. Through this instability and multiplicity, superhero comics, as this collection suggests, invite all kinds of identification from their readers. In *Origin Stories: Fans, Scholars, and the Superhero Comics That Shaped Their Identities*, a diverse group of scholars, writers, and comics fans tell their own stories about the comics they loved and how those comics intersected with their lives. Weaving together personal narratives and critical analysis, in a kind of hybrid form made up of its own unstable molecules, the essays examine how readers from widely different backgrounds find reflections of their own experiences in the wildly protean forms of superheroes. But as each essay also vividly demonstrates, that sense of identification becomes even more powerful when comics readers—like everyone in this collection—feel themselves, in some ways, to be outsiders from a larger public sphere. Sometimes that sense of marginalization is shaped by the pressures of identity categories like race, ethnicity, sexuality, class, disability, and, often, the intersectional connections between them. And sometimes, comics fans—again, like the ones gathered here—can feel like outsiders because of what they experience, what they perceive, and what they desire. But *always*, as the essays here all demonstrate, that sense of somehow being outside the mainstream of the dominant culture can be reflected and explored in the larger-than-life worlds of superhero comics.

The theoretical groundwork for this collection builds on a set of suggestions made by Ramzi Fawaz and Darieck Scott in "Queer about Comics," the introduction to a special issue of the journal *American Literature*, which itself builds on Fawaz's book *The New Mutants*. Drawing on Michael Warner's notion of discourse publics to conceptualize the relationship between readers and the fantasy content of superhero comics, Fawaz and Scott remind us that while superhero comics have been historically pigeonholed as simple normative fantasies of armored bodies enacting nationalist agendas, they've also often been characterized as a marginalized medium for marginalized audiences. Dismissed over the years by all kinds of social crusaders as childish, delinquent, and antisocial, comic books are consumed by a diverse audience of fans, who, for much of the history of the medium (at least before the conquest of popular culture by Marvel Studios and other superhero franchises in the twenty-first century), were themselves commonly stereotyped as backward, strange, and perverse—particularly the most ardent fans, whose fervent attachment to comic books functioned as a marker of their alienation from the cultural and social mainstream. In this interaction between a medium that was marginalized for much of its history and readers who often felt like outsiders too, comic book stories could function, in Michael Warner's term, as a counterpublic, a self-consciously marginal discourse space capable of generating all kinds of fantasies about "deviant" bodies and identities, fantasies that were consumed by an audience of outsiders in a process that could shape the way those readers saw themselves, the world, and the way they existed in that world.

The essays in *Origin Stories* are loosely modeled on the brief personal/analytical descriptions of their early attachments to superheroes that Scott and Fawaz provide in "Queer about Comics," which illustrate how comics initiate readers into nonnormative counterpublics. The collection builds on what is demonstrated, for instance, by Scott, who describes his childhood fascination with the Black Amazon Nubia, a "dark-skinned, glamorous, powerful black woman warrior" he remembers seeing for the first time on the cover of *Wonder Woman* #206 in 1973 (205). Through an analysis of Nubia that reveals the character to be a fantasy of "black power and beauty" that lived on for decades in Wonder Woman fan communities and scholarship (before being reintroduced in comics in recent years), Scott argues that his identification with the character marked his initial experience of queer self-recognition (205). For Scott, a boy living in a predominantly straight white society and not yet even capable of articulating his own desires, Nubia instantiated "black and queer as objects of desire" and helped him come into being as a queer Black man. Through an affirmation of the power and pleasure of his body and his desires, such fantasies helped him resist the racism and homophobia of a white, heteronormative social order.

This collection is also predicated on the idea—as many scholars, fans, and comics creators have long argued—that the very nature of comics as a form invites an imaginative and deeply subjective interaction between the reader and the work. In her essay in this collection, Anna F. Peppard cites "Scott McCloud's seminal theories of 'closure' (63) and 'amplification through simplification' (30)" as formal elements in comics that foster a reader's "participatory investment" in the images, characters, and storyworlds of comics (107). Samantha Langsdale, John Edward Martin, and Michael Kobre in their respective essays cite Frederick Luis Aldama's assertion that comics readers "*co-create* the story" (91). As Aldama himself writes in *Latinx Superheroes in Mainstream Comics*: "Co-creating is the mental process involved in the audience's apprehension then emotion and cognitive meaning making of the comic book storyworld. Indeed, it is the wonderfully generative capacity of this co-creating potential in comic book readers that not only allows readers and audiences to imagine movement and three dimensions in the static, two-dimensional in-print comic book storyworld spaces, but allows them to feel and think about identities and experiences distant from their own" (90–91). Through this process of co-creation, through the reader's participatory investment in the story, comics readers, as this collection demonstrates, can find worlds to which they belong, worlds in which they see themselves reflected and affirmed in fantasies about the power and pleasure of perceived deviance and difference. These are also worlds that offer them community, providing them membership in fictional coalitions (super teams) and fan subcultures that are often formed through shared experiences of social estrangement.

To cite just one example of the complex interaction between comics, the readers' co-creation, and the communities that comics fans can form, consider the reaction of fans in 2024 when Marvel Comics phased out its yearslong "Krakoa" storyline in its *X-Men* titles, in which the long-persecuted mutants who inhabited the Marvel universe had formed their own nation, with its own utopian ideals, culture, and customs, and, inevitably, its own internal conflicts too. As perhaps the quintessential example of an outsider community in superhero comics, the X-Men had long been embraced by all kinds of marginalized readers, particularly in the LGBTQ community, and for these readers the mutant counterculture of Krakoa—with its joyous fluidity of relationships, genders, and even bodily forms—represented a kind of freedom and acceptance that couldn't be found outside the pages of a superhero comic. After the storyline ended, as the company mandated a return to a more traditional status quo in the comics' continuity (in preparation apparently for the next screen adaptation of *X-Men*), many of these fans expressed both their disappointment at the company's decision and, likewise, the passionate attachment they'd felt to the storyline and the fan communities it generated. Writing on the ComicsXF site, Anna F. Peppard, who explores her intense connection to the X-Man Nightcrawler in this collection, recalled that her initial concerns about the Krakoa storyline were eased by the response from other fans and the robust conversation surrounding the comics. "What eventually sold me on the era was the fan community surrounding it," she wrote. "The passion people had for this era transformed it, for me, into something transformative." As another ComicsXF contributor, Jude Jones, observed in a critical forum on a 2025 issue in which the mutants had gathered to memorialize their lost homeland of Krakoa, the creation of the ComicsXF site itself, as an online community of writers and readers, was at least in part a response to the storyline. "The current iteration of ComicsXF in large part exists because of Krakoa," Jones wrote, before going on to make an even more emphatic claim. "I, in large part, exist because of ComicsXF . . . Krakoa is why I'm here," he wrote, linking his words to another ComicsXF article in which he'd confessed that the opportunity to write about Krakoa for the site and share his responses with other fans had literally saved his life as a Black man struggling with depression. "Without Krakoa," Jones said, "I might not be alive."

Superhero comics then, through this process of co-creation and the passionate responses that particular stories and characters engender, can function as counterpublics—discourse spaces, in Michael Warner's terminology, which exist on the pages of superhero comics, in the minds of readers, and in the communities that readers and creators form. Moreover, within these counterpublics, comics fans and outsiders of all kinds can, to use a familiar trope from those comics, reveal their true identities. And that, of course, is exactly what the contributors to this collection do in their individual essays, in which they combine detailed, deeply researched readings of superhero stories with personal narratives about family relationships, transgressive desires, and the uncertainties and dangers of navigating boundaries of race, gender, sexuality, and multiple forms of difference.

In the first section of this collection, "Secret Identities," the essays describe ways that comics shape identity in childhood and adolescence. For John Edward Martin, "a 'poor' kid" uncomfortable with conventional notions of masculinity, the mask of Spider-Man mirrors his own sense of difference and his wariness of self-exposure. In Jose Alaniz's essay, presented in comics form itself, the Hulk's uncontrollable rage reflects Alaniz's older brother's chronic anger and abusiveness, while the Hulk's shifting skin color (green, white, grey, red) offers a means of identification for a light-skinned Chicano like Alaniz. Michael Kobre, continuing an exploration of some of the signature characters of Marvel Comics, details how Jack Kirby and Stan Lee's presentation of the Thing in *Fantastic Four*, a character who was later canonically identified as Jewish, embodies aspects of Kobre's experience as a child in an insular American Jewish community in the 1960s. Extending forward to the 1990s and the debut of the Vertigo imprint from DC Comics, Michelle Bumatay explores the way Peter Milligan and Duncan Fegredo's revisionist superhero series *Enigma* mirrored her own sense of difference as a child of white and Filipino parents who was continually perceived by others as racially ambiguous, an enigma herself.

In the second section, "Transformations," comics characters and images generate more fluid and liberated understandings of gender and sexuality. For Anna F. Peppard, the exuberant sexuality of Kurt Wagner, Nightcrawler in the X-Men, inspires "a sensuous if sometimes uncomfortable tryst" between objectification and identification, a desire simultaneously to have and to be the character, even as his appearance as a blue-skinned, demonic-looking mutant subverts the conventional border between monstrosity and beauty. For Samantha Langsdale, Terry Moore's independent comics series *Strangers in Paradise* employs "the rhetoric of the superhero genre" to create complex characters whose fluid sexuality mirrors Langsdale's own increasing awareness of her bisexuality and "the expansiveness of [her] desires." In Peter Nagy's essay, Superman's pal Jimmy Olsen's repeated affinity for cross-dressing in his own title in the 1960s "spoke to, or perhaps instilled" Nagy's own impulse to push the boundaries of gender identity and occasionally transform himself with make-up, jewelry, and skirts.

The essays in the final section, "Masks," explore the way that masks are assumed in and outside of comic books to enable characters and readers to negotiate a threatening and sometimes hostile world. Alison Wellford tells a harrowing story of being stalked by a sexual predator and finding power and freedom afterwards by modeling her appearance on Death of the Endless in Neil Gaiman's *Sandman* series, in which the power to reap countless human lives is gendered as "an unassuming goth woman" indifferent to the male gaze and any conventional expectations of female beauty or deference. In the punning, allusive voice of his essay—a complex rhetorical strategy that functions almost like a mask itself—Sheng-mei Ma explores both his own unease as an immigrant "caught in a perpetual arriving, never quite there" and the various masks assumed by Gene Luen Yang's characters in *The Shadow Hero* and, particularly, *American Born Chinese*, where the Monkey King of the sixteenth-century Chinese classic *Journey to the West* is reimagined as a protosuperhero. In Sika Dagbovie-Mullins's essay, a Wonder Woman costume that her daughter wears to a preschool Halloween party, in which the only two Black girls in the class are both dressed as Wonder Woman, invites a meditation on "the metaphoric mask Black girls are forced to wear" and "the significance of Black girl superheroes in a culture that denies Black girls their full humanity."

In all these essays, the unstable molecules that make up the superhero genre are reconfigured to reveal more complicated truths, as familiar tropes of the genre—secret identities, transformations, masks—become parts of different kinds of origin stories. In sharing these stories, the essays collected here speak to each other too, as they all explore the forces, in our culture and in ourselves, that instill a sense of difference and marginalization, that tag us somehow as outsiders from the mainstream of a larger public sphere. But in their own ways, these essays also all affirm the power of a passionate reader's imagination to co-create out of the most fantastic images and words an alternate sense of identity and a different kind of space in which to exist, where difference and marginalization can be reimagined as strength and freedom. And in sharing these stories and these possibilities, the different voices in this collection also form a kind of counterpublic of their own, a community of readers and writers within these pages in which feeling different and loving the wildest, most improbable characters and stories can be celebrated and affirmed—a community, in fact, that's waiting for *you*, the person reading these words now, to join it too.

Works Cited

Aldama, Frederick Luis. *Latinx Superheroes in Mainstream Comics*. U of Arizona P, 2017.

Burt, Stephanie, Austin Gorton, Dan Grote, Anna Peppard, Adam Reck, Scott Redmond, Rob Secundus, Sean Dillon, Jake Murray, and Latonya Pennington. "The ComicsXF Bullpen Share Their Favorite Krakoa Memories." *ComicsXF*, 21 June 2024, comicsxf.com/2024/06/21/goodbye-krakoa/.

Fawaz, Ramzi. *The New Mutants: Superheroes and the Radical Imagination of American Comics*. NYU Press, 2016.

Jones, Jude. "Krakoa Was for Lovers: How the Last 5 Years of X-Men Stories Helped Save One Writer's Life." *ComicsXF*, 6 June 2024, comicsxf.com/2024/06/06/krakoa-was-for-lovers/.

Lee, Stan, and Jack Kirby. "Captives of the Deadly Duo!" *Fantastic Four Epic Collection: The World's Greatest Comic Magazine*, Marvel Worldwide, 2014, pp. 130–54.

Lee, Stan, and Jack Kirby. "Questions and Answers about the Fantastic Four." *Fantastic Four Epic Collection: "The Master Plan of Doctor Doom,"* Marvel Worldwide, 2017, pp. 46–47.

Morrison, Grant. *Supergods*. Spiegel & Grau, 2012.

Peppard, Anna, Jude Jones, Adam Reck, Austin Gorton, Tony Thornley, and Jake Murray. "X-Men: The Hellfire Vigil Is One Weird Wake." *ComicsXF*, 5 July 2025, comicsxf.com/2025/07/06/xmen-hellfire-vigil-2/.

Scott, Darieck, and Ramzi Fawaz. "Introduction: Queer about Comics." *American Literature*, vol. 90, no. 2, June 2018, pp. 197–219.

Sturm, James, and Guy Davis. *Fantastic Four: Unstable Molecules*. Marvel Comics, 2005.

PART 1

SECRET IDENTITIES

1

CLIMBING THE WALLS

How I Got Bit and Turned Spider-Man into Me

John Edward Martin

I can't remember a time in my life when Spider-Man wasn't there. First, as an eerie, voiceless figure dancing across the screen of *The Electric Company*'s "Spidey Super Stories" (1974) to spray some unlucky miscreant with a thick, rope-like webbing. Later, the jazzy theme song of the *Spider-Man* (1967) animated series, dragging me out of bed on those early mornings as my parents prepared for work: "Spider-Man, Spider-Man, does whatever a spider can." Still later, just learning to read, I'd follow along in the book that accompanied a record, *The Amazing Spider-Man: Mark of the Man-Wolf* (1974), entranced by words and sounds and pictures that made me feel a part of the story. And of course, there were the toys ("It spins real webs!"), the Spider-Man bedding, and the Spidey Underoos (my Gen-X readers will understand)—all before I even discovered the Spider-Man of the comics. But man, when I did . . . when I learned that Spider-Man wasn't just a faceless superhero or even a man—he was a kid! What's more, he was a working-class kid, or to use the word my family more often used for ourselves, a poor kid. Like me, too, he was a city boy, a nerd who wore glasses, got bullied, and liked to read, an introvert who didn't know how to talk to girls, or anyone else for that matter, a weirdo, a freak, a kid uncomfortable in his body and his environment. He was, in many ways, *me*.

Of course, none of this ubiquitous presence or even my feelings of identification with this character, who was already among the most popular figures in comics history, was an accident. Even a casual look into the history of Marvel comics, and Spider-Man in particular, reveals the fact that he was created with me in mind—or rather, with kids like me in mind. The great innovation that ushered in the Marvel Age in the early 1960s was the company's recognition (either prophetic or just timely, depending on your source) that American audiences, particularly young audiences, longed for heroes who were less distant, idealized, and morally certain than those of earlier ages—heroes who were more like themselves (Wright 210). Stan Lee says as much directly through the voice of the narrator at the end of *The Amazing Spider-Man* (hereafter "*ASM*") #9, where he informs us that in the next issue we'll get "more fascinating details about the life and adventures of the world's most amazing teen-ager—Spider-Man—the superhero who could be—YOU!" (Lee and Ditko 162).

Early reactions to Spider-Man seem to affirm Lee's intuition. In a fan letter from *ASM* #13, a young Marine Corps service member, Charles M. Wisnewski, writes, "Instead of the usual superhero who is never wrong and is indestructible, I was glad to see a down-to-earth human (Spider?). Passed it along to the squad and everyone enjoys it" (216). In that same issue, reader Dave Catena, notes that "as the story went on, I really felt that I was in the story, living it with Peter Parker instead of just being on the outside looking in—that's what makes Spider-Man so wonderful—his reality" (216). And in issue #14, another fan, Mark Meed, writes, "You've come up with a super-hero who is, of all things, human. Spider-Man is the only super-hero who makes mistakes—bravo!" (241). His humanity, his mistakes, his reality and the ability to imagine one's *self* in the story—these were what made Spider-Man different for these readers. Interestingly, none of these fans were, apparently, children or even adolescents, but mostly young adults, perhaps not much older than Peter Parker. Bradford Wright suggests that this college/military/young adult demographic was an emerging audience for comics at this time, particularly those produced by Marvel, which targeted this age group as one that might identify with the outcast, persecuted, antiestablishment types of heroes that Marvel was pioneering, just as they did with the popular music and films of the period (Wright 223).

A cynical view might be that heroes like the Fantastic Four, the Incredible Hulk, the X-Men, and the Amazing Spider-Man were simply a clever marketing ploy designed to appeal to just the sort of youth who were likely to be browsing the racks at their local newsstand or convenience store for something new, hip, and identifiable. But hold on a minute. Marketing ploy or not, Spider-Man was more than just a product or entertainment for me, more than a status symbol or marker of my hipness—or rather, "coolness," by my era. If anything, he was the opposite of all that. He was a reminder of my lack of status, coolness, or even participation in a community of fans, which I wouldn't discover until long afterward. And yet, he would become an indispensable part of my early life and as central to my intellectual, emotional, and social development as any friend or teacher that I had until well past my teenage years. It was from Spider-Man that I learned words like *agility*, *biochemistry*, and *photojournalist*; learned that "With great power there must also come—great responsibility" (Lee and Ditko 11); and, most importantly, learned that with some combination of intelligence, determination, and luck, one could actually climb out of the most difficult situations and *gasp* maybe go to college, find a girlfriend, get a cool job, be a hero. If Peter Parker as a teenager was me, perhaps I could be Spider-Man as an adult.

Whatever their intentions, Stan Lee and Steve Ditko, along with their creative partners before and after, created something in Spider-Man that transcended the marketing and the profits, at least for those of us who found traces of ourselves and our experiences reflected there. This is probably the case with most pop-culture icons or franchises that have garnered a following, but I think it's important to distinguish between what Spider-Man represents for the industry or even the history of comics and popular culture and what he represents for several generations of readers, not all of them kids or boys, who found something deeper and more personally meaningful in the idea of a superhero who made us feel seen.

That's what Spider-Man did for me—and apparently, I'm not alone in that more personal connection. Jason Reynolds, in his foreword to the recent Penguin Classics Marvel Collection of *The Amazing Spider-Man*, describes his own and, more significantly, his older brother's identification with Peter Parker, not just as a heroic figure, but as one who struggles with loneliness, awkwardness, a lack of confidence, and the need to escape—that is to say, as someone recognizable to them: "Peter Parker was my brother, Allen. Allen was Peter. And because of that familiarity, that representation, Allen could then become Spider-Man" (Lee and Ditko, Foreward, xx). As the younger sibling, Reynolds both admired and struggled to understand his older brother until he, too, was introduced to Spider-Man, who became the emotional bridge between them. Similarly, Gary Jackson asserts that "his normality is what draws us to him; it's why we see him as more complex than other superheroes. He reminds us too much of ourselves. It's why we love him. It's why I love him" (Afterword 249). Familiarity, representation, becoming—*love*. Those are words that go beyond just appreciation for a cool character or an exciting story, even beyond the recognition of his "normality" or his humanity. To these readers, as for me, Spider-Man and Peter Parker became something more intimate than just another man on the street. We *loved* him—we *became* him, or vice versa.

I want to explore why and how this is. But before I do that, there's another important dynamic revealed in the quotes above that only becomes apparent if you know something about the authors. Though I don't know much about those early fan-letter writers beyond their names, I know that in my case and in the cases of Jason Reynolds and Gary Jackson, our identification with Spider-Man/Peter Parker crosses racial, ethnic, and cultural lines—certainly geographical ones. Reynolds is a Black poet and novelist from the Washington, DC, area who has written, among other things, two Miles Morales novels for Marvel, *Miles Morales: Spider-Man* (2018) and *Miles Morales: Suspended* (2023). I'll return to Miles and his significance later on. Jackson is a mixed-heritage Black and Korean poet from Topeka, Kansas, who has published several books of poetry that include superhero themes and characters, most notably *Missing You, Metropolis* (2009) and *origin story* (2021), which explore his own intimate relationships with superheroes and with his personal and family history. I'm a mixed-race Mexican Irish American academic and librarian from Houston (sadly, I've never written a Spider-Man book). Each of us have lives and experiences that would likely feel as strange and unfamiliar to Peter Parker as his own experience as a white, orphaned, superpowered teenager from Queens, New York, not to mention a photographer, scientist, and eventual corporate executive, might seem to us. Yet somehow, Spider-Man has become not just a hero or a symbol for me and other readers, but in some ways, an alter-ego—another version of us—regardless of our race, gender, class, sexuality, or other distinctive aspects of identity. What allows for this kind of identification, and why with Spider-Man?

Maybe it's just aspiration or, rather, desperate escapism. Gary Jackson suggests as much in one of his poems from *Missing You, Metropolis*, "Upon Seeing Spider-Man on My Way to Work" (26). The speaker of the poem recalls seeing Spider-Man swinging overhead during his own long, cold commute to work and feeling a twinge of both anger and envy at the web-slinger's apparent freedom and ability to avoid the mundane frustrations of going to work or earning a living:

> What I wouldn't give to be up there in some red-
> and-blues, slingshotting between skyscrapers,

ready to swing in and save some beauty getting
mugged. I'd take out the thugs with an uppercut,
a flick of webs and a one-liner." (26)

Of course, that's the heroic fantasy—one we're likely to feel in the presence of any larger-than-life figure who appears to have powers and freedoms that we don't possess. But this speaker has more specific complaints. He has to walk home in "the goddamn New York cold" because his car is broken down and he can't afford to fix it because he's just a high school teacher and "rent costs a grand" (26). What Spider-Man seems to offer isn't just a faster way home or an exciting life of adventure, but an escape from what we are: "I'd trade my job, my BA, // hell, even my wife, anything to climb walls, / spin webs, touch rooftops with toes" (26).

We all want to be someone else now and then, especially someone extraordinary, someone not burdened by our problems, our frustrations, our limitations. But the irony of Jackson's speaker is that it's precisely those kinds of problems and frustrations, those failures and limitations, that seem to make Spider-Man so identifiable to Jackson himself and to other fans. Of course, Jackson is aware of this, assuming his reader is also a reader of the comics. It's an in-joke just for us, because we know that if that is Spider-Man up there, he's likely worried about his own rent, rushing off to get photos he can sell to his penny-pinching boss, J. Jonah Jameson, or worse, on his way to the bedside of his always-ill Aunt May. We know that, at times, Peter would gladly trade his powers for the education that he's always wanted, a real job with a salary and benefits, a wife and kids, maybe even a cold commute that brings him home to something stable and safe—something he's never had. Brilliantly, Jackson is counting on the fact that some of us will read this poem as the man on the street, cold and cranky and envious, while others will read it as the man (or boy) swinging overhead, lost in his own troubles and anxieties, alone and alienated, despite his extraordinary gifts. But does it matter if one of us is Black or Brown and the other white, if one is male and the other female or nonbinary, one straight and the other gay or bisexual? Yes, of course it does. It always matters.

Not where you thought I was going? Me neither. Not in the beginning anyway. My early recognition of myself in Spider-Man was based on those things that immediately connected us—our class, age, gender, personalities, social standing, the common dilemmas and anxieties of a teenager and an introvert, our shared aspirations for an education and, through that, an escape. I, like Jason Reynolds and Gary Jackson, wanted and needed to see myself in Peter—so I did. But not quite. For one thing, I wasn't white—or, at least, not entirely. I didn't live in the kind of strangely homogenous neighborhood that early Spider-Man artists conceptualized as Queens, where everyone looked and acted as if they were from Riverdale. I wasn't an orphan raised by an elderly aunt, but by two working class parents in a mixed-race household. I didn't lose someone tragically to violence at an early age, though I knew plenty of kids who did. I wasn't a genius, either. Smart maybe, and certainly nerdy enough to be identified as such, but not smart enough to build a web-shooter from scratch or outsmart a super-villain with my scientific knowledge. Most importantly, I had no powers, literally or metaphorically. At least none that I could identify after much experimentation, trial, and mostly error (sorry, Mom). All of which is to say that no matter how much I identified with him, there would always be a chasm between me and my greatest hero, just as there is between Jackson's man on the street and the mysterious figure swinging overhead. At times, I felt that as a real loss, an alienation from myself, in a sense—the other me who I could never be. He wouldn't be the last hero to leave me feeling that way. And I wouldn't be the only kid who felt keenly the distance between themselves and their chosen heroes.

And yet, here I am at 52, still thinking and writing about what Spider-Man means to me. I'd like to understand why. How is it that I and other readers, like Gary Jackson, Jason Reynolds, and countless others, were able to imagine our way past the obvious differences and distances between ourselves and the selves we only dreamed of becoming? Maybe fantasy is enough, or empathy, or desperation. Those can be powerful tools of self-creation—though not always in a positive direction. And why would those things be directed toward something so unlikely, so strange, so childish? Is that all it is, the flexibility and openness of the childhood imagination and its ability to embrace the impossible?

Maybe. But I think back to the intentionality of all this. Not just the intentionality of Stan Lee and Steve Ditko, who targeted not just children but teenagers and young adults in their storytelling, but also the intentionality of decades of artists and writers who followed them and found other audiences and points of recognition; the intentionality of fans who continue to read and buy and build relationships around these comics; and the intentionality, if we can call it that, of the medium itself. How do comics, as a form, superheroes, as a genre, and Spider-Man, in particular, produce the necessary conditions for the kinds of intimate identifications that some of us have found there—identifications that reach across class, race, gender, sexuality, culture, geography, and other boundaries of selfhood?

Frederick Luis Aldama, in *Latinx Superheroes in Mainstream Comics* (2017), suggests one possible mechanism that is both inherent and intentional to the comics medium in his notion of co-creation. For Aldama, "co-creating is the mental process involved in the audience's apprehension then emotion and cognitive meaning-making of the comic book storyworld" (Aldama 90). That is to say, it is the active process of making meaning through our reading of the words, images, movement, and structure on the page—a process that is integral to comics. For Aldama, this isn't just a cognitive or rational process, but an emotional one. We don't just think our way into identifying with a character, but feel our way into it through a complex, nuanced process of imagination and identification. It is our capacity to co-create, rather than to just passively receive meaning, that "allows Latinos to imagine beyond the boundaries of Anglo superhero comics; even if Batman doesn't look like us, we can imagine ourselves as Batman" (91). Or Spider-Man.

However, this process of co-creation on the part of the reader still requires a map or blueprint (Aldama's term) to follow and enough visual and verbal markers to allow us to build our own story from that of the storyworld provided by the creators. The more such markers they provide—consciously or unconsciously, but preferably the former—the more we are able to co-create those stories with them. Those markers can come in the form of images that we immediately identify as meaningful to us (say, a crucifix or an album cover or a pair of bell-bottoms), words that carry specific cultural or subcultural significance (hip, gangsta, madre), or even themes and stories that reflect something in our own lives. When co-creation happens, "we become chiasmic transformers, all while not changing the DNA of the story itself" (91). He's suggesting here that our transformation of comics characters into a version of ourselves, and vice versa, isn't a misreading or alteration of the blueprint, but rather, a powerful and purposeful implementation of it: "Due to the wondrous plasticity of the mind and expansive imaginative functions, we co-create from that which is least like us, and in ways that can be empowering" (94).

What Aldama gives us isn't just a mechanism for understanding how cross-cultural identifications might work in comics, but also a lens through which to read the specific elements of Spider-Man—the words, images, themes, stories, and narrative structures—that have allowed me and other readers to co-create those worlds in which we become Spider-Man. It also offers an implicit call-to-action for creators to participate in this process by providing the kinds of blueprints that allow for broader identifications and co-created worlds. It also opens the door for considering how more explicit forms of representation—like, say, a Black or Latino Spider-Man who speaks Spanish—work together with the more subtle, nuanced, sometimes hidden or coded elements of the comics medium that may have allowed diverse audiences to identify with Spider-Man long before they could literally see themselves on the page. In the following sections, I want to dig a little deeper into the web of influences that have kept me and others entangled in the world of Spider-Man.

Spider-Man Is Weird

This is a loaded question: What is the first thing you notice about Spider-Man? The answer may vary by reader but let's look at some of the obvious possibilities. The mask? That iconic image of a red-faced, black-webbed pattern extending back over the whole head, the large white, reflective eyeholes, and—nothing else. No mouth, nose, ears, skin, facial hair, or other recognizable features. No tattoos, jewelry, piercings, or makeup (that we can see). Nothing that would indicate race, age, gender, or cultural identity. It is a mask designed to evoke mystery, anonymity, and strangeness, even inhumanity. Who could possibly identify with such a face?

According to Steve Ditko, the original series artist and designer of Spider-Man's iconic look, the answer is virtually anyone. "I wasn't sure Stan would like the idea of covering the character's face, but I did it because it hid an obviously boyish face. It would also add mystery to the character and allow the reader/viewer to 'draw' his own preferred expression on Parker's face and, perhaps, become the personality behind the mask" (quoted in David, Greenberger, and Manning 16). Here again is that intentionality on the part of the artist: on the one hand, creating a unique and unusual identity for his new superhero and, on the other, providing a virtual blank slate for the reader to co-create a face, an expression, a personality. It's interesting that part of Ditko's purpose here is to hide the boyish face of the hero. The tension between that face and the name "Spider-Man" adds a hint of deception to the concept. Indeed, a mask is always a deception and an invitation to speculate, infer, or invent an identity. In this case, Peter himself is inventing an identity that must serve as his public self, his powerful self, his heroic and/or criminal self (depending on one's perspective), but one that must remain a secret for the sake of his loved ones and his own security. It's also one that allows him to masquerade as the adult hero that he wants to embody but rarely feels himself to be.

While this purposeful deception has a logical reason within the story, it also creates a dynamic that might be recognizable to readers, especially those who, for whatever reason, feel a tension between their public and private selves: the faces they show to their closest friends and family, and the ones they wear for everyone else. I certainly understood its purpose fairly instinctively as a child, because it reflected my own innate sense of the dangers of self-exposure, especially to those who posed a potential threat to me: adults, bullies, strangers, crushes. As I grew into an adolescent and then a teenager, the need for some veil between my inner and outer lives became even more urgent, especially in a household where privacy was a fraught and contentious subject (both because of our close quarters and a father who didn't see privacy as either a right or a necessity for children), as was the dawning awareness that I was different, not only from many of my peers, but even from my family and friends. I wasn't a mutant or an alien, but I might as well have been, at least in my own mind. I didn't share their interests, their beliefs, their priorities, or their assumptions about who and what I was supposed to be, especially their assumptions about masculinity and what it might mean to be "a man." I'm not talking specifically about sexuality or gender-identity, though both are relevant, but about the broader assumptions about masculinity or femininity that come with being a teenager, or, indeed, any age, in our culture. I, like Peter Parker, learned to wear certain masks—I played sports (badly), told sexist and homophobic jokes (shamefully), occasionally fought or got in trouble (angrily)—but always with a sense that *this wasn't really me*, just a character I had to assume in order to survive, though admittedly, more of a villain than a hero to my adult sensibilities.

Similarly, Peter Parker's long habit of hiding parts of himself, especially socially uncomfortable or embarrassing parts, extends even into his life as Spider-Man. If Peter is masquerading as an adult man in his superhero guise, he is also masquerading as a masculine one. Peter, with his gawky, skinny frame, awkwardly large head, owlish glasses, and introverted personality, stands in marked contrast to the muscular, handsome, commanding alpha males, like Flash Thompson, who embody the masculine ideal, particularly in the pages of most superhero comics. He is frequently reminded of these deficiencies in his interactions with other men, even after he gains powers that would allow him to humiliate such archetypal males. Unlike other comic book heroes, his transformation into a superpowered being doesn't immediately come with an accompanying change in his physique. Thus his strangely awkward, angled poses, diminutive size, and deceptive strength, all features of spiders, no doubt, but also of supposed wimps. But when he puts on the costume and leaps into action, these physical traits are suddenly obscured by his incredible physical feats and heroic actions, so much so that even Flash Thompson becomes an ardent admirer; in fact, he becomes the founder and president of the Spider-Man Fan Club! (*ASM* #17). The mask and the costume allow for this transformation in the eyes of other people as well as in his own. The mask—and indeed, the whole costume with its intricate webs and bright colors—are just the visual metaphor of a life already marked by obfuscation and misdirection for the sake of self-protection.

I should note that the image of Spider-Man and Peter Parker outlined above is distinctively that of his first artist, Steve Ditko. Later versions of Spider-Man, drawn by other artists, notably John Romita Sr., offer a more traditionally heroic and masculine physique. Indeed, it was these later incarnations that I first encountered as a Spider-Man reader, beginning in the late 1970s and early '80s. It was only after I became a true devotee and collector during my teenage years that I went back and discovered Ditko's earlier version of the boy hero, but that discovery only sealed my love for and identification with Spider-Man. It gave me a more intimate and visceral sense of what Peter was hiding behind that mask: a deep insecurity and uncertainty about his own masculinity and manhood that he would carry with him even as he later came to visually embody the hero within. The anonymity of the mask remains an important mechanism for negotiating those dual identities.

However, while anonymity allows for a certain degree of safety and protection from social scrutiny, this impulse exists in tension with another that is just as strong, particularly in young people: the need to be recognized, acknowledged, seen. Indeed, for Peter Parker, the latter often overpowers the former, as we see him, time and again, especially in the early years, seeking out attention and recognition or, more dangerously, feeling compelled to reveal his secret identity to those closest to him, an act that inevitably puts him and them in danger, just as he always feared. But this confessional

Figure 1.1. Stan Lee and Steve Ditko, *The Amazing Spider-Man* #1, Marvel Comics, March 1963, 1.

impulse is almost an inevitability, given that the mask at once has the effect of obscuring and creating identities. To some, Spider-Man is a hero and a familiar presence ("your friendly neighborhood Spider-Man"), while to others, as we see in the splash-page (figure 1.1), he is a "freak," "menace," stranger, even in his own neighborhood. The tension between these public perceptions reflects the tension between Peter's own inner and outer lives, even when he's not in costume. With both identities, there are the competing desires to remain hidden or to come out, to preserve a necessary illusion or to reveal a dangerous truth.

The costume isn't Spidey's only mask, of course. Another iconic feature might be his unique sense of humor in the heat of battle: his ability to disarm opponents with, as Gary Jackson put it, "a flick of webs and a one-liner." In stark contrast to the silent mime of "Spidey Super Stories" or the reticent Peter Parker that we see in most of his civilian incarnations, Spider-Man

Figure 1.2. Stan Lee and Steve Ditko, *The Amazing Spider-Man* #4, Marvel Comics, March 1963, 17.

is a merciless wit, especially toward his overly serious and self-important villains. In the early days, that wit generally takes the form of distracting bravado—bragging about his powers or cleverness—or insults and mockery of his opponents. Other times we see it in clever, if silly, strategies and visual gags, as in *ASM* #4 when he stages a battle with a bucket of sand tossed into the air because he forgot to take pictures of his actual battle with the Sandman (figure 1.2), which he desperately needs to sell to the *Daily Bugle*.

Spidey's quick-thinking and verbal wit often seem to be as much a superpower as his heightened reflexes and agility, and like those powers, they manifest more fully when he's in costume than out of it. They are yet another distinctive aspect of Peter/Spider-Man's dual nature and conflicting identities. We might also recognize the purpose of this sometimes inane and often irritating banter: not just to distract and frustrate his opponents, but more importantly, to distract himself from his own fears and uncertainties. It is the strategy of many a "nerd" or "wimp" when confronted by a bully to use the only weapons they typically have available to them: their intelligence, wit, and self-effacing humor. These were certainly weapons that I employed early and often, sometimes to the point of being called out and disciplined by parents or teachers for overindulging in sarcasm or mockery of others, especially those I felt threatened by. But in Spider-Man, I found a sympathetic peer—one who understood the need for laughter in the face of terror or helplessness—and like many readers, I responded with an even deeper attachment to the "web-zinger."

One thing I discovered, as Peter does in time, is that humor might be employed not just as a defense against bullies, but as a way of being seen, recognized, or even liked. Although I, too, was an introvert by nature and throughout my early childhood, by high school I had discovered that self-effacing jokes, witty jabs at authority-figures, sarcasm in the face of things other kids found tiresome or boring, or mockery of the things and people we all found threatening, allowed others, especially my peers, to see me in a different light. I wasn't just the silent geek, reading comics in the corner, but a clever observer of our shared situation or anxieties and a (sometimes) fearless voice of resistance to those things. I could call them out, laugh them off, and share a sense of camaraderie with my fellow sufferers. And those shared anxieties weren't just about bullies, but about other very real dangers in our lives: family violence, poverty, racial tensions, AIDS, fears about nuclear war, or, more intimately, fears about our own inadequacy to face the world of adulthood. Humor, and other people's appreciation of it, made me feel stronger, or at least braver, in the face of all these things and allowed me an entry point into a social world that I had long felt excluded from.

Humor as a means of coming out might also resonate with other readers who, like Peter Parker, have hidden behind masks both literal and metaphorical for their own and others' protection, but who also feel an urge to be known. Humor, we know, can be defensive, but it can also be a weapon or a tool, much like Spider-Man's web-shooters. It allows him (or us) to fight in creative and unexpected ways, to distract, to connect with others, or to entangle them in hopeless repartee, to confuse opponents, or to counter our apparent strangeness with something familiar and relatable. The effect depends upon the audience and the intention. For many a young person struggling with a sense of identity, self-confidence, or uncertainty about whom to trust or how to share themselves, humor may be the only tool they have. Spider-Man's adeptness with this tool, over the course of several generations and incarnations, suggests the centrality of that power, both for the character and his audience.

I was reminded of this during a more recent encounter with Spider-Man on my own campus, where he has become something of a familiar presence, as you'll see below. Spider-Man, it seems, has followed me even here.

For every first-generation college student who's been stuck without funds for books or food or web-fluid, Spider-Man remains our voice and our champion. And working, as I do, on a majority-minority, heavily Hispanic college campus, I feel he gives particular voice to the realities of those

Figure 1.3. John Edward Martin, Facebook post, April 16, 2019.

students, whether the person under that mask is really one of them or not. He has been seen at campus socials, charitable events, student rallies, protests, and other places where a hero is needed, always with his characteristic wit and fearlessness on display. I have even seen him pursuing the black-clad Venom across campus, on my way to the library, hurling insults as they went. There is, in fact, more than one Spider-Man in our neighborhood. The so-called Denton Spider-Man, who appeared shortly after the COVID-19 pandemic began, has been seen around town spreading the messages of "masking" for safety, antibullying, and community-building (Carter, 2024). Yet another, commissioned by a local comic shop, has been immortalized on a variant cover of *The Amazing Spider-Man* #001 (October 2015) swinging above the Denton County courthouse (Friedman, 2015).

I can never be certain which Spider-Man I may have seen on a given day, or who they really are, though their true identities are perhaps less important than what we all see and know: that he is simply Spider-Man, and he is ours.

One last weird, if iconic thing about Spider-Man, though this one may prove controversial: his deep sense of moral responsibility. Anyone familiar

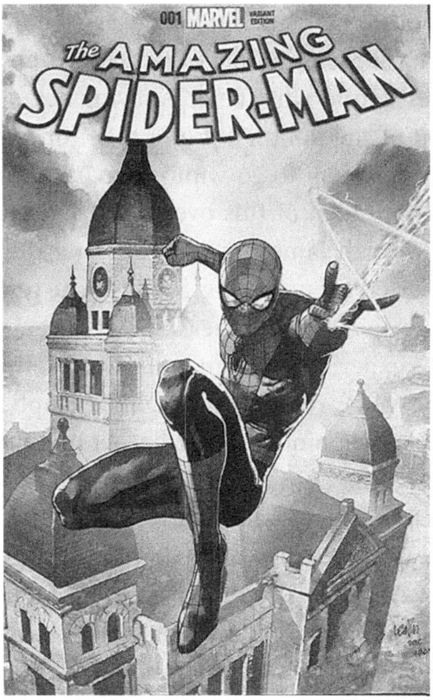

Figure 1.4. Leinil Francis Yu, *The Amazing Spider-Man* #001, Marvel Comics, October 2015, variant cover.

with Spider-Man's origin story knows that his most famous mantra, "With great power, there must also come—great responsibility," is a lesson learned from his Uncle Ben, who is tragically murdered by a robber that Spider-Man earlier allowed to escape from the police (Lee and Ditko 11). In that famous moment of failed responsibility, Spidey tells the pursuing officer, "Sorry, Pal! That's **your** job! I'm **thru** being pushed around—by anyone! From now on I just look out for number one—that means—**ME!**" (8, emphasis in original). Just a few panels later, he revises this sentiment somewhat, saying of his Aunt May and Uncle Ben, "They're the only ones who've ever been kind to me! I'll see to it that **they're** always happy, but the rest of the world can go hang for all I care!" (10, emphasis in original).

Generations of Spider-Man readers and fans, and for that matter Peter himself, have been conditioned to read these scenes as moments of profound selfishness—the moral failure at the heart of Spider-Man's origin story and the source of that driving guilt that will later define his heroic mission: "great responsibility" (11). But I've always been vaguely uncomfortable with this reading, for reasons that weren't always obvious to me. So, let's reread, or rather, relisten to what Peter is saying here. First, that catching criminals is the job of the police, not of a man (or rather, a teenager) in a costume. That would seem to go without saying, although Spider-Man will be frequently reminded of this over the years, usually by the police themselves or by J. Jonah Jameson, when he later decides to do exactly what he's been criticized for not doing. Secondly, he reminds us that being scolded by a policeman is just another version of "being pushed around" (10), something he's experienced from bullies and authority figures all his life. The anger in his voice, revealed through the emphasis in the lettering as well as the exclamation points, marks a deeper trauma than just inconvenience or selfishness. Finally, in narrowing his concerns to himself and his loved ones, he is reminding us where he feels his ultimate "responsibility" (11) lies: with those who have shown him kindness, not with "the rest of the world" (10). Indeed, where else should his responsibility lie?

The traditional reading of Spider-Man's origin suggests that it should be read as a moral tale of the dangers of power without responsibility, to emphasize our obligation to others, especially those who are weaker or more vulnerable than ourselves. But really, who is more vulnerable than Peter at this point in his life? While he has been given extraordinary abilities, through no fault or intention of his own, he is still, for all intents and purposes, a child. What's more, he's a child who has been repeatedly traumatized—by the death of his parents, by poverty, by social marginalization, personal humiliations, and his own feelings of inadequacy. Yet his first impulse upon gaining his spider-powers isn't to take revenge on his bullies or go battle supervillains for the sake of humanity; it's to take care of his elderly aunt and uncle by earning some money to help them out of their financial troubles. In doing so, he consciously rejects some larger notion of heroism, in favor of a more understandable, if ultimately tragic, focus on a more localized suffering: his own and his family's.

It's easy to criticize these sentiments coming from a supposed superhero, because, as Ben Saunders notes (citing Peter Coogan), the notion of superheroes as selfless and driven by a heroic mission has been central to the genre from the beginning. Saunders writes that "superheroes are supposed to understand themselves as playing a selfless role within society; they are not supposed to be interested in personal gain because that, by definition, would not be heroic" (Introduction xxvii). Easy to say when you're the heir to a family fortune, a god-like alien, an Amazonian princess, or even an adult super-soldier; but how is that a reasonable expectation for a working-class, teenage nerd (or really, anyone else)? Saunders elsewhere notes that Spider-Man's origin story shatters this expectation, and that his future struggles to live up to his heroic mission, over the course of decades, marks a departure from the superhero archetype (*Do Gods Wear Capes?*). But the mythos still holds this mission up as not only the heroic ideal, but as a moral obligation: "With great power, there *must* also come—great responsibility" (Lee and Ditko 11, my emphasis).

Must it, though? My early unease with this assertion may have just been a result of my sympathetic identification with Peter and with the unfairness of the guilt he is made to feel forever after this one tragic event. But as I've grown older, I see other possible dangers in the supposed lessons of Spider-Man's origin, because it suggests that even a moment of self-interest, of negligence, or of anger and indignation, can have tragic consequences and lasting moral implications. It condemns, almost criminalizes, the notion of seeking material rewards, recognition, or even acknowledgement of one's efforts and sacrifices in a public way (thus the need for a secret identity). Worst of all, it encourages the values of martyrdom, self-sacrifice, anonymity, and self-renunciation, all of which Ben Saunders rightly points out are traces of a distinctly religious, even Biblical notion of moral obligation (*Do Gods Wear Capes?* 61). And there's the rub, for me at least. Because at about the same age that Peter is undergoing his traumatic coming-of-age (fifteen, sixteen-years old?), I was also struggling with a deeply conflicted and antagonistic relationship with religion, spirituality, and guilt, which left me in much the same mood as Peter when confronted by the authoritarian police officer: angry, defensive, indignant, and dismissive. Was I, too, abandoning my responsibilities? Was I, too, bound to be punished for it? This seemed to be the lesson I was supposed to take from the famous mantra.

If so, I did a pretty shit job of it. At age thirteen, I was baptized in my grandparents' Baptist church, while living temporarily in the same small town where they and my father had been born (once again, for financial reasons). I got baptized not primarily because it was the right thing to do, or because I had found God, but because it was one of the only ways to be socially recognized or respectable in a place where I was a stranger. Worse, I was a city boy, a poor kid, a mixed-race kid, already overweight, geeky, and deep in the throes of adolescent rage and resentment. I thought that maybe God and the church would ease some of the latter and maybe make my peers forget about the rest. But, like Peter, I learned that the world around us doesn't change just because we experience some extraordinary change of our own—or, at least, try to. I didn't gain any amazing powers, or anything else apparently, through my baptism, nor did I gain much social acceptance or respite from being pushed around or marginalized. I was as much an outsider after my supposed spiritual transformation as before. Needless to say, my rage and resentment only grew deeper and found a new target: the church itself. By the time I was Peter's age (fifteen or sixteen), I was an avowed agnostic, a bitter opponent of evangelicalism, and a vocal critic of any authority figures who reminded me of the failed promises of religion. And yet I still felt a deep sense of guilt because I knew what a disappointment it must have been to my grandparents and, to a lesser extent, my parents and others in my life who were believers. I also suspected that I might have been to blame for my failed conversion: maybe I didn't believe hard enough, maybe I was too wicked, maybe I was too selfish and irresponsible. Hadn't I been given a great gift, and therefore a great responsibility? In rejecting that, wouldn't I deserve any punishment that came as a result? These were doubts that would follow me far beyond my adolescent and young adult years.

These are just some of the things I likely read into Spider-Man's origin story, whether I was aware of it or not. They were part of an unconscious co-creation that was happening as I transferred my own blueprint onto Peter and vice versa. I understood both his resentment and his guilt, even as I consciously accepted the overt message of the story: that Peter (and I) had a responsibility that we failed to live up to. In retrospect, this seems like a particularly insidious moral burden to place on an orphaned teenager who is economically disadvantaged, soon to be living in a single-parent home and already suffering from a sense of his own invisibility among his peers (yes, I mean Peter, in case the lines have blurred!). The idea that such a child somehow owes the world more self-sacrifice because of some cosmic accident or exceptional abilities seems unreasonable. What's more, as Saunders again points out, for Peter it leads to a lifelong cycle of anxiety, neurosis, guilt, remorse, and even repeated renunciations of his identity as Spider-Man, all because no amount of martyrdom can ever make up for that initial mistake. That's because this particular manifestation of the heroic mission is ultimately a repression of a deeper truth: that "no amount of earthly power could entirely mitigate human suffering or prevent injustice" (*Do Gods Wear Capes?* 62). And neither can any amount of guilt or self-sacrifice.

I would argue that Peter's ongoing struggle with responsibility is ultimately the greatest nemesis of his life, both as a superhero and as a man. Certainly, it does more damage to his body, mind, and soul than any villain he ever faces. While cast in the mythos as a heroic mission, I tend to agree with Saunders view of it as something closer to a heroic pathology. But as with many of Peter's other character traits, it's one that I reluctantly identify with, because really, who doesn't? We are all martyrs to our own ideals and aspirations, no matter how unfair or self-destructive they may be.

I've left some things out, of course. There are other qualities of Spider-Man that you or I might notice and co-create an identity from: his wall-crawling, his web-spinning, his Spidey sense, among others. The point is that these surface features are always more than they appear, always part of that complex blueprint that allows us to co-create a shared identity, regardless of how different we might actually be from the hero on the page. Much of what I saw of myself in Spider-Man as a young person came intuitively and emotionally, not rationally. Only as an adult, and one trained in close reading and analysis, can I pull the threads that reveal some of the deeper currents and meanings at work both in the comics and in my own responses to them. But do we really need to work so hard to find ourselves in the pages of a comic book? Am I stretching its potential meaning too far, or am I just longing for something that isn't there? Anyone who's ever taught literature or popular media has no doubt faced these questions and, frankly, they're not irrelevant. Why shouldn't we expect to see ourselves more directly represented in our heroes, at least in the pages of a comic book?

"Told You Spider-Man Was Black"

Spider-Man has been through a lot over the years, but I have to admit that I haven't been there for a lot of it. I was there as he grew up and went to college, became a freelance photographer for the *Daily Bugle*, married Mary Jane Watson, got whisked away to another world to face the Beyonder, acquired his new black symbiote costume, fought alongside other stars of the Marvel universe, and developed into a full-fledged superstar on page and screen. But then, we parted ways. Like many early fans, I gave up comics for a long while, sometime in the early 1990s, to pursue other, more serious things, much like Peter did: college, graduate school, a career, relationships, setbacks, transitions, etc. In most of those contexts, my love of comics and Spider-Man were, at best, topics of nostalgic conversation or, at worst, embarrassing remnants of a childhood that I'd just as soon forget. Sure, I watched the Sony movies with Tobey Maguire and Andrew Garfield with interest and affection and was thrilled by the appearance of Tom Holland's more boyish and wittier Spidey in the MCU; but none of these told me anything I didn't already know about my old friend, and none made me feel the need to return to the comics. It would be more than twenty years before I came back to comics as a scholar and librarian and to Spider-Man as a reader and fan. Wow! Was I in for a few surprises!

In that time, new Spider-Men (and Spider-Women) were born, some of them with even more connections to my own life and experiences than Peter Parker. Spider-Man, it seems, had begun a strange journey back to me entirely of his own accord. He would travel to the future and become a Mexican Irish geneticist, Miguel O'Hara, reflecting my own heritage, if not my career choices. Later, he would return to the present as an Afro-Puerto Rican teenager, Miles Morales, in a more diverse and multicultural neighborhood than the one Peter Parker inhabited but very like the one I grew up in. He would even become a woman (several, in fact), a little girl, a giant robot, a punk rocker, and an animated pig. Eventually Spider-Man would inhabit an entire multiverse of identities, localities, and experiences that came to reflect not only my experience, but that of an entire fandom who no doubt reveled to see themselves in him, or rather, to see him in themselves.

For some, this emergence of a more multifaceted and diverse Spider-Verse has been nothing short of a blessing and an emotional catharsis. For others it's been an ambivalent or even cynical development. For still others, a blatant imposition of unwanted "wokeism" in their beloved canon of Spider-lore. Nowhere are these mixed feelings more apparent than around the issues of race and cultural representation. Brian Montes (2016) examines some of the controversy surrounding the introduction of Miles Morales as the new Ultimate Spider-Man in 2011, which included not only the predictably hostile backlash from conservative commentators, who saw it as multiculturalism and political correctness run amok, but also from some Afro-Latino and other readers of color, who saw the representation of his cultural background as weak and sanitized. Montes notes that Miles, at least early on, had few markers of his Afro-Latino identity other than his name and skin color. He didn't speak Spanish often, didn't have a lot of Latino friends, and didn't reflect much on his cultural heritage or traditions (Montes 273–75). Both Montes and Kathryn M. Frank also suggest that in placing Miles Morales in an alternate universe from the one occupied by the canonical Spider-Man, Marvel at once tried to appeal to a more diverse market while also appeasing those fans who refuse to accept a Black or Latino version of the character as the "real" Spider-Man. Similarly, placing Miguel O'Hara in a futuristic timeline also serves to marginalize and give second-tier status to this new hero, while preserving the status quo of the mainstream Marvel universe (Frank 141–42).

In time, some of these critiques were taken to heart by the creators involved in writing and drawing these comics, as both Miles and Miguel were eventually allowed to cross over into the mainstream Marvel continuity and to overtly embrace more of their respective ethnic and cultural heritages. This was particularly noticeable in the recent films, *Spider-Man: Into the Spider-Verse* (2018) and *Spider-Man: Across the Spider-Verse* (2023), where we see Miles Morales's Afro-Latino identity, community, and family more clearly represented, both visually and aurally, through the images, language, music, and style of the production. Even here, critics like Isabel Molina-Guzmán see some cynical pandering on the part of Marvel and the creators in pursuing what she calls "color-blind cinematic practices"—that is, emphasizing the universality and familiarity of Miles's values and experiences rather than their specificity to his racial and cultural identity (Molina-Guzmán 229). Nevertheless, Molina-Guzmán acknowledges that there is the possibility of a "critical celebratory" response to the film and the character through two mechanisms that she calls "self-recognition" and "optimistic reimagining." (Molina-Guzmán 232). In other words, through co-creation—in this case, with a more complex and nuanced blueprint that provides more specific markers for identification by Afro-Latino and mixed-race audiences: "Miles Morales's non-white, mixed-race identity produces a transformative moment of sonic, visual, and cultural recognition for a range of communities often left off Hollywood movie screens and soundtracks—African American, Latina/o, Afro-Latina/o, and mixed-race audiences" (233).

I find all these critical responses legitimate and valuable. But as with my earlier relationship to Peter Parker as Spider-Man, my encounters with Miguel O'Hara, and especially with Miles Morales, have been more personal, based less on my training as a literary scholar or a cultural critic, and more on my experience as a reader and as a Latino man who has long felt an attachment to Spider-Man. Of the two, it might make sense that I'd identify more strongly with Miguel O'Hara, a character who shares my somewhat unusual (except in Texas) ethnic heritage—Mexican Irish—as well as my adult perspective and my Gen-X sensibilities (he was introduced in 1992, when I was a sophomore in college). As Frank notes, he was the first Latino Spider-Man, and he came along during the era of dark and gritty comics of the early nineties, characterized by its cyberpunk aesthetic and more adult themes, including violence and sexuality, trauma, death, and psychological tension—all things that certainly appealed to me at the time (Frank 243).

But, unfortunately, I didn't encounter him at that time. In fact, I was introduced to the character through the second *Spider-Verse* (2023) film and only recently went back to read some of the earlier comic books. At this point in my life, I find him less engaging than I might have at twenty years old—still cool and interesting, no doubt, and a wonderful addition to the larger Spider-Verse that has evolved in the wake of his first appearance. But maybe time and distance, not to mention changes in my own emotional and artistic needs, have made Miguel less an object of identification. His vampiric appearance, his Día de los Muertos–inspired costume, and his anticorporate heroic mission are all undeniably important and culturally significant. He has much to tell us about the relationship of Latinos, now and in the future, to social status, power, resistance, and cultural embodiment. And yet, nothing in *Spider Man 2099* moves me in quite the same way that Miles Morales has moved me, and other readers, in the decade or so since his introduction. Why is that?

I think part of the answer lies in Miles's reformulation of the Spider-Man origin story and his embrace of his own heroic mission. Before the *Into the Spider-Verse* films, this story is told in the pages of *Ultimate Comics: Fallout* #4 (August 2011) and continued in the relaunched title, *Ultimate Comics: Spider-Man* #1 (September 2011), both created by writer Brian Michael Bendis and artist Sara Pichelli. Unlike the orphaned and tragic Peter Parker, Miles grows up with both of his parents, in a mixed-race, lower-middle-class household that provides stability, love, and support for him. His African American father and Puerto Rican mother encourage his education and try to instill both a sense of responsibility and autonomy in their son. Though they also worry about money and the dangers he may face out in the world, there is never any sense of imminent danger or some cynical view of a crime-infested urban landscape. That's not to say that Miles doesn't eventually face violence, tragedy, and loss—he certainly does, most notably the death of his universe's Peter Parker—but he does so from a place of security that Peter never really had. And when he does eventually acquire his spider-powers, Miles's first instinct isn't to hide them from everyone in his life, but to immediately share them with his best friend, Ganke, who will become one of the most important and charming sidekicks in recent comics history. While Miles does decide to hide his identity from others in his life, for their own safety, it's notable that when he does reveal it to a few trusted people, the results are not an immediate tragic death. In fact, he eventually forms a close-knit cohort of allies and friends who provide a support network that Peter Parker rarely experiences. I found all this both refreshing and reassuring, especially as a mixed-race, urban product myself.

Of course, Mile's racial identity is also important here, although he will struggle at times with his desire to be seen, not as the Black Spider-Man—or, as he repeatedly reminds Ganke, also Latino—but simply as Spider-Man. Early in his first series, *Ultimate Comics: Spider-Man* #3 (2011), before he has even assumed his Spider-Man identity, Miles is called upon to use his new-found abilities to save a family from a burning building. As he leaps overhead after the spectacular rescue, costume-less and barefoot, a Black fireman glances up and then says to his partner, "Told you Spider-Man was black." It is an astounding moment, not just for its acknowledgement of the new Spider-Man's racial identity, but for the revelation that some observers, like this firefighter, suspected it along. That is, that there has been a conversation about that identity even before there *was* a Black Spider-Man!

It might lead us to wonder why he or others would have constructed a Black or Latino identity for Spider-Man before this moment. For me, it led me to consider all those elements of the canonical Spidey stories that, when read through the lens of race, might be recognizable to audiences of color: his locality and identification with the neighborhood, in this case Brooklyn, a diverse and multiracial community; his concern for the street-level problems often ignored by the more globe-trotting heroes; his frequent harassment by police and other authorities; his need for a hidden identity to protect himself and his family; perhaps even his luchador-like costume. But these are markers, not evidence; they can be read as indicators of racial or cultural identity, but don't have to be, unless you're looking for that.

Which brings me back to intentionality, to co-creation, and to the need that some of us feel to see ourselves in our heroes, whether they affirm our need or not. In this case, that need is met directly and powerfully through the appearance of a hero who affirms the existence and legitimacy of those Black and Latino viewers longing for identification and representation. That we actually see another fan, the firefighter, with a similar need, also on the page is yet another affirmation that we're not alone in imagining such a possibility.

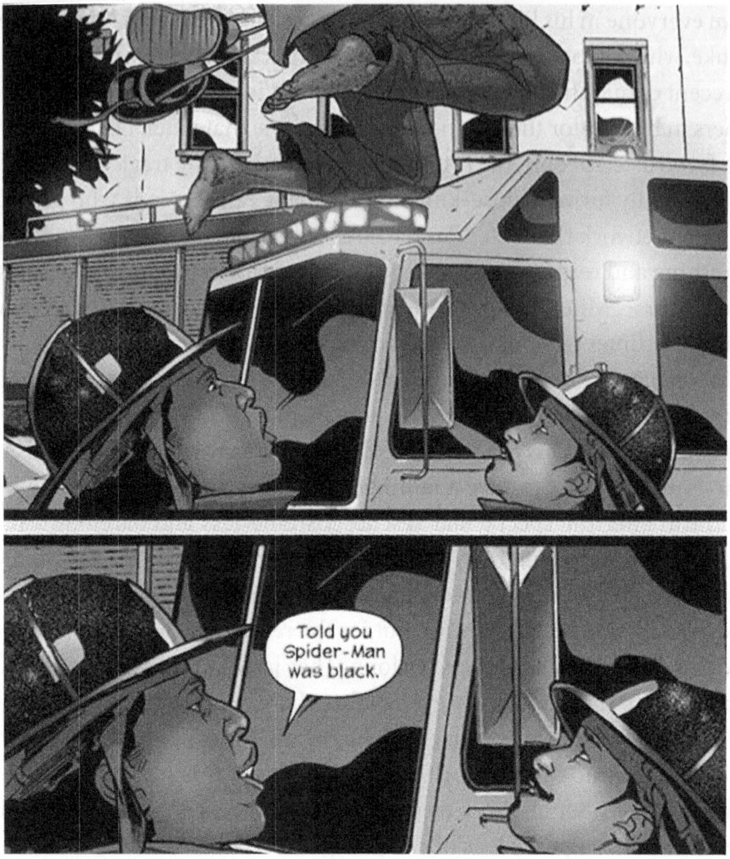

Figure 1.5. Brian Michael Bendis and Sara Pichelli, *Ultimate Comics: Spider-Man* #3, Marvel Comics, October 2011, 51.

In his review of *Spider-Man: Into the Spider-Verse* (2018), David Betancourt, a comics artist, longtime Spider-fan, and a man of mixed Afro-Puerto Rican heritage himself, writes that, "I saw the movie and connected with Miles instantly. Finally, the real me in a movie—*where the real me is Spider-Man* [my emphasis]. It was thrilling. I got lost in the sauce of being a superhero. . . . However Miles hits the screen, I'll be right there. Vicariously web-swinging through him." Similarly, the novelist and comics writer Victor LaValle, also of mixed-race heritage and a native of Queens, penned a moving and personal fictional letter to Miles himself in the pages of *The New York Times Style Magazine* following the release of the film. I quote it at length here, but encourage you to read the full letter:

Dear Miles,

My kids think you're great, but I'm the one who loves you. I'm 47, my son is 7 and my daughter is 5, but at the end of *Spider-Man: Into the Spider-Verse*, I'm the only family member who sat there in tears . . .

I spent 39 years without you, but you've been a part of my kids' imagination for their whole lives. They didn't get emotional because, for them, a brown-skinned Spider-Man with big, beautiful curly hair is a commonplace. NBD. Other people may take it for granted that they have a face like a superhero's. I'm happy my kids get to feel that way. I spent too long without such a thing; my big feelings about you reflect how much I needed it.

So I apologize that at the cookouts and family reunions you'll have to put up with uncles and aunties who pull you close and hold you too tight and get a little teary-eyed when you come around. We're just so proud of you. Forgive us. Or don't. I don't care. You're still getting hugged. (LaValle)

Both men's words recall those early fan letters to *The Amazing Spider-Man* almost sixty years earlier and their language echoes the feelings that those first fans expressed toward this new, more familiar, more personal superhero who inspires not just admiration or identification, but *love*—love and gratitude and a sense of recognition. Spider-Man is family. Spider-Man is *me*.

And for myself? Nothing captures my own feelings about my return to Spider-Man, via Miles Morales, more than an image drawn by artist Sara Pichelli as a variant cover for *Spider-Men* #2, the limited series which sees the original Peter Parker (from the Earth-616 mainstream Marvel Universe) meeting Miles Morales in his own universe and effectively "passing the torch" by giving Miles his blessing to become Spider-Man in his own right (figure 1.6). The image of the two heroes unmasking each other carries so much history, so much emotional, cultural, and symbolic weight that it brings me to tears. I see in it, not just two iterations of Spider-Man literally *seeing* each other for the first time, but two halves of myself being unmasked and vulnerable, though ultimately affirming of one another. Sentimental, much? Sure. But this has always been Spider-Man's greatest power: to make us true believers in our own inherent heroism and in the meaningfulness of our unique experiences. That Miles (or Miguel or Spider-Gwen or Spider-Punk) still possesses this power is a testament to the character and the artform.

Figure 1.6. Sara Pichelli, *Spider-Men #2*, *The Art of Sara Pichelli*, Marvel Monograph, November 2019, variant cover.

Works Cited

Aldama, Frederick Luis. *Latinx Superheroes in Mainstream Comics*. U of Arizona P, 2017.

Bendis, Brian Michael, and Sara Pichelli. *Ultimate Comics Spider-Man*. Marvel Comics, 2011.

Betancourt, David. "Miles Morales Is a Spider-Man Who's Biracial like Me. So Why Wasn't I More Excited for His Movie?" *The Washington Post*, 13 Dec. 2018, www.washingtonpost.com/arts-entertainment/2018/12/13/miles-morales-is-spider-man-whos-biracial-like-me-so-why-wasnt-i-more-excited-his-movie/.

Busato, Joselyn, and Clara McCormick. "Interview with Gary Jackson." *West Branch*, Spring/Summer 2023, westbranch.blogs.bucknell.edu/an-interview-with-gary-jackson/05/2023/.

Carter, Simone. "Denton Spider-Man Casts Web of Joy over North Texas." *Dallas Observer*, 26 Nov. 2020, www.dallasobserver.com/news/the-denton-spider-man-casts-web-of-cheer-over-north-texas-11964964/.

Children's Television Workshop. "Spidey Super Stories." *The Electric Company*, PBS, 1974–1977.

Conway, Gerry, et al. *The Amazing Spider-Man: The Mark of the Man Wolf.* Power Records, 1974.

Coogan, Peter. *Superheroes: The Secret Origins of a Genre.* MonkeyBrain, 2006, pp. 29–31.

David, Peter A., Robert Greenberger, and Matthew K. Manning. *Spider-Man: A History and Celebration of the Web-Slinger, Decade by Decade.* Epic Ink/The Quarto Group, 2022.

Frank, Kathryn M. "Everybody Wants to Rule the Multiverse: Latino Spider-Men in Marvel's Media Empire." *Graphic Borders: Latino Comic Books Past, Present, and Future*, edited by Frederick Luis Aldama and Christopher Gonzalez, U of Texas P, 2016, pp. 241–51.

Friedman, Nicholas. "Spidey Swings to Denton Square in Variant Cover for 'Amazing Spider-Man' #1." *The Dallas Morning News*, 15 Sept. 2015, www.dallasnews.com/arts-entertainment/pop-culture/2015/09/15/spidey-swings-to-denton-square-in-variant-cover-for-amazing-spider-man-1/.

Jackson, Gary. "Upon Seeing Spider-Man on My Way to Work." *Missing You: Metropolis*, Graywolf Press, 2009, p. 26.

Jackson, Gary. "Afterword." *Web-Spinning Heroics: Critical Essays on the History and Meaning of Spider-Man*, edited by R. M. Peaslee and R. G. Weiner, McFarland, 2012.

LaValle, Victor. "How Miles Morales Changed the Spider-Verse." *The New York Times Style Magazine*, 14 Feb. 2019, www.nytimes.com/2019/02/14/t-magazine/miles-morales-spiderman.html.

Lee, Stan, and Steve Ditko. *The Amazing Spider-Man.* Penguin Classics Marvel Collection, 2022.

Marvel Comics Group. *Spider-Man.* ABC, 1967–1970.

Montes, Brian. "The Paradox of Miles Morales: Social Gatekeeping and the Browning of America's Spider-Man." *Graphic Borders: Latino Comic Books Past, Present, and Future*, edited by Frederick Luis Aldama and Christopher González, U of Texas P, 2016, pp. 269–79.

Molina-Guzmán, Isabel. "Into the Spider-Verse and the Commodified (Re)imagining of Afro-Rican Visibility." *Mixed-Race Superheroes*, edited by Eric Berlatsky and Sika Dagbovie-Mullins, Rutgers UP, 2021, pp. 220–42.

Saunders, Ben. "Ch. 3: Spider-Man: Heroic Failure and Spiritual Triumph." *Do Gods Wear Capes? Spirituality, Fantasy, and Superheroes.* Continuum, 2011, pp. 61–83.

Saunders, Ben. "Introduction." *The Amazing Spider-Man*, by Stan Lee and Steve Ditko, Penguin Classics Marvel Collection, 2022, pp. xxiii–xxix.

Slott, Dan, et al. *Superior Spider-Man.* Marvel NOW, 2013.

Straczynski, J. Michael, and Joe Quesada. *Sensational Spider-Man, Second Series.* Marvel Comics, 2006.

Wright, Bradford W. *Comic Book Nation: The Transformation of Youth Culture in America.* Johns Hopkins UP, 2003.

2

MAN OR MONSTER OR . . . IS HE BOTH?

Hulk *en el Valle*

José Alaniz

12¢
MAN
THE STRANGEST MAN OF ALL TIME!!
FANTASY AS YOU LIKE IT!
IS HE MAN OR MONSTER
OR...
IS HE BOTH
OR... IS HE
OR MONSTER
BOTH
BY JOSÉ ALANIZ
HULK EN EL VALLE
OVER THE YEARS, I'VE SEEN MY OLDER BROTHER PEDRO IN THE SMOLDERING GAZE OF OLIVER REED, IN THE RAGGED SWAGGER OF MICKEY ROURKE, IN THE GLOWERING NO CHINGES OF DANNY TREJO (A CHICANO, AT LEAST). BUT MOSTLY– SINCE FOREVER– HE REMINDS ME OF THE HULK. GROWING UP IN THE RIO GRANDE VALLEY OF SOUTH TEXAS, ALONG THE BORDER WITH MEXICO, AN INVETERATE GOBBLER-UPPER OF SUPERHEROES-ESPECIALLY MARVEL–WHAT OTHER FRAME OF REFERENCE COULD I HAVE HAD FOR PEDRO'S UNADDRESSED MENTAL HEALTH ISSUES,* HIS ANGER MANAGEMENT PROBLEMS, HIS JUVENILE DELINQUENCY, HIS EXPLOSIONS OF VIOLENCE TOWARDS ME AND OTHERS? AS THE COVER OF THE INCREDIBLE HULK #1 PUT IT (I PARAPHASE): WAS HE MAN OR MONSTER – OR WAS HE BOTH? HE CAME FROM THE SAME WOMB AS ME, BUT ALWAYS STAYED A MYSTERY. A SCARY MYSTERY.
*A LOT OF THAT IN LA FAMILIA.
?

CA. 1978. I AM TEN OR SO YEARS OLD. THE HOUSE I GREW UP IN, ON KUHN. I THINK I'M ALONE. THEN I HEAR HIM. LOOKING AROUND A CORNER, KID THESEUS SPIES THE MINOTAUR—WITH IT'S BACK TURNED!
AT LAST, I COULD GET BACK AT HIM... FOR SO MANY THINGS. I SAW MY CHANCE—AND TOOK IT.
I KNEW I'D ONLY EVER HAVE ONE SHOT.

AY CHINGAO
I GAVE IT ALL I HAD.
DID I KNOCK HIM DOWN?
I THINK SO.
I DIDN'T STICK AROUND TO FIND OUT.
WITHOUT LOOKING BACK, I RAN LIKE HELL TO MY GRANDPARENTS', A BLOCK AWAY.
IN MY PANIC, I COULD'VE EASILY GOTTEN RUN OVER BY A CAR.*

DENIAL, SHAME, GASLIGHTING, THROWING AROUND HIS BIG FOOTBALL-PLAYER BODY – MY VERY SMART BROTHER PEDRO USED EVERY TRICK HE COULD TO COVER UP THE TRUTH. TO WIT:
SPLAT
HE BEAT ME. EVEN WHEN I WAS STILL IN THE CRIB. ONCE I WAS LYING ON MY STOMACH ON THE FLOOR (PROBABLY READING COMICS) AND HE PUT HIS FULL WEIGHT DOWN ON ME. I FARTED LOUDLY; HE LAUGHED.
ME WATCHING THROUGH THE FRONT WINDOW, THE FIRST TIME I SAW HIM BROUGHT HOME BY COPS
BY HIS EARLY TEENS HE WAS ALREADY GETTING ARRESTED: FOR BREAK-INS, THEFTS, FIGHTS, DRUNKEN AND DISORDERLIES... LATER HE TOOK TO HUNTING AND TORTURING STRAY CATS WITH A BOW AND ARROW. DAD WOULD BELT HIM AFTER EACH INFRACTION, BUT IT DIDN'T DO ANY GOOD. NOTHING DID.

PEDRO HAS ACCUMULATED OVER FOUR DECADES OF MUG SHOTS. AN ADDICT IN AND OUT OF PRISON, HOMELESS IN A FARAWAY TOWN, LIVING IN DENIAL, ONLINE MUG SHOTS ARE AT LEAST A WAY TO KEEP TRACK OF HIM.
THE MADDER HE GOT -- THE MADD
OF COURSE, IN THESE PICTURES HE LOOKS WORSE AND WORSE WITH EVERY PASSING YEAR. BUT HE ALWAYS REFUSES PLEAS TO GET TREATMENT. "IT'S OKAY," HE TELLS MY SISTER. "I LIKE MY BEERS." OR ELSE HE'LL REPEAT, OVER AND OVER: "I LIKE MY PLEASURES, YOLI, I LIKE MY PLEASURES." I.E. WHATEVER GETS HIM HIGH. AT TIMES, I'VE CONFRONTED HIM ABOUT SOME OF THIS. (FORTUNATELY, I THINK HE FORGOT ABOUT THE DROPKICK INCIDENT.)

ONCE I WAS GIVING HIM AND HIS COOLER OF BEER A RIDE. HE SEETHED WITH HATRED AS I TOLD HIM:
YOU CAN'T JUST LIE TO ME, PETE. I'M NOT YOLANDA. I SEE THROUGH YOU. EVERYBODY DOES.
YOU NEED HELP. THERAPY.
OF COURSE IT WAS THE WRONG APPROACH. THAT NIGHT, AT OUR UNCLE CRUZ'S, PEDRO GLARED AT ME THE WHOLE TIME, UNTIL:
YOU THINK YOU'RE SO SMART, HUH? WELL, I'LL KICK YOUR ASS RIGHT NOW...
...WIPE THAT SMILE OFF YOUR FACE...
HEY, HEY, CALM DOWN!
IT'S OKAY, CRUZ...
LATER WE ALL WENT TO BED. IN THE DARK I WATCHED, MESMERIZED, AS MY BROTHER POUNDED AND POUNDED ON THE COUCH, 'TIL HE FINALLY DOZED OFF. I GOT THE SENSE THAT HE WAS POUNDING AWAY AT SOMETHING OTHER THAN THAT COUCH.
BUT THAT HAPPENED LATER, IN OUR FORTIES. (HE'S FIVE YEARS OLDER THAN ME.) HOW WAS I TO PROCESS, AS A VERY YOUNG CHILD, WHO PEDRO WAS?
WHAT HE WAS BECOMING?

IS IT ANY WONDER THAT I WOULD GROW TO LOVE THE HULK, A CHARACTER INSPIRED BY FRANKENSTEIN'S MONSTER AND JEKYLL & HYDE (LEE, "ORIGINS: 75; CAPITANIO, "THE JEKYLL"); WHO, AS CHRIS GAVALER REMINDS, "IS NOT WHITE!" ("HULK"); WHO IN FACT LITERALLY CHANGES COLORS OVER HIS HISTORY; WHO MADE THE U.S. SOUTHWEST - NOT NEW YORK - HIS REGULAR STOMPING GROUNDS; WHO HAS A SPLIT PERSONALITY; AND WHO ROUTINELY ERUPTED IN UNCONTROLLABLE RAGES, LASHING OUT AT ALL AROUND HIM? IS IT SURPRISING THAT MY CHILDHOOD DRAWINGS LOOKED LIKE THIS? REALLY, IS IT AT ALL STRANGE THAT I WOULD COME TO SEE MY FAMILY'S DYSFUNCTION AND SLOW-MOTION TRAGEDY WITH PEDRO, THE SON AND BROTHER WHO SLIPPED AWAY ...
... THROUGH THE SUPERHEROES THAT I LOVED SO MUCH?

HELL, STARTING IN THE MID-80s THE HULK SERIES ITSELF GOT RETCONNED INTO A STORY ABOUT FAMILY DYSFUNCTION; BRUCE BANNER'S CHILD ABUSE AT THE HANDS OF HIS FATHER LED TO A FORM OF METAHUMAN POST-GAMMA BOMB DISSOCIATIVE IDENTITY DISORDER. DANIEL STEIN WRITES THAT THE SUPERHERO IS "AN INHERENTLY AMBIGUOUS CREATURE, SIMULTANEOUSLY MOVING AND UNMOVED THROUGH THE INTERPLAY OF STASIS AND SEQUENTIAL SUCCESSION IN A PERMANENT STATE—AN ETERNAL MEDIAS RES—OF BODILY TRANSITION" ("BODIES": 18). "OL' GREENSKIN" INCARNATES THAT QUEER ESSENCE MORE THAN MOST, THROUGH RADICAL MENTAL/CORPOREAL TRANSFORMATION. HE IS AN ANGRY CHAMELEON (GREY, NO GREEN, NO RED): THE PERFECT POP CULTURE (MIS)FRAMING TO SHAPE SUBJECTIVITY AT A TENDER AGE, A VESSEL BIEN PADRE FOR THE UNEXAMINED PAIN THAT COMES FROM HAVING SOMEONE IN YOUR LIFE, THAT YOU LIVE WITH CLOSELY, WHOM YOU LOVE AND FEAR, QUE TE LASTIMA YET IN WHOM YOU SEE A DISTORTED REFLECTION DE TI MISMO. ALL THIS AS I WAS GROWING UP EN EL VALLE, A REMOTE BORDER REGION, AS A MEXICAN-AMERICAN (CHICANO, ESE!), LIGHT-SKINNED WHERE MY BROTHER WAS DARK, TRYING TO FIGURE OUT QUIEN CHINGAOS ERA. (AH, SHIT, I THINK QUIÉN HAS AN ACCENT.) TRYING TO UNDERSTAND WHY THEY CALLED ME "GÜERITO" AND "BOLILLO" WITH CONTEMPT, EVEN

AS MY LIGHT SKIN GAVE ME ALL SORTS OF ADVANTAGES OVER THE "PRIETOS." (YA!) SO DID MY GOOD GRADES. (JOTO!) I DIDN'T CHOOSE THEM! (YA CÁLLATE LO SICO!) THEY JUST HAPPENED! IT WASN'T MY FAULT I HAD ALL THIS UNEARNED PRIVILEGE! (DESGRACIADO!) LEAVE ME ALONE, CABRONES! I'LL SMASH YOU! ¡VÁYANSE A LA CHINGADA! I'LL SMASH AND SMASH AND SMASH HASTA QUE TODOS USTEDES PENDEJOS ME DEJEN EN PAZ

IS IT ANY WONDER, EN FIN, THAT I WOULD GRAVITATE TO THIS?
DISIDENTIFICATION IS ABOUT RECYCLING AND RETHINKING ENCODED MEANING. THE PROCESS OF DISIDENTIFICATION SCRAMBLES AND RECONSTRUCTS THE ENCODED MESSAGE OF A CULTURAL TEXT IN A FASHION THAT BOTH EXPOSES THE ENCODED MESSAGE'S UNIVERSALIZING AND EXCLUSIONARY MACHINATIONS AND RECRUITS ITS WORKINGS TO ACCOUNT FOR, INCLUDE, AND EMPOWER MINORITY IDENTITIES AND IDENTIFICATIONS. THUS, DISIDENTIFICATION IS A STEP FURTHER THAN CRACKING OPEN THE CODE OF THE MAJORITY; IT PROCEEDS TO USE THIS CODE AS RAW MATERIAL FOR REPRESENTING A DISEMPOWERED POLITICS OR POSITIONALITY THAT HAS BEEN RENDERED UNTHINKABLE BY THE DOMINANT CULTURE.
(ST. MUÑOZ : DISIDENTIFICATIONS : 31)
ANY WONDER THAT I WOULD DEEPLY, FATALLY (DIS)IDENTIFY WITH THE HULK, THAT PILLAR OF 1970s POP CULTURE, TO TRY TO WRAP MY HEAD AROUND THE PAINFUL INTERPERSONAL CONFLICT BETWEEN MY OLDER BROTHER AND ME. OR THAT, IN MIDDLE AGE, I WOULD FLAIL AWAY AT THIS BACK-HANDED TRIBUTE TO HIM, WHO FIRST TAUGHT ME TO DRAW, WHO HIMSELF DREW QUITE WELL, WHO SPIRALED OUT OF MY LIFE LONG AGO LEAVING ONLY CRATERS, PUNCHED WALL-HOLES AND (EMOTIONAL) DEVASTATION IN HIS WAKE.
FOR PEDRO, MI HERMANO, WHO I FOREVER SEE AS MY ALL-TIME FAVORITE SUPERHERO: MY BELOVED, TRAGIC MAN-CHILD HULK.
THE NEW INCREDIBLE HULK
TO BE CONTINUED

Works Cited

Alaniz, José. *Puro Pinche True Fictions.* FlowerSong Press, 2023.

Alaniz, José. "'The Monster's Analyst' and the 'Binomial Self.'" *The Ages of the Incredible Hulk*, edited by Joe Darowski, McFarland, 2016, pp. 62–77.

Capitanio, Adam. "'The Jekyll and Hyde of the Atomic Age': The Incredible Hulk as the Ambiguous Embodiment of Nuclear Power." *The Journal of Popular Culture*, vol. 43, no. 2, 2010, pp. 249–70.

Gavaler, Chris. "Hulk Is Not White!" *The Patron Saint of Superheroes*, May 2022, thepatronsaintofsuperheroes.wordpress.com/2022/05/02/hulk-is-not-white/.

Lee, Stan. *Origins of Marvel Comics.* Simon & Schuster, 1974.

Muñoz, José Esteban. *Disidentifications: Queers of Color and the Performance of Politics.* U of Minnesota P, 1999.

Stein, Daniel. "Bodies in Transition: Queering the Comic Book Superhero." *Navigationen-Zeitschrift für Medien-und Kulturwissenschaften*, vol. 18, no. 1, 2018, pp. 15–38.

3

"IT'S A JEWISH THING"

Monstrosity and Jewish Identity in *Fantastic Four*

Michael Kobre

The first issue I remember seeing was #7, "Prisoners of Kurgo, Master of Planet X." But something about its cover disturbed me in a way that the other comics on the spinner rack in the drug store that day—sometime in July 1962—didn't. Was it the images of the members of the Fantastic Four on a billboard declaring them "WANTED DEAD OR ALIVE," with four solemn headshots of our heroes looking vaguely guilty and oppressed below those words, the Thing's head canted slightly to one side and partly in shadow, at an angle that emphasized the rough edges of the orange rocks that made up his skin? Or was it the mob with torches and clubs clustered beneath the billboard, one man's fist raised in the air as he proclaimed in a speech balloon, "Down with The Fantastic Four!!"? I wasn't disturbed, I knew, by the flying saucer blasting into the night sky away from the mob, because I'd seen lots of other spaceships before on other comic book covers. Was it the word balloon clearly emanating from inside the flying saucer and obviously spoken by one of the members of the Fantastic Four? "We escaped just in time! We can't remain on Earth any longer! We've *got* to head for *Planet X*!!" Something about those words, with their claims of desperate flight and exile, seemed to amplify the force of the mob's hatred and the solemn expressions of the Fantastic Four on the billboard.

By then, even as a five-year-old child just beginning to read, I was already under the spell of all those primary colors and fantastic creatures waiting on the comics rack in the drug store or the five-and-dime. I begged my parents every week to let me buy a few, two or even three at a time if I was lucky, at 12 cents each, so I had to choose carefully. I liked DC titles well enough, but

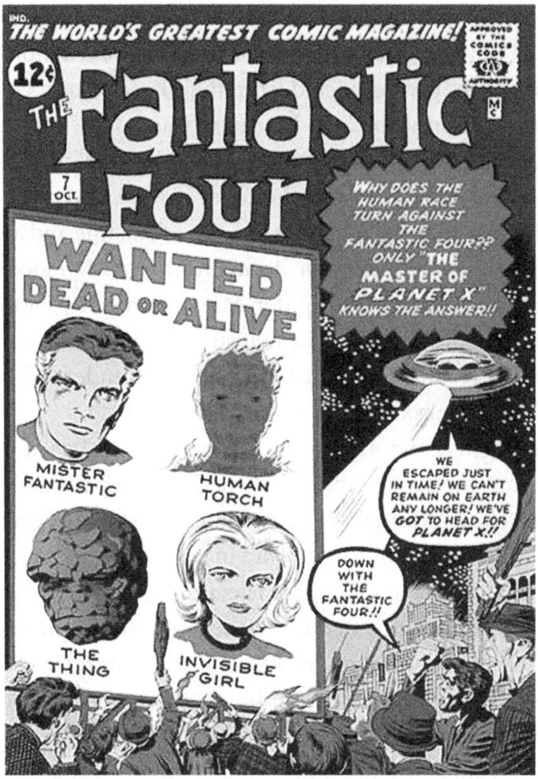

Figure 3.1. Stan Lee and Jack Kirby, *Fantastic Four* #7, Marvel Comics, July 1962, cover.

there was something almost stately about Superman, who always seemed to be a reassuring father figure, and the other members of the Justice League of America had colorful costumes yet bland personalities, a genial group of earnest scientists and test pilots who never lost their tempers.

But those *other* comics, with no publisher's logo until Marvel would introduce its iconic corner box on each cover in February 1963, were different somehow, in ways that compelled and disturbed me: *The Fantastic Four* and *The Incredible Hulk*, drawn and coplotted by Jack Kirby and scripted by Stan Lee, and later *The Amazing Spider-Man*, drawn and coplotted by Steve Ditko and scripted by Lee.[1] Unlike all those upstanding citizens in DC comics, these heroes were routinely mistrusted, denounced, and surrounded by angry mobs. Panicked solders on the cover of *The Incredible Hulk* #3 pointed to the Hulk leaping above their heads—"Look! Nothing can stop him now! *He can fly*!"—and fired their weapons at him as even a missile veered toward him. On the cover of *Fantastic Four* #9, a mob jeered at the Fantastic Four as they were evicted from their headquarters for not paying rent, while their enemy, the Sub-Mariner (was *he* the architect of this?), leered in triumph. "*Heroes* one minute—bums, the next!" the Thing says, but no matter how carefully I studied the cover I could never understand why a financial disaster should be a cause of so much shame and anger. For that matter, virtually every issue of *The Amazing Spider-Man* took as one of its central themes the suspicion of Spider-Man inflamed by J. Jonah Jameson, publisher of the *Daily Bugle*, and the nearly crippling anxiety suffered by Peter Parker as a result of that mistrust, a feeling rendered in every one of Steve Ditko's jittery, almost expressionist lines.

Inside *Fantastic Four* #7 too, in the very first Marvel comic I ever owned, I felt an unsettling emotional chaos. The opening pages focused on Kurgo—a yellow-skinned, vaguely Asiatic dwarf with a giant cranium—reclining on some wildly futuristic divan in one of Jack Kirby's characteristic alien landscapes, using a kind of space television to spy on the Fantastic Four. But these images only captivated me in the way other comics routinely did. From the first sequence, though, as the Fantastic Four quarrel over whether or not to attend a state dinner in their honor, there were emotional currents that I felt powerfully but didn't really understand. Unlike Reed Richards—the stretchable Mr. Fantastic and nominal father-figure of the team, a thoughtful, pipe-smoking scientist who might have stepped out of the hero's role in a 1950s science fiction movie—the others only feel anxiety about being shunned and embarrassed at the dinner. Johnny Storm, the Human Torch, worries about his fear of public speaking causing him to "burst into flame" at the podium, while his sister Sue, the Invisible Girl, imagines becoming "flustered" and vanishing when she has to make conversation with "all those important people" (152–53). Yet as always the locus of shame and anxiety is Ben Grimm, the Thing, who envisions himself arriving at the dinner with his monstrous form—an assemblage of orange rocks with vaguely simian features—concealed beneath a heavy trench coat, a scarf bundled tightly around his throat, and a hat pulled low over his eyes, before that concealment is literally torn from his body by photographers and he erupts in rage and destroys the room. If Johnny's and Sue's anxieties are reflections of immaturity and social awkwardness expressed in an inability to control their own impulses, Ben experiences a deeper self-loathing, a punishing awareness of a kind of difference that can't be concealed or contained.

As the plot unfolded, other things bothered me. Kurgo, we learn, wants to summon the Fantastic Four to Planet X to stop an asteroid from crashing into his world, and he sends his robot servant—a giant metal man with what looks like a car's grille for a face, who's clearly modeled after the robot Gort in the 1951 science fiction classic *The Day the Earth Stood Still*—to travel to Earth and capture the Fantastic Four. All this was more or less typical comic book stuff, and no reader would ever single out "Prisoners of Kurgo, Master of Planet X" as one of the standout stories in Kirby and Lee's genre-defining run on *Fantastic Four*. But what unsettled me most was Kurgo's scheme to have his robot transmit a "hostility ray" across the earth and turn the world's population against the Fantastic Four (158). First, the diplomats at the state dinner denounce the Fantastic Four as "menaces" (158), and then the team has to flee from rioting crowds everywhere, only to find the robot waiting for them on the roof of their headquarters at the Baxter Building in New York City. "No matter where you go, no matter what continent you flee to, you will be hunted by your fellow humans as though you are four monsters," the robot tells them in a caption above a panel that shows the Fantastic Four running down a dark cobblestone street in some European city as jackbooted soldiers chase and shoot at them (163).

I suppose, looking back at those pages now, it was *that* panel which bothered me the most. Because even then, barely starting my Jewish education, I'd seen images like it in Hebrew school when my parents dropped me off at the temple on Sunday mornings. Of course, I was still too young in 1962 for one of the Holocaust films to be shown in any of my classes, yet somehow, as I try to piece together these memories now, the images seem as if they were always present, seared into the consciousness of my Jewish identity from the start. Maybe I just caught a glimpse of the film by accident, walking down one of the cinderblock hallways in the temple annex that housed the Hebrew school. We'd take any excuse to get out of class after all—a trip to the bathroom, a drink of water, anything. Maybe I happened to glance through the open doorway of a classroom filled with older students, and there it was, projected on a screen in front of the room: the black and white footage of a steam shovel hauling up another load of skeletal bodies from a mass grave.

To be a child in the American Jewish community at that time, like I was in July 1962 when *Fantastic Four* #7 was published, was to experience your Jewish identity at a particular historical moment, in the aftermath of two seismic events: the Holocaust and the establishment of the state of Israel.

Figure 3.2. Stan Lee and Jack Kirby, *Fantastic Four #7*, Marvel Comics, July 1962, 13.

By the early sixties, a general knowledge of the Holocaust—a term that only began to be used in the late 1950s—had reached new levels throughout American culture after the publication of *The Diary of Anne Frank* in 1952 and its subsequent stage and film adaptations and after excerpts from the trial of Adolf Eichmann in Jerusalem in 1961 had been broadcast on American television networks. The creation of Israel in 1948 had electrified the American Jewish community too. In his graphic memoir *Not the Israel My Parents Promised Me*, Harvey Pekar recalls his father's joy at what seemed a miraculous event. "I'm just so happy I was alive at the time when the state of Israel was reborn," Pekar's father told him (122). Within the American Jewish community—among the families in my neighborhood or the members of the congregation at our temple, and far beyond as well—these events were understood as a mythic narrative of horrific tragedy followed by redemption, a covenant fulfilled at last, in a drama uncomplicated by politics or the history of colonialism, decades before anyone I knew ever heard the Palestinian name for these events, the *Nakba*, the catastrophe. To hear some adults and the teachers at Hebrew school talk about it, the ovens that had consumed so many grandparents and uncles and aunts and distant cousins had hardly cooled. And our brothers and sisters in the Middle East were heroic pioneers, we were told, making the desert blossom, a tiny nation ringed about by hostile neighbors. In Hebrew school, we would hand over all our spare change, pocketfuls of pennies and nickels, to transform the desert alongside those brave pioneers and plant trees in *Eretz Yisrael*. Within a few years, though, this simple narrative would reach its apogee in Israel's sudden and seemingly miraculous triumph over its enemies in the Six-Day War, and then begin to crumble during the long, increasingly oppressive occupation of the West Bank and Gaza.

Growing up in the shadow of all this history, I lived in a community that was at once cautiously proud, a little more open about their Jewish identity than their parents and grandparents had been, yet wary and often insular as well, all too aware of the painful facts of that history. In July 1962, when I'd discovered Marvel Comics with *Fantastic Four* #7 and *Incredible Hulk* #3, which also came out that month, my family was living in the Virginia Leigh apartments in Columbus, Ohio, a complex of sixteen narrow brick townhomes across the street from my elementary school, filled with Jewish families and developed by a former clothing salesman, Bernard "Bunny" Ruben, who would later command a real estate empire and become one of the most important philanthropists in the Columbus Jewish community. It was a Jewish place owned and operated by a Jewish company, our own little *shtetl* in an otherwise gentile neighborhood.

My family, like many of the others around us, wasn't particularly observant. We went to temple on High Holy Days, of course (although my sister and I would always beg our mother to just let us stay home instead and not waste a precious day out of school sitting through those interminably long services). We got presents for Hanukkah. We went to Passover seders. On Tuesday and Thursday afternoons, after I'd started first grade in 1963, my sister and I would be part of a whole group of kids from the neighborhood waiting grudgingly on a corner after elementary school for another school bus to pick us up and take us downtown to the temple for two long hours of Hebrew school, which in winter didn't even end till after dark. Like every family in our neighborhood, we owned a copy of the Broadway cast album of *Fiddler on the Roof* and the Leon Uris novel *Exodus*, a heroic retelling of the foundation of Israel with blockbuster sales that rivalled the success of *Gone With the Wind.* Once in a while too, when there was a bar or bat mitzvah of someone we knew, my family even went to Shabbat services.

In some ways, I wore my Jewish identity lightly as a child. We just had different customs and celebrated different holidays than other people—although Hanukkah, even with eight nights of candles and presents (which got smaller as the days ticked down), was always filled with an anxious sense of compensation, an inferiority complex to the far more glamorous and festive Christmas season bursting with light, color, and song all around us. I was much more interested in comics and superheroes and old Tarzan movies on TV than the prayers we were taught in Hebrew school and the scraps of Jewish history that accompanied them (usually some tale of persecution and the heroic Jews clinging to their faith in the face of it). Yet my mother had once told my older sister and me how she'd been fired from her first job, right after high school, as a secretary in a New York advertising agency, when her supervisor found out she was Jewish. And my father who "looked Jewish," with the kind of classic beaked Jewish nose that had inspired a German Jewish doctor in the nineteenth century to invent a new surgical procedure to cure "nostrility," had hinted at worse things growing up in the South.[2] So I was aware too, even as a child, of constantly negotiating a sense of difference that defined me, a difference that could seem benign most of the time, but could also, in the past at least, hurt you and even threaten your life. Just day to day, being Jewish was confusing sometimes. How enthusiastically was I supposed to sing the Christmas songs at my elementary school's annual holiday assembly? What was I supposed to do with my hands when a guest speaker at one of those assemblies asked us all to bow our heads as he led us in prayer that morning in Jesus's name? The Jewish kids might play games on the school playground with the gentile kids, but no one from one group ever invited anyone from the other to their home.

And somehow all of this spilled over into the comics I read, particularly *Fantastic Four* and, especially, those parts of the stories about Ben Grimm, the Thing. It wasn't just the effects of Kurgo's "hostility ray" in #7 that formed this connection. (Did it really take some alien signal from outer space to unleash so much suspicion and hatred inside so many people?) In a process that Frederick Luis Aldama has described as "co-creation"—which John Edward Martin and Samantha Langsdale also discuss in this collection—my imagination brought to life the static images and words on the page, making them cohere into a story, in an effort that was even more interactive for a child like me still learning to read. I'd lay the comic book open flat on the edge of my bed and stand over it, studying each panel in turn, piecing out whatever words I could, and half-chanting under my breath some version of a TV soundtrack to underscore the action. And through what Aldama calls "the wonderfully generative capacity of this co-creating potential in comics readers," that sense of difference I felt was reflected and magnified in the forms on the page, especially Ben Grimm (90–91). Reed, Sue, and Johnny, after all, could pass as normal if they didn't use their powers, and they looked like the same kind of ethnically undifferentiated characters you'd find in most superhero comics. But Ben's difference was inescapable. He could try to cover it up, as he'd imagined in #7, under a heavy trenchcoat, a scarf around his neck, and a hat pulled low over his face, but no disguise ever worked for long. He was defined by his difference, as I was too, even if, looking at me, I didn't appear all that different from the other boys at my school. Still, my Jewish identity structured my world: where I lived, who I played with, the traditions I'd inherited, the things I was supposed to believe. Even the way I looked wouldn't necessarily conceal my difference. When I was a little older, my mother would tell me how in her nightmares as a girl in the Bronx during World War II, the Nazis invaded America, and not even her red hair and freckles could stop them from knowing she was Jewish.

Of course, the Fantastic Four, as far as I knew, weren't Jewish, and I had no idea then that their creators, Jack Kirby and Stan Lee, the former Jacob Kurtzberg and Stanley Lieber, like so many of the first generation of American comic book creators, were Jews. The only explicitly Jewish character I could identify was Izzy Cohen in Marvel's war title, *Sgt. Fury and His Howling Commandos*, and Izzy's Jewishness was never particularly emphasized, except as just another coloration in a squad of ethnic stereotypes: a romantic Italian American movie star, a blustering Irishman, a jazz-playing Black man, among others. More often, in fact, Izzy was simply referred to as the "Brooklyn-born Howler" (Friedrich 8). None of Marvel's other characters, as far as its readers could know, were Jewish or professed any particular faith at all, other than acknowledging the Norse gods who occasionally walked the earth in *The Mighty Thor*.

But that inchoate connection I felt between my Jewish identity and Ben Grimm's monstrous form wasn't completely imagined either. In 1975, five years after the end of his epic run on *Fantastic Four*, Jack Kirby, an observant Jew who occasionally read Torah portions at *Shabbat* services at his temple and later fulfilled a lifelong dream when he joined a congregational trip to Israel, drew a picture of the Thing on a Hanukkah card that showed Ben dressed for *Shabbat* services himself, in a coat and tie and wearing a yarmulke and prayer shawl.[3] Kirby liked the image so much that he hung a copy on the wall of his studio. When guests would ask him about it, as his friend and biographer Mark Evanier remembered, Kirby would just say, "It's a Jewish Thing" (212).

It's revealing, though, that Kirby's image of a Jewish Thing was created to be circulated privately and then displayed on the wall of his studio, and certainly not to be printed in an issue of *Fantastic Four*. Judaism exists as a kind of lacuna in both Kirby's and Lee's published work, a fact of both men's backgrounds that's conspicuous by its absence. In a sequence in a concentration camp in *Sgt. Fury* #2, for instance, the careful omission of any reference to Judaism must be a calculated editorial choice by Lee; none of the prisoners in this sequence is seen wearing a yellow Star of David or is identified in the dialogue or captions as Jewish. Even a late autobiographical story by Kirby, "Street Code" from 1983, which is set in the Lower East Side of his youth, has no images of Jewish life or references to Kirby's Judaism.

Of course, as first-generation American Jews, Kirby and Lee, like virtually all of their generation, strove to assimilate and be fully embraced as Americans. In *World of Our Fathers*, a history of Jewish immigration to America from Eastern Europe, Irving Howe says of younger Jewish immigrants and their children, "To be an American, dress like an American, look like an American, and even . . . talk like an American became a collective goal" (128). And, naturally, this was mirrored in the comic book industry too, a junk trade largely created by American Jews. So Jewish artists and writers created characters with square jaws, blue eyes, and goyish names like Clark Kent, Bruce Wayne, and Steve Rogers (the creations respectively of Jerry Siegel and Joe Shuster, Robert Kahn and Bill Finger, and Hymie Simon and Jacob Kurtzberg). As Kirby recalled in a 1978 interview, "In the '40s, the best thing to be was an Anglo-Saxon Protestant. Comics have to reflect the society in general on the level that [what] we admired was Anglo-Saxon. Everybody else was an immigrant" (quoted in Baron-Carvais).

And yet, as many writers and scholars have long argued, there were Jewish subtexts to some of these characters.[4] In "The Minsk Theory of Krypton," Jules Feiffer's 1996 remembrance of Jerry Siegel, the cocreator of the most archetypal superhero of all, Feiffer describes Superman—a refugee from a doomed world who arrives in the American heartland and becomes a quintessential American—as "the ultimate assimilationist fantasy. . . . It wasn't Krypton that Superman came from; it was the planet Minsk or Lodz or Vilna or Warsaw." Similarly, in *Men of Tomorrow*, Gerard Jones suggests that scrawny Steve Rogers's metamorphosis through the agency of a super-soldier serum into Captain America is also a concealed narrative of "the underfed ghetto kid transformed into a roof-rattling power by seizing American opportunities, the world-weary old-country survivor reborn as the new fighting Jew through the crucible of American freedom and violence" (201–2).

In much the same way, if Jack Kirby's Jewish identity is reflected at all in the character of Ben Grimm, it's coded, inscribed as a subtext to be deciphered later. "My generation lied to survive," Kirby told a group of fans in a 1970 conversation when he was asked to explain why he changed his name from Jacob Kurtzberg. "When I tell you my generation lied or died, I'm not kidding," he said, going on to explain how he was perceived as "a total alien" by the kind of men from the Midwest or Texas whom he served with in the army, even citing one soldier from a small rural town who refused to believe Kirby was Jewish because he didn't have horns ("Shel Speaks (Kirby Too)!"). Like his Americanized name, Kirby's avoidance of any explicit Jewish content in his published work might have been another of those "lies," concealing a deeper truth beneath the surface.

Certainly, no other character in all of Kirby's work embodies that sense of feeling like "a total alien" as much as the Thing, whose very name as a superhero denies his humanity. For that matter, even if Benjamin Jacob Grimm—whose name is a conflation of Kirby's own, Jacob, and his father's, Benjamin—was never formally identified as Jewish in Kirby and Lee's run on *Fantastic Four*, he's infused with much of Kirby's own personality. "Everybody seemed to associate me with the Thing because he acted like a regular guy," Kirby said in a 1989 interview. "I suppose I must be a lot like Ben Grimm. I never duck out of a fight; I don't care what the hell the odds are, and I'm rough at times, but I try to be a decent guy all the time" (quoted in Groth 41). Like Kirby too, who was driven to support his family by working twelve to fourteen hours a day turning out page after page of artwork in a basement studio that his family called "the dungeon," the Thing was the workhorse of superheroes, often depicted lugging gigantic pieces of machinery around the Fantastic Four's headquarters for Reed Richards's futuristic technology or bearing the brunt of the team's battles, as in his epic slugfest with the Hulk in #25, after all the other members of the team were weakened or wounded. In one of Kirby's last stories for Marvel, "What If the Fantastic Four Were the Original Marvel Bullpen?" published in 1978 in issue #11 of Marvel's anthology title exploring parallel realities, *What If*, Kirby even drew himself as the Thing, imposing his own features, complete with a cigar jammed in the corner of his mouth, on the Thing's rock-like façade. So if Jack Kirby was Jewish and the Thing was like Kirby, was the Thing Jewish too? At least on the wall of Kirby's studio, and, I suppose, in my imagination as well.

For me, as a child, the Thing's monstrousness was an emblem for the sense of difference that structured my world, and his struggle to be more than just a monster compelled and fascinated me. Although the Thing had a girlfriend, the blind sculptor Alicia Masters, the daughter of the Fantastic Four's enemy the Puppet-Master, the precise nature of their relationship was unclear. The implication, of course, was that she could only love him *because* she was blind, like the old blind De Lacey, who is the monster's only friend in Mary Shelley's *Frankenstein* (or like the blind hermit onscreen in James Whale's *The Bride of Frankenstein*, a more likely influence on Kirby and Lee since both acknowledged the Frankenstein movies as an inspiration for the Hulk). Even as a child though, I wondered about what, if any, intimacy they could possibly share. Could the Thing's blunt, rock-like fingers—with only four on each hand, instruments of destruction that could tear through solid steel—even touch her without hurting her? Could he brush her cheek or feel her skin at all? And later, in adolescence, I'd wonder what was under the blue trunks that functioned as his costume. Was his whole body made of orange rocks?[5]

But nothing affected me as powerfully as those sequences when Ben would briefly turn back into his human form and then, inevitably, become the Thing again. It was a kind of ritual agony he would experience over and over. In "The Battle of the Baxter Building!" in #40, midway through an extended storyline in which, at first, the Fantastic Four had lost their powers and Ben was human again, Reed invents a new device to restore their abilities after Dr. Doom has invaded their headquarters. "But—mebbe I don't *wanna* become the *Thing* again!!! I'm finally *normal*—like anyone else!" Ben says, when Reed turns his invention on Ben too. Then, in a three-panel sequence that takes up a whole page—a formal decision which announced, even to a child like me in 1965, the gravity and pain of the moment—Kirby presents what's perhaps his greatest and most tragic transformation sequence.

In the opening two panels, which occupy the top half of the page, we first see Ben lying on the floor propped on the palms of his hands with his face down. Then, in the second panel, the transformation begins: he looks up as the T-shirt he's been wearing in his human form starts to tear and split open and as the outlines of orange scales appear on his skin, with his features shifting too—a ridge forming above his eyes, his nose flattening, his mouth getting wider, his hair fading away and leaving only a few wisps on the top of his head—while one enormous hand reaches forward with blunt, square fingertips. The third panel completes the sequence and takes up the entire bottom half of the page. Now he rises to his knees, fully transformed, with his fists on the floor to bear what is clearly the massive weight of his body, surrounded by the shreds of his clothing and back in the familiar blue trunks that he must have been wearing beneath them, as he stares out from the page directly at us, almost accusingly (perhaps because, at some metatextual level, he's condemned to exist as the Thing for the readers' pleasure too). His jaw is thrust forward. His eyes, two small circles with tiny black dots for pupils, look out coldly from under the great ledge of his forehead. Deep shadows across his chest and arms highlight the rough-edged plates of the rocks that form his skin.

Kirby in drawing the Thing had always emphasized the cumbersome, ungainly quality of his body; the very first time he appears in issue #1 he smashes through a doorway that's too narrow for him. By contrast, the Hulk could leap through the air despite his size, and Ditko's Spider-Man was a lithe, graceful acrobat. But the Thing was always earthbound, weighted down both physically and emotionally by his responsibility and sacrifice. In this transformation sequence in #40, as his humanity is sacrificed again, we see more vividly than perhaps anywhere else in Kirby's run on the title the unbearable weight of being trapped in the Thing's body and the force of his own self-loathing.

That torment at being trapped in a monster's body also functions as a distorted reflection of culturally inscribed internal conflicts that had been passed down over generations of European and American Jews. In his sense of alienness and his deep discomfort in his own body, the Thing evokes aspects of the cultural legacy of those first-generation American Jews, the descendants of the *shtetls*, who created the comic book industry. Like the parents and grandparents of Jacob Kurtzberg and Stanley Lieber, from Austria and Romania respectively, Ben Grimm exists in a world where he's constantly reminded that other people view him as grotesque and monstrous, reinforcing his self-loathing and unease in his own body—as, for centuries, from the Middle Ages onward, monstrous images of Jews

Figure 3.3. Stan Lee and Jack Kirby, *Fantastic Four* #40, Marvel Comics, April 1965, 14.

pervaded European culture and were internalized, in turn, by Jews themselves. As Sander Gilman details in his groundbreaking study *The Jew's Body*, Jewish bodies were routinely represented throughout Europe as stunted, misshapen, diseased, and weak. "There is no category of supposed human beings which comes closer to the Orang-Utan than does a Polish Jew," an eighteenth-century Viennese intellectual declared, "covered from foot to head in filth, dirt and rags, covered in a type of black sack . . . their necks exposed, the color of a Black, their faces covered up to the eyes with a beard . . . the hair turned and knotted as if they all suffered from the 'plica polonica' [a dermatologic disease endemic to Eastern Europe]" (quoted in Gilman 172). Immersed in a culture in which such images were pervasive, Jews began to believe them too. "The Jew's experience of his or her own body," Gilman writes, "was so deeply impacted by anti-Semitic rhetoric that even when that body met the expectations for perfection in the community in which the Jew lived, the Jew experienced his or her body as flawed, diseased" (179). They were monsters, in a way, like Ben Grimm, who, no matter how many heroic deeds he performed, would always be just a Thing. "Maybe this is the *real* me!" he wondered at the end of one of Kirby and Lee's most iconic stories, "This Man . . . This Monster!" from *Fantastic Four* #51. "Maybe *Ben Grimm* is nothin' more than—a *dream*!"

Who knows how this heritage of internalized difference and body shame was felt by Kirby and Lee? In Abraham Josephine Riesman's biography of Stan Lee, *True Believer*, Riesman documents the pogrom that Lee's father lived through as a child in Romania, amidst a resurgence of anti-Semitism, and observes that "The impact of such trauma on a human being and its reverberations in that person's children should never be underestimated" (21). Did Kirby and Lee inherit some trace of the internal divisions and body shame described by Gilman, a generational trauma brought to America by Jacob Kurtzberg's and Stanley Lieber's parents, packed away with whatever other rags and keepsakes they could carry? If so, then perhaps this legacy, the inherited weight of all those cultural images speak through that silence on the page about Kirby and Lee's Jewish identities by taking the warped and mutated forms of the Thing and so many other outcast heroes in the Marvel Universe—including Spider-Man, the Hulk, and the X-Men, who were themselves a feared minority of mutants. Mistrusted, denounced, and often perceived as monsters, these characters at once internalize these perceptions and drive themselves to rise above them, trying again and again to show the very people who fear them that they are not so different and that they can even be heroes too, trying in their own ways to assimilate, like the American Jews of Kirby and Lee's generation.

If the origins of Superman in 1938 and Captain America in 1940 are myths of successful assimilation and Americanization, Marvel's characters in the 1960s can't hide or escape from the difference that separates them from a "normal" world that they desperately want to accept them. That difference is written on their bodies, and any attempt to repress or transform it inevitably fails. Yes, sometimes they might be celebrated as heroes, but that status is never secure. There's a current of suspicion and fear that won't go away just beneath the surface of the world, an ember of hatred in human hearts waiting to be inflamed by a signal from space or some less fantastic earthly means. If they find any lasting community at all, it's only among their own kind, those others transformed by cosmic rays or radioactive spiders or mutant genes triggered by birth in the atomic age.

Did I recognize any of this as a child, lost in another issue of *Fantastic Four* or *Spider-Man*? Not consciously, no. But there was a tension I felt in my world too, a palpable sense of separation that defined its borders, inscribed in the names of the families in our neighborhood: the Rosens, the Feinsteins, the Cohens, the Kobres. There was an otherness that was manifest in where we lived, how we socialized, in the holidays we celebrated, and in that strange, uncomfortable way I felt every year singing Christmas songs in school assemblies. If, as I got older, I let myself think that Jewish identity in America hardly mattered any more, history would prove me wrong after neo-Nazis and white supremacists marched in Charlottesville, Virginia, in 2017, chanting "Jews will not replace us"; after a mass shooting in 2018 at the Tree of Life synagogue in Pittsburgh, only a few miles from my sister's home; and after another shooting at a synagogue in San Diego in 2019. And yet being Jewish has become more complicated too as I write this now, as the war in Gaza rages on after the horrors of the October 7, 2023, attack in Israel by Hamas, with tens of thousands of civilians in Gaza killed and starved in a siege campaign directed by an extremist Israeli government that looks nothing like the heroic pioneers my Hebrew school teachers talked about, a government whose most virulent members openly call for ethnic cleansing and annexation, echoing the oppressors that Jews had fled to Palestine to escape. In the wake of protests against the carnage in Gaza, even the charge of anti-Semitism has become a political weapon in the United States, used cynically to restrict free expression by the administration of a president who called the neo-Nazis in Charlottesville "very fine people."

In some ways, my Jewish identity was simpler as child. The community I lived in, as I had been made to understand, was different, and its history was often tragic. And in a way I felt but couldn't articulate, the sense of difference that defined my world was reflected for me on the pages of my comic books, transformed and intensified in the larger-than-life forms of superheroes. In *Hellboy's World*, Scott Bukatman says of his study of comics, "I give myself up to the drift of the text, letting it take me where it wants to go, remaining attentive not just to what the text says, but how it feels" (18). Judaism isn't the subject of Marvel comics or even *a* subject, except in the most glancing ways. Yet that inchoate identification I felt as a child is clearer today and its pull is as strong as ever. Part of the reason for this, of course, comes from my understanding now of how the comic book industry was largely created by Jews, who toiled in a ghettoized trade and created work dismissed as junk, with the same heritage of conflict and exile as me. But there's something more as well. Because among the many powers of superheroes is their ability to sustain multiple meanings and foster all kinds of imaginative transactions, a protean quality that arises in part from their long narrative lives over many decades, reinterpreted continuously by many generations of creators and fans. So why couldn't a man trapped in a body of orange rocks and always achingly aware of his own difference be like me too? Wasn't he also the hero after all, no matter how he looked or how outcast he felt?

Forty-one years after his introduction in *Fantastic Four* #1, in a 2002 story written by Karl Kessel and drawn by Stuart Immonen, one of the many subsequent creative teams since Kirby and Lee had left the series, the Thing would finally come out as Jewish. In a story full of the kind of braided history that all those different creative teams over the years had added retroactively to the ongoing narratives of enduring characters like the Fantastic Four, the Thing goes back to Yancy Street where he grew up to return a Star of David necklace to a Jewish pawnbroker whom a teenage Ben Grimm had stolen it from to win his membership in the Yancy Street Gang (a group of mostly unseen background characters, first introduced in the earliest issues, who regularly tormented the Thing with practical jokes). But when the pawnbroker, Mr. Scheckerburg, is injured on the sidelines of a battle between the Thing and an entirely forgettable supervillain who's forcing the Yancy Street businesses to pay protection, the Thing is helpless, once again a prisoner of his own monstrous form. "Me giving him CPR could *crush* him," Ben says, and so, hesitantly at first—"Lessee. . . . Been a while . . . ," he admits—he prays instead, reciting the words of the Shema, that central prayer to all Jewish services, which, as my Hebrew school teachers said, had been the last words of Rabbi Akiva in the second century, recited by dying lips as Roman soldiers flayed his skin for the crime of teaching Torah. When Scheckerburg recovers and asks if Ben is "ashamed" of his identity—"All those years in the news, they never mention you're *Jewish*," the pawnbroker says—Ben's response is telling, as he seems to acknowledge, in a sideways fashion, the long history of depicting Jewish bodies as monstrous.

Figure 3.4. Jack Kirby, Hanukah card to David Folkman, 1975. First published in *Kirby: King of Comics by Mark Evanier*, Abrams, 2008, 212.

"It's just . . . I don't talk it *up*, is all," he says. "Figure there's *enough* trouble in the world without people thinkin' Jews are all *monsters* like *me*." In later issues too, other creators would build on his Jewish identity. In 2006, the Thing would celebrate his bar mitzvah, thirteen years—in story time, that is—after being transformed into a monster. And in a 2018 issue, he would marry his girlfriend Alicia in a Jewish ceremony, in which he was pictured on the cover as Kirby had drawn him for that 1975 Hanukkah card, in a coat and tie, wearing a yarmulke and prayer shawl.

He was apparently, as I'd always somehow sensed, another nice Jewish boy, part of my community. In a way too, he represented the best kind of Jewish identity to me. He might have been misunderstood, feared sometimes, but life was sacred to him, and he always fought for others, even when the odds were against him, whether it was the Hulk rampaging through New York City or Galactus threatening to eat the whole planet. He might have been a tough guy too, but he wasn't afraid to show his emotions. You could see him tearing up after Sue and Johnny's father was killed in #32 and when Reed and Sue announced that their son Franklin's middle name was Benjamin in #94. The Thing was, to use a Yiddish term, a *mensch*. As

Kirby said in 1989, "He was always a human being, despite his physical change" (quoted in Groth 41). *Mazel tov*, Ben Grimm. *Yasher Koach*, may you always have strength.

Notes

1. Parsing out how to attribute creative credit for Marvel Comics in its early years has generated fierce arguments for decades. In what Stan Lee called "the Marvel Method," artists didn't work from complete scripts but from plot descriptions generated in loose conversations that may or may not have ever been written down. After something resembling a story conference, which was sometimes just a quick phone call, the artists would create finished pages that Lee would add dialogue and captions to later. Given this method, I believe that Kirby and Ditko were the primary creators behind *Fantastic Four*, *Spider-Man* and other core Marvel titles and characters, with Lee in a vital role establishing the tone of individual comics in his scripting and shaping the connective tissue across the whole line as its editor. As Charles Hatfield says in his book on Kirby, *Hand of Fire*, the Marvel method "placed the cartoonist in the driver's seat narratively, calling on them to break down plots and lay out pages on their own without minute, page-by-page input from another [creator]" (90).

2. That operation to cure "nostrility" became better known as "the nose job." The information on its creator, the surgeon Jacques Joseph, born Jacob Joseph, comes from *The Jew's Body* by Sander Gilman, pages 181–88.

3. The information on Kirby's membership in Temple Etz Chaim, in Thousand Oaks, California, is drawn from the article "You Don't Know Jack" by Michael Aushenker, published in *Jewish Journal* on August 23, 2001, and from the article "Circle of Friends," published in *Jack Kirby Collector* #78, Winter 2020.

4. To be sure, some of these arguments for Jewish subtexts are a little forced. Is Superman's motto, "Truth, Justice, and the American Way," introduced in the opening of his radio show in 1942, really an echo of a passage from ancient rabbinical literature, the *Mishnah*, as Simcha Weinstein suggests in *Up, Up, and Oy Vey!* (28)? Arguments like this, which seem more willed than grounded in fact, encourage skepticism, like Sean Guynes and Martin Lund's dismissal of "the so-called Jewish comics connection" in the introduction to their edited collection *Unstable Masks* (10). But that connection and the subtexts it inspires derive from the historical facts about the backgrounds of so many key comic book creators in the early years of the industry and from the culture of Ashkenazi Judaism, with all its internal conflicts and contradictions, which they inherited as first-generation Americans—as I argue in this essay.

5. In Ramzi Fawaz's queer reading of *Fantastic Four* in *The New Mutants*, Fawaz describes the Thing as "the neurotic subject of failed masculinity" (76). Yet Fawaz also argues that this seeming failure transforms the Thing into an icon of a queer counterpublic: "Ben is paradoxically unable to perform the assumed functions of hard masculinity—obtaining a job, getting married, having sex—which makes him a 'sissy.' Rather than a cautionary tale, however, it was The Thing's neuroses that audiences identified with, similarly encouraged by the logic of the comic book to refuse identification with normative masculinity" (77).

Works Cited

Baron-Carvais, Annie. "Jack Kirby Interview." *The Jack Kirby Collector*, vol. 4, no. 16, July 1997, pp. 16–23.

"Bernard R. Ruben Obituary." *The Columbus Dispatch*, 13 Mar. 2007, www.legacy.com/obituaries/dispatch/obituary.aspx?n=bernard-r-ruben&pid=86779721/.

Bukatman, Scott. *Hellboy's World: Comics and Monsters on the Margins*. U of California P, 2016.

"Circle of Friends." *Jack Kirby Collector*, vol. 27, no. 78, Winter 2020, pp. 63–64.

Evanier, Mark. *Kirby: King of Comics*. Abrams, 2008.

Fawaz, Ramzi. *The New Mutants: Superheroes and the Radical Imagination of American Comics*. NYU Press, 2016.

Feiffer, Jules. "The Minsk Theory of Krypton." *The New York Times*, 29 December 1996.

Friedrich, Gary, Dick Ayers, and John Severin. "Izzy Shoots the Works!" *Sgt. Fury and His Howling Commandos*, vol. 1, no. 54, May 1968.

Gilman, Sander. *The Jew's Body*. Routledge, 1991.

Groth, Gary. "I've Never Done Anything Halfheartedly." *The Comics Journal Library: Jack Kirby*, Fantagraphics, 2002, pp. 18–49.

Guynes, Sean, and Martin Lund. "Introduction: Not to Interpret, But to Abolish: Whiteness Studies and American Superhero Comics." *Unstable Masks: Whiteness and American Superhero Comics*, edited by Sean Guynes and Martin Lund, Ohio State UP, 2020, pp. 1–16.

Hatfield, Charles. *Hand of Fire: The Comics Art of Jack Kirby*. UP of Mississippi, 2011.

Howe, Irving. *World of Our Fathers: The Journey of the East European Jews to America and the Life They Found and Made*. Harcourt, 1976.

Jones, Gerard. *Men of Tomorrow: Geeks, Gangsters, and the Birth of the Comic Book*. Basic Books, 2004.

Kessel, Karl, and Stuart Immonen. "Remembrance of Things Past." *Fantastic Four*, vol. 3, no. 56, Aug. 2002.

Kirby, Jack. "Street Code." *Kirby: King of Comics*, by Mark Evanier, Abrams, 2008, pp. 24–33.

Lee, Stan, and Jack Kirby. "The Battle of the Baxter Building!" *Fantastic Four*, vol. 1, no. 40, July 1965.

Lee, Stan, and Jack Kirby. "Prisoners of Kurgo, Master of Planet X." *Epic Collection: The World's Greatest Comic Magazine*, Marvel, 2014, pp. 155–79.

Lee, Stan, and Jack Kirby. "This Man . . . This Monster!" *Fantastic Four*, vol. 1, no. 51, June 1966.

Pekar, Harvey. *Not the Israel My Parents Promised Me*. Hill and Wang, 2012.

Riesman, Abraham Josephine. *True Believer: The Rise and Fall of Stan Lee*. Crown, 2021.

Weinstein, Simcha. *Up, Up, and Oy Vey! How Jewish History, Culture and Values Shaped the Comic Book Superhero*. Barricade Books, 2006.

4

THE *ENIGMA* OF ALWAYS BEING OTHER

A Path Toward Research and Reflection

Michelle Bumatay

At about thirteen, I stumbled on an intriguing text at a going-out-of-business sale while I was with my family on our annual Thanksgiving trek from my Southern California beach-city hometown to visit relatives in the state's central valley. My family, which consists of avid readers, decided to check out the soon-to-be-closing bookstore to stock up on reading material, willing to take risks thanks to the extremely discounted prices. I remember a sense of sadness at the loss of a bookstore coupled with the anticipation of acquiring hours of entertainment for next to no cost. Outings to large chain bookstores had already become one of our regular pastimes. Under the pretense of needing to pick up the newest publication by some well-known author, my parents would drive us to Barnes and Noble, Borders, or Crown Books, and each of us would disperse upon entry to our own beloved sections and inevitably meander through the entire store. On such occasions, it was rare that we all left with something. Unlike many of my friends' parents, my mom and dad found it easy to say no to frequent purchases. This is not to say that they didn't spoil me and my older sister on holidays and birthdays. Rather, it demonstrates how they taught me that though I might want something, it did not mean that I would get it, and also that browsing was a magical form of discovery laced with the heady potential of unforeseen surprises (lessons that were further strengthened by their love of antiquing). Thus, when we drove up to the bookstore in front of which were folding tables covered with piles of books, and my parents told us we could each get at least one book, I tried to temper my giddiness by telling myself that I had an important decision to make.

I can't remember if my parents bought me more than one book because the only one that matters—and which set me on a specific path—was the trade paperback of Vertigo's *Enigma*. The mystery of the title drew me in despite its deliberate obviousness; being the puzzle-lover I am, I couldn't help but pick it up. The juxtaposition of the title with the cover design forecasted an unexpected adventure à la Alice in Wonderland (an emblematic favorite of mine at the time). The front of the multilayered purple cover of the 1995 trade paperback version of Peter Milligan and Duncan Fegredo's *Enigma* miniseries, with moody and dynamic colors by Sherilyn Van Valkenburgh, features a partial mask meant to cover the top half of one's face (an integral accessory for the title character) superimposed over a sea of wriggling lizards of various colors and white curlicues. The back cover presents a three-quarter portrait of Michael Smith, the series's protagonist, covered in lizards as he holds the mask out in front of his face while looking directly at the reader with eyebrows raised. His anticipatory look invites the reader to join him in seeing where the wearing of this mask might lead him.

Flipping through the pages as I stood there, I was immediately struck by the visual chaos of the layouts and artwork, for they were wildly beyond what I knew of comics then, which was not much beyond a tertiary awareness of superhero comics from avid fans among my friend group. It was unclear who the main character was or what the major action of the plot would be, but the bleeds, splash pages, and embedded monthly covers, elegant in their multimedia makeup and beckoning in their abstracted and symbolic composition, convinced me that I would not regret joining Michael on his way down the rabbit hole. That, perhaps like him, I wouldn't be the same on the other side of his journey, which, according to the blurb on the back cover, would be "a tale of sexual obsessions, flying lizards, and superheroes." I added my find to my family's growing pile and anxiously awaited reading it. Though I was cognizant of a major change after finishing *Enigma*—namely, that I had fallen head-over-heels for it, much as Michael falls for the Enigma—I could not have predicted what came next. Looking back, the allure of *Enigma*'s postmodern embrace of alterity for someone like me, someone who has always been "Other," seems blatantly self-evident. Much less obvious is how falling and purposefully climbing down rabbit holes with Michael and the Enigma would eventually lead me back to myself by way of Africa triangulated through France.

Much more recently, during a phone call with my parents on March 19, 2021, in addition to our weekly check-in made even more crucial going into the second year of the COVID-19 pandemic, my mom gave me unsolicited advice, which was not unusual in itself.[1] Yet on that particular day, the advice she provided, seemingly out of the blue, reveals much about our different experiences as Americans. "Don't show your Filipino side as much over there," she told me. This abstract instruction was delivered in the same tone as if she were doling out gardening or baking tips. And though nothing in our conversation up to that point had ventured anywhere near the ever-increasing daily reality of gun violence in the United States, my mom's instruction was undoubtedly her way of demonstrating concern for me in the wake of the gender-based mass shooting in Atlanta, Georgia, just three days prior on March 16. On that Friday, a young white man legally bought a gun and, since Georgia does not have a waiting period to purchase firearms, that very afternoon drove to three separate spas and massage parlors and killed eight people, six of whom were women of Asian descent. He was captured by police a few days later while on his way to Florida (where I live), supposedly to commit more violent murders (Fausset et al.). Though the murderer claimed his actions were not racially motivated, his premeditated killing spree marks a particularly devastating point in an ongoing sharp increase in anti-Asian hate crimes provoked by political rhetoric that scapegoats Asians and Asian Americans for the pandemic and its multifaceted fallout. Like many Americans, I was simultaneously outraged by the magnitude of this tragedy and numb from the regularity of such gun violence.

Since I had spent years learning how to read, or rather listen, between the lines when conversing with my mom, I could nimbly jump with her to new topics, well aware of the unspoken subtext; in this case, the subtext was obvious in spite of the vague language. She lived in southern California in the same house where I grew up, whereas I had moved multiple times further east and south as a result of different academic positions. I thus knew that "over there" meant both that she was worried about my geographic proximity to where the shootings had taken place and that she felt powerless to do more to protect me from regions less culturally diverse than California. The order to be judicious about how I presented myself in public was equally linked to her overall concern, but the tension in her use of the imperative (to not show my Filipino side as much) spoke to a subtext that was much more opaque. It hinted at the complex ways in which race operated differently for each member of my close family (my parents, me, and my older sister) and illustrated how discussing such complexities among ourselves has long been coded, paradoxically both out in the open and not.

Both my parents were born in the United States during World War II to working-class families, an important fact that meant that they shared an awareness of scarcity and rationing as well as a strong belief in education as the most effective vehicle for social mobility. And yet their experiences were drastically different. In the early 1960s, at twenty years old, my white mom moved to California from Ohio, where the majority of both sides of her family had lived since the Revolutionary War. Her upbringing was staunchly anchored in Midwest American culture, yet her move to the West Coast as a young adult tested and tempered her values due to California's diverse population. There she met my dad, born in Delano in the central valley to Filipino migrants who moved to the United States in the 1920s when the Philippines were still an American colony. Born into a migrant family, my dad worked as a child and was repeatedly told by others that success was not for him. When my sister and I would ask about when he was little, he would jokingly respond that he was never little. We would always giggle at his retort's surface-level implication that since he had been a large child, he had therefore never been little. Looking back, his response's deeper purpose comes into focus. He does not have fond memories of his childhood, and he did not want his past to tinge our lives as kids. It wasn't until I was in high school that he told us about how, as a child, he picked grapes and was paid by the crate over a decade before Cesar Chavez helped successfully organize farm workers in the Delano grape strike, which improved farm labor locally and nationally. By ten, even though he was underage, my dad drove a delivery truck, making rounds before heading to school. Forestalling any discussion about his childhood while my sister and I were young allowed him the necessary distance to create a different environment for us. Like most parents, he and my mom worked to provide better circumstances for us, which involved conscientiously shielding us from their respective hardships, different as they were, and from the discrimination they both faced as a mixed couple who had been together since the early 1960s.

Throughout my childhood, the cultural differences between the two sides of my extended family were downplayed and framed as differences between the state of Ohio (read conservative Midwest) and the state of California (read liberal West Coast), but I vaguely knew there was more under the surface than what was discussed openly. Obviously, I recognized that the two sides of the family looked different and had different dietary preferences, but as a child, it made sense due to the diversity within my own nuclear family unit. We all had different skin colors, tanned at different rates (my sister always being the lightest), and stood by our favorite ice cream flavor. Moreover, we all had our own interests and, since both my parents worked, we all helped out with chores. Without explicitly telling me, my family taught me the value of individuality within a community of equals. Neither race nor gender ever seemed important, at least not as important as the personality, talents, and passions of each member. Unsurprisingly, school was where I would learn how unlike those around us we were.

My internal logic that each person is unique, a banal yet crucial foundational belief, influenced how I understood my grade-school classmates. It made sense that some of my peers excelled at math or art while others dominated at games during recess. Yet I quickly realized that diversity and uniqueness were not the norm for everyone. Living in a predominantly white neighborhood and attending a predominantly white school in a Southern California beach city, I was introduced to and repeatedly reminded of whiteness's intersection with cisgender heteronormativity and bourgeois middle-class values. Many of the boys were interested in becoming professional surfers, while the girls were categorized as either blond or brunette. Additionally, most of my classmates' moms didn't work and not only walked their child to school but were often there to volunteer or bring cupcakes to the whole class for their child's birthday. My parents, both teachers, left early each day to commute to cities in opposite directions, my mom to an affluent region of southern Orange County and my dad to a richly diverse area inland with a high density of several diasporic Asian communities (primarily Vietnamese and Korean). As a result, I walked to school with other neighborhood kids, and after school, I took a shuttle with only two other students (both of whom were also not white) to the Boys & Girls Club to be picked up hours later by one of my parents. Though having to wait for the shuttle as my friends' parents picked them up was not what I wanted as a kid, once at the Boys & Girls Club, I played and, thanks to my parents' practicality and involvement with the club's board, took lessons in dance, music, and art. To be sure, I was often too busy and in too much of a rush to be concerned about my difference.

Around the age of seven, I started to notice the yearly standardized tests we had to take. Through these institutional data-gathering and measuring practices I became aware of how out-of-sight, nameless, faceless adults prescribed a system for articulating difference. Each year, when the teachers read over the test instructions, I was reminded to use a No. 2 pencil, to write my name clearly, to completely fill in one oval per question, to check the box for my sex, and to check the box for my race. And each year, without hesitation, I checked the box for "Other." None of the other options available came close to describing my situation, and so I did not select them, nor did I identify with them. To be sure, the options in the 1980s were far from extensive, yet I didn't consider myself white or Asian, and neither did those around me (a social reality with a deeper history I only recently uncovered). While I can't quite recall the exact conversations with my family about this, my impression is that when I mentioned my choice ("Other"), we all laughed quite similarly to how we would when my dad insisted that he had never been little. With each year and round of tests, my identification with the category "Other" only became stronger, yet I never considered it negative in the slightest. Conversely, though "Male" and "Female" were the only options for sex, and though I chose "Female," I didn't feel particularly aligned with either choice. Whereas the large majority of my classmates fell easily into one category, my practical bowl haircut and overalls, when coupled with my racial ambiguity, contributed to me often being misgendered when out with my family (figure 4.1). It definitely didn't help that for my third-grade play about the solar system, while other kids got to be a planet, the sun, or famous comets, I was assigned the abstract concept of friction.

As a kid I didn't know how all this would impact my decisions and sense of self, but it also didn't matter. This transitory fluidness allowed me to take on the identity of any character with relative ease, but it's no wonder that my strongest preference was for equally elastic (Alice) and ambiguous (Yoshi and Link from Zelda) characters in unstable, malleable worlds. Through reading and video games, I took on whatever other personality I wanted, which primed me to fall hard for *Enigma* when I selected it from the going-out-of-business bookstore. Its unabashedly postmodern narrative resonated with my adolescent indifference toward origins and ownership. Though I loved my extended family and enjoyed visiting them in different parts of California and across the nation (from Hawaii to Ohio and Florida), I was uninterested in any sense of competitive pride in one's place of birth. My young-person logic told me that everyone came from somewhere, but that was not the same thing as who that person was.

Peter Milligan and Duncan Fegredo's *Enigma*, released in 1993 as an eight-issue limited series, helped launch Karen Berger's DC Comics imprint

Figure 4.1. Author's personal archive.

Vertigo, which was geared toward more adult content and played a crucial role in radically changing mainstream Anglo-American comics.[2] Though the disclaimer on the back of the 1995 trade paperback version—"Suggested for mature readers"—alerted would-be purchasers to the series's deviation from typical mainstream comics that adhered to the Comics Code Authority's standards, this was not alarming for me. I had already consumed much adult content by then, reading as much Stephen King as I could get my hands on and watching television series and films (such as *Jacob's Ladder* and *The Rocky Horror Picture Show*) with my older sister without a thought for whether or not they were appropriate. What did intrigue me was the series' postmodern approach and grappling with existential questions, though at that age I had no idea what either postmodernism or existentialism were. Recounted by a wry narrator revealed on the last page as a talking lizard, *Enigma* centers on Michael Smith (whose name literally spells out his mundaneness) as his average life in Pacific City, California, is turned upside down by a spate of crimes carried out by people transformed into outlandish supervillains from his favorite childhood comic,

Enigma. Following a floating lizard, Michael becomes victim to one of the characters, the Head, and though he is rescued by the comic's eponymous superhero the Enigma, he remains in a coma. Just as the doctors are about to take him off life support, Michael thrashes awake with the realization that the Enigma must have the answers. In a feverish quest to learn the truth, Michael seeks out Titus Bird, author of the comics, who also doesn't know the origins of the bizarre appearances. While discussing possibilities, Titus hits on Michael, who immediately punches him in the face hard enough to knock him off his stool. When Titus tries to apologize, Michael angrily chastises him for assuming he was queer. However, as the two continue on their journey to uncover the truth, Michael starts to change. He has an erotic dream about the Enigma, nervously ventures to a gay bar on his own, and breaks up with his girlfriend. These important steps precede when he finally comes face to face with the Enigma while looking for answers in his destroyed childhood home. In an emotional discussion on a rooftop, Michael inquires after the Enigma's secret identity just before stepping off the edge of the roof of his own volition (figure 4.2). Of course, the Enigma uses his superpowers to save him, thus confirming Michael's suspicions that he is a superbeing. The scene ends with another fall, but this time it is a metaphorical one; Michael lets himself fall for the Enigma and the two become lovers. In a heated argument during the denouement, Michael asks the Enigma to remove his mask to tell him the truth; he finally learns that the Enigma used his superpowers on him like he did on other creatures. Having been abandoned in a well as an infant by his mother, another superbeing, the Enigma learned to cast his consciousness into other beings. Ultimately, his loneliness prompted him to create the villains and make Michael fall in love with him. Despite being angry at first, Michael embraces being gay, his own figurative mask gone as well. The story ends with him, Titus, and the Enigma walking hand in hand to face the Enigma's violent mother set on killing her son. On the last page, the three walk out of view, and the story hones in on a lizard transformed by the Enigma, who finishes telling the story only to restart it again for the unaltered lizards listening to him.

Though the opening narration lays out the banality of Michael's routine heteronormative life, Fegredo's early chaotic style heavily laden with pen and ink lines created an atmospheric buzzing that I instantly recognized. From the first time we see Michael on page three, his reality already felt like a sham or a mask to me because there were other, more real forces just under the surface that one could almost make out (figure 4.3). It was the same feeling I

Figure 4.2. Peter Milligan, Duncan Fegredo, and Sherilyn Van Valkenburgh, *Enigma: The Definitive Edition*, Berger Books, October 2021, 153.

Figure 4.3. Peter Milligan, Duncan Fegredo, and Sherilyn Van Valkenburgh, *Enigma: The Definitive Edition*, Berger Books, October 2021, 10.

got watching the work of David Lynch and Tim Burton, and, when I first saw *The Matrix* by the Wachowskis, it was almost like watching *Enigma* on screen. In fact, the immediate tension generated between the matter-of-factness of Michael's quotidian experience and Fegredo's densely packed, supercharged artwork drew me in much more than the spate of comic book characters made flesh who started appearing and wreaking havoc.

As many have pointed out, *Enigma*'s main thrust revolves around "the nature of identity—both how it's formed and what it means" for Michael as well as the Enigma (Carey). Though the refinement of Fegredo's style and page layout was a byproduct of his becoming more skilled at working with pen and ink and not intended from the start, it naturally supports Michael's shifting sense of self, an aptly fortuitous development for the series as the creators have pointed out (Milligan 5; Fegredo 215). Indeed, *Enigma*'s magnetic charm is its beautifully chaotic ability to operate simultaneously on multiple levels. In addition to being about Michael's discovery and acceptance of being gay and about the Enigma's struggle against existential loneliness, it is also a story about stories and their impact on the nature of identity. As Isabelle Licari-Guillaume eloquently puts it,

> *Enigma* locates itself in the work of the "revisionist" phase of the superhero genre, which questioned the politics and aesthetics of hero figures, notably by encouraging metatextual engagement with the genre's history. Moreover, Milligan and Fegredo's deviation from genre conventions directly corresponds with their main character's quest for individual identity, as Michael swerves from the straight line of social and sexual orthodoxy to reassert his agency over his own life: by accepting to hold a *decentered* or *marginal* position in society (both as a homosexual and as a comics fan), Michael reclaims his body as the perceptual, subjective *center* of his life. (46–47, emphasis in the original)

The multipronged questioning of politics, aesthetics, and identity from a doubly marginal position undoubtedly struck a chord with me. Equally important, *Enigma*'s metatextual relationship with comics gave me an opening into a world that I had only previously glimpsed and about which I was apprehensive. My exposure to comics culture up to then led me to believe that it was an exclusively masculine space with a high entry threshold based on encyclopedic knowledge of superheroes and their abilities. Since Michael was a proxy for the reader and since his transformation was woven from comics' past, I could vicariously take on having always been an avid comics reader, thereby bypassing such a threshold. Furthermore, with *Enigma*, Milligan and Fegredo showed me how readers' responses could and often did deviate from authors' intentions; how, unlike the lizards listening to the narrator, we, like Michael and the Enigma, have the agency to interpret stories and decide what meaning they hold for us; and how comics themselves could be a powerful form of worldbuilding, storytelling, and identity formation.

Had it not been for my encounter with the trade paperback of *Enigma*, it is likely I never would have started down this particular path. As my first taste of what comics could be beyond the funnies and superhero comics, *Enigma* spoiled me by generating a hungry expectation for intoxicating, labyrinthine narratives powered by energetic in-your-face artwork and colors. At the material level, this version cued me in to the episodic nature of monthly issued comics while allowing me to experience the arc in a holistic, self-contained way. The format helped me appreciate the narrative playfulness of serialization and *mise en abyme*, which made the twinned evolutions of Michael's transformation and Fegredo's artwork easily legible over the course of the series. Rather than reading the cliffhangers as motivation for me to purchase the next month's issue, I considered them pregnant pauses, which resulted in my admiration of Milligan's temporal jumps as innovative narrative devices ripe with efficient yet rich worldbuilding. Not to mention I didn't have the means to keep up regularly with graphic novel and trade paperback series, let alone monthly comics. My monthly allowance of $20 was precious for potential larger purchases (a couple years prior I had saved for months to buy my very own Super Nintendo Entertainment System), and public libraries were still years away from collecting comics, graphic novels, and manga. I also lacked transportation to large chain bookstores, and on the rare occasions I had been inside specialty comics stores, I had felt intimidated and, more significantly, ignored and unwelcome. That I lacked knowledge of superheroes and their powers and that I didn't care who would win in a fight precluded me from any conversations, while my ethnic and gender ambiguity rendered me invisible to store employees.

During subsequent family bookstore trips, I thus gravitated toward other punchy graphic novels and trade paperbacks, which meant that I cut my teeth on Frank Miller and Alan Moore before stumbling quickly onto Neil Gaiman's *The Sandman*. Though I had no idea at the time that Vertigo's issuing of *The Sandman* trade paperbacks was "dictated by market demands" such that the second story arc was the first to be released (Round 18), I nevertheless had an atypical reading experience. Due to the infrequency of my purchases, I started with the ones that most appealed to me visually and thus read *The Kindly Ones* and *The Wake*, the last two volumes, before understanding who everyone was. But this bothered me not in the slightest and seemed entirely natural. Consequently, when I took an undergraduate course on French and Belgian *bandes dessinées* a handful of years later in college, I felt right at home even though the context had shifted. And when we read the album version of Moebius's *Arzak*, I fell in love once again. I relished his trailblazing style and aestheticized approach to page layout, and I connected right away with the elasticity of his storytelling exemplified by the various spellings of Arzak/Arzach.

This course became the catalyst for me to apply to graduate school to work on Jean Giraud a.k.a. Moebius, *Le Métal hurlant*, and other influential cartoonists of the 1960s and 1970s. In 2004 when I started applying, I didn't know if my proposed project to work exclusively on *bandes dessinées* would be accepted by any French graduate program, as comics studies was still in its infancy despite the wide support in academia for film studies, media studies, and cultural studies. Yet having always considered myself "Other" meant that I wasn't compelled to reproduce what existed. Since no categories, official or not, seemed to fit me, I assumed both that they weren't for me, or at least I wasn't their target audience; and that they were constructs made by people and could just as well be changed. Way before reading anything by Francophone Caribbean theorists such as Frantz Fanon and Édouard Glissant, I was hard-pressed to put any stock in value systems meant to preserve origins and uncritically reproduce traditions. Luckily, though I had already made plans B and C, both of which included reapplying the following year, I was accepted, much to my dad's delight, to the French and Francophone Studies program at the University of California Los Angeles (UCLA)—his undergraduate alma mater. Not knowing what was in store or where I would land, like Michael in *Enigma*, I let myself fall. While I lacked Michael's certainty that a gorgeous mystery man would save me, my decision to go off into the unknown echoed his choice at the end of the story in that it was a step toward a different me, a becoming, a transformation, with no clear path in sight.[3] How could I have known that a blazing path would emerge almost immediately and that through its twists and turns, it would illuminate everything that had led me there and, in a way, teach me a different way to understand one's origins?

I arrived at UCLA with the intention of studying social and cultural changes in France via experimental, trippy, and adult-oriented *bandes dessinées*, and in less than four months, I was unflinchingly committed to working on *bandes dessinées* by cartoonists from Africa and of African descent. Thanks to hindsight, the links between antiestablishment French cartoonists in the 1960s and 1970s and Francophone cartoonists from former French and Belgian colonies make perfect sense. Undergirding both contexts is my interest in how cartoonists play with identity and reality while exposing and challenging systems of power through the elastic system of comics. It was wondrous to discover that there were passionate cartoonists working throughout Francophone Africa, the French Caribbean, and the Indian Ocean. I was blown away by the sheer diversity of comics already in existence in 2005, and it was only the tip of the iceberg. I initially thought I would be researching African French-language comics with an eye toward national and periodization trends. Other researchers—Christophe Cassiau-Haurie, Alain Brezault, and Sandra Federici—have already made great strides along such lines of inquiry, sketching a rich landscape of comics production since the 1960s. However, to my eyes, the lasting imprint and effects of European colonialism, specifically French and Belgian cultural imperialism, were the instant matrix I sensed within which such comics were crafted. In Francophone Africa the Franco-Belgian mainstream standard of hardback albums with high-quality glossy paper is a luxury well beyond the financial means of local readers to purchase and for cartoonists to produce, a reality aggravated by the fact that the former metropoles' publishing industry easily outperforms and undercuts African publishers. As a result, locally produced comics were, for a long time, often ephemeral objects: daily strips, weekly publications, and self-published zines with limited print runs. This model rarely results in sustainable careers for cartoonists. Like their literary counterparts, many African Francophone cartoonists thus look to European publishers who, in turn, often opt for stories able to attract a wide readership. Looking at the content of the first European-published *bandes dessinées* by African creators such as the early volumes of *Aya de Yopougon* by Marguerite Abouet and Clément Oubrerie, the two-volume *La vie de Pahé* by Pahé (Patrick Essono), and *Malamine, un africain à Paris* by Christophe Edimo and Simon-Pierre Mbumbo, the primary concern, without doubt, is the question of one's identity in a postcolonial setting.

Despite being born and raised in Southern California and only learning French starting in high school, I instantly recognized my experiences in the trials and tribulations of the main characters of these *bandes dessinées*, especially in scenes set in France where the French Republic's colorblind ideology clashed (sometimes violently) with the reality of structural racism carried over from the colonial era. The French state refuses to recognize race or ethnicity as meaningful categories, yet, as Jean Beaman and Amy Petts point out, "race, though repeatedly denied, is nonetheless omnipresent throughout French society" (Beaman and Petts 5).[4] Many scholars of contemporary France and the Francophone world have meticulously demonstrated how this present reality stems from the ad hoc sociopolitical, economic, and military strategies of the French to either maintain the colonial status quo or negotiate decolonization with an outcome as close to the status quo as possible.[5] At the same time as France maneuvered to sustain its imperial might, it actively recruited manpower from the soon-to-be and former colonies first to fight in both World Wars and then, from the 1940s until the 1970s, to rebuild and modernize the country.[6] Due to the twin projects of strategic decolonization and modernizing the nation, there was a steady rise of French subjects and citizens of non-European descent in mainland France whose legal status shifted but whose national belonging remains undermined. In spite of the French Republic's insistence on universal rights for all its citizens, French universalism has been repeatedly called out for its implicit and extreme bias for a white French Catholic identity as the not-actually-neutral standard.

The American Dream and French universalism are powerfully seductive myths that, when coupled with the need for cheap labor throughout the twentieth century, have increased diversity in both countries and consequently generated all sorts of enigmas linked to (im)migration, belonging, and identity. Without realizing it, when I read *Enigma*, I already understood it as an allegory of postcolonialism. Michael's discovery of constructed realities and different kinds of masks was intimately familiar, as was his realization that the real story begins when we decide what value, if any, such constructs and masks have for ourselves. Later, what seized my attention in African Francophone *bandes dessinées* was the exploration of the lived experiences of characters with strong senses of self who were nevertheless enigmas to others, including those closest to them. My instant identification with them had everything to do with the messy unevenness of postcoloniality without actual decolonization—that is, legal and (sometimes) political changes without shifts in ideology or sociocultural norms. I understood on a deep level their experiences of cultural hybridity, repeated unbelonging, and the friction generated by having a fluid identity that continually bumps into external obstacles or, put another way, that misaligns with existing masks. State-crafted definitions of identity that, far from being static, change over time as a function of the confluence of politics, economics, and ideologies. Socially and culturally constructed definitions that are often at odds with legal ones. Interactions with head-spinning bureaucracy, institutional gatekeepers, and all manner of customs and border agents. Like many non-white French people, I have long been an enigma to others who are more invested in placing me than in me. What I look like (at any given time), what I say and how I say it (or don't), what passport I hold, and my actual name all, unsurprisingly, influence how others interact with me and what they say to me. From a lifetime of informally gathering and comparing interactions across contexts, I have learned much about others, their assumptions and preoccupations, and that for them, identifying masks and trying to get behind them are not priorities.

At fifteen, I took a driver's education course through my high school, which included a test drive in groups of three with a certified instructor. When it was my turn behind the wheel, the instructor guided me through checking the mirrors, starting the car, and driving out onto the street. After telling me where to go, he asked me where I was from. While he hadn't asked either of the other kids where they were from and even though I considered myself just as American as them, I knew what his question meant. By that time, I already had a patterned response to such questions, which I knew weren't about my nationality. I told him I was half Filipino, even though both my parents were American from birth. Immediately, the instructor asked if my mom was a nurse and I said, "No, she's a teacher." Since I was focused on not crashing with fellow classmates in the car, I didn't say anything else though I was confused by the specificity of his question. At dinner, when I told my parents what had happened, they cracked up at the blatant stereotypes encoded in his line of questioning, and I laughed with them, but I didn't know why and they didn't explain. A couple of years later I realized that he had obviously assumed my mom was Filipino (and therefore a nurse) and that my dad was white.

In my twenties, when it was my turn to approach the customs agent on my first trip to the United Kingdom, I was curious to see how the mechanisms of categorization and border control would compare with those in France with which I was already familiar. My interaction with the older white British customs agent was short but packed a punch. He looked over my passport with the same blank, stern expression I recognized from France and the United States that implied serious scrutiny was taking place. Without looking up from my passport, he asked how long I intended to stay and what the purpose of my visit was (I was there for a week-long comics conference). He then looked up at me, pronounced my last name, and declared that his housekeeper was Filipino before telling me to enjoy my stay. Obviously he knew I was American since he had just been holding my passport. Yet he was compelled to out me, or at least out the heritage of my family name. But to what end? Though his comment could have been an attempt to generate a connection through his recognition of a Filipino last name, it wasn't. As a declarative statement about his reality, it was not an invitation for dialogue. It was a demonstration of a sort of satisfaction at being able to place me into a container familiar to him. According to his logic, that I was a woman with a Filipino last name trumped (and always would) my Southern California accent and American passport. Similarly, as with the driving instructor, I was cast in a domestic care-giving role, lumped together as an object resembling other objects.

Knowing more about the ongoing mixed legacies of European and American imperialisms has shed light on such encounters, but does not mean that I'm done bumping into obstacles. Quite the contrary. Now, all interactions, big and small, teeter on the edge of becoming a freefall toward more questions. Returning to the phone call with my mom in the spring of 2021 and her instruction ("Don't show your Filipino side as much over there"), how could I follow her advice? Which side? Front, back, left, right? Was it my nose that we all jokingly tried to straighten when I was little by pinching the bridge so I wouldn't look too Filipino? (I only recently found out that this was not unique to the quirkiness of my family!) My brown skin and dark hair that, in Southern California, telegraphed that I must be Latinx, especially since I easily outgrew my Filipino grandma at the age of ten? Or if she didn't mean that I should downplay any physical features, which are rarely read as Filipino, what constitutes my Filipino side? Is it a language I don't speak (Tagalog), or an accent I don't have? My nostalgia for adobo, even though I've been vegetarian since I graduated high school? Do I even have a Filipino side to show? Instead of asking my mom what she thought constituted my Filipino side and what concrete steps she'd suggest for me to not show it as much, as usual I made a joke out of it, asking whether she meant the front or back of me. In my attempt to be a dutiful daughter and allay her worrying in place of following her advice, I reminded her that since no one knew what I was anyway, I was nonthreatening and out of harm's way. And while I have developed a range of survival strategies based on my ability to read the deep structure of various sociocultural contexts, this is not true.

Though becoming a bilingual chameleon (one might even say a talking lizard à la Milligan and Fegredo) helps me discern matrices around me, it is also a source of intense unbelonging. As mentioned, in Southern California, others have always assumed that I am Latinx and that I therefore speak Spanish, which I don't. Though my parents studied various European languages in high school and college (my mom even majored in French), both only spoke English growing up; we were thus a monolingual household. For me, though Spanish would have been much more practical in Southern California, like my mom and my sister before me, I chose French as my second language in high school as it was an abstract way of connecting with my mom's ancestry. However, whenever people spoke Spanish to me, most often without asking if I spoke Spanish, I did my best to listen for cognates and leverage what vocabulary I knew. Inevitably, instead of being perceived as a lack of language proficiency, my inability to communicate was regularly read as a refusal to speak Spanish in an effort to deny what was assumed to be my cultural and ethnic background. While some people scoffed at me, others would shame me for rejecting what wasn't even part of my family's heritage. It wasn't until college that I was frequently around other Filipino Americans and Filipinos. At first, it was a delight to be with so many others that looked like me, and I was curious to compare notes about our lived experiences. It thus initially came as a shock to once again be subjected to scoffs and shaming with the addition of others' pity when they learned that I didn't speak Tagalog and neither did my dad, because his parents pushed him and his siblings to assimilate. Due to such encounters, when I first read Frantz Fanon's *Black Skin, White Masks*, it made perfect sense to me that he would devote the first chapter to the various individual and communal anxieties around language. Put another way, like Michael, I learned the value of identifying masks and getting at what is behind them.

Studying the intersection of race, postcolonialism, and immigration in France has helped me better understand my interactions with others, as well as the generational differences between my paternal grandparents, my dad and his siblings, and my sister and me; but it has also prompted me to dig more into my own context. In episode six of *Enigma*, appropriately titled "The End of the World," Michael's drive to uncover the truth takes him back to his childhood. We learn that his West Coast home collapsed into a dangerous pit during an earthquake and that his father's body was never recovered from the sunken structure. It is also the episode in which the Enigma first discusses his own origin of having grown up in a well and Michael shyly recounts his first steps exploring his homosexuality. This dual descent into the past with new eyes marks a pivotal shift for both characters. Like them, a descent into my past with a new perspective recast what I thought I knew. For instance, when I was young, my dad would share large black and white photographs with us as he proudly explained how his cousins were extras in Hollywood films from the 1930s playing Chinese peasants, Native Americans, and Mexican cowboys. When I was younger, I understood this as similar to my own tendency to select the box for "Other" on standardized tests. I didn't learn until recently that since the Philippines was still an American colony at the time, our cousins (and my grandparents) weren't American citizens and that there were laws preventing them from owning land (Tamayo Lott 12). As a workaround, some Filipinos would leverage their Spanish last names (resulting from the previous imperial occupiers of the Philippines since the 1500s) to pass for Mexican in order to purchase land (Rock and Yeh). Potential residual resentment that some Filipinos could pass in a way that (im)migrants from other Asian countries couldn't back then might partially explain why other Asian Americans, even in my close friend group, have never considered me Asian.

Paradoxically, in California, Filipinos have been too Asian, not Asian enough, Latinx-adjacent, and, more recently, white. These complex twists and turns bubble up in unexpected ways in my own life. I've always loved hearing about how my parents met and when they started dating. During a group outing to a concert, they squeezed into a tiny car with a comedic number of other young adults and though they were with others, the two of them talked only to each other the whole night. Soon after, my dad called my mom and left a message with her roommate, but since my mom's Mormon roommate never delivered the message because she didn't think they should date, my mom assumed my dad was uninterested. Luckily, they lived in a small town, and the odds of running into each other again were high. In their stories, the next couple of years were full of fun and adventures through a long engagement. When I was little, it didn't occur to me that they would be apprehensive because of the unevenness of state and federal antimiscegenation laws. In 1933, due in part to the Watsonville Anti-Filipino Riot just three years earlier in which Filipino men were attacked for ostensibly stealing work and white women from white Californians, the state added Filipinos to the existing antimiscegenation laws.

California was one of the first states to strike down all antimiscegenation laws in 1948, yet my parents waited. They didn't wed until a couple of years after the *Loving v. Virginia* supreme court case in 1967, which declared all laws banning interracial marriage a violation of rights. Of course, neither of my parents ever framed their stories through a political lens, which has made learning about California's legal history a kind of out-of-body experience. Just as laws in the past sought to limit my relatives' access to social mobility, they have shaped my trajectory. When I was four, "Filipinos were eliminated from affirmative action recruitment and admissions programs in California . . . they [thus] technically [fell] out of the 'other' category, suffering the brunt of being mistakenly included in the majority" (Maramba and Bonus xv–xvi). This means that while I was checking the box for "Other," I should have been checking the box for "White." Looking back, it seems appropriate that I would misidentify myself just as everyone else does.

Instead of trying to fit into a matrix that wasn't intended for me and that recalculates in an ad hoc manner, I am all for leaning into the messiness and walking off into the unknown. Deciding to fall with Michael Smith and walk off into an unknown future with him and his chosen family, the Enigma and Titus, allowed me to see comics as an infinitely rich multimodal site for experimentation and worldbuilding. Continuing down the rabbit hole by way of other series, I found my way to *bandes dessinées* by African Francophone cartoonists exploring questions of postcoloniality, identity, and belonging. That life writing in comics has only flourished in the decades since I started on this path speaks to the power of this medium to engage deeply with crucial questions and facilitate new understanding. Indeed, as *Enigma* demonstrated decades ago, reading comics helps us identify masks, interrogate them, and get behind them to see through others' eyes in the name of better understanding those around us and ourselves.

Notes

1. I would like to dedicate this chapter to both my parents and especially my mom, who instilled a love of reading in me, who encouraged my curiosity, who let me go on adventures even when they took me far from her, and who passed away in the time between when I started writing this chapter and when I finished it.

2. For more on Vertigo's impact under editor Karen Berger, see Julia Round, "'Is This a Book?'"; Christophe Dony, "The Rewriting Ethos of the Vertigo Imprint"; and Isabelle Licari-Guillaume, *Vertigo Comics*.

3. As education was of prime importance in my family, there was never any question as to whether I would go to college. Both my parents and my sister earned undergraduate degrees, as did both of my maternal grandparents, but not my paternal grandparents. My dad and his siblings were the first in his family to attend college. As a sort of echo, I was the first to go on to earn a doctoral degree. Hence, while I felt well-informed going into my undergraduate experience, I was dramatically under-prepared for and often comedically confused about graduate school.

4. For more on the friction between France's ethos of colorblindness and the reality of race in France, see *Race in France: Interdisciplinary Perspectives on the Politics of Difference*, edited by Herrick Chapman and Laura L. Frader; and *Black France / France Noire: The History and Politics of Blackness*, edited by Trica Danielle Keaton et al.

5. For key studies, see Michel-Rolph Trouillot, *Silencing the Past*; Todd Shepard, *The Invention of Decolonization*; and Emily Marker, "Obscuring Race."

6. For a detailed cultural analysis of this period, see Kristin Ross, *Fast Cars, Clean Bodies.*

Works Cited

Abouet, Marguerite, and Clément Oubrerie. *Aya de Yopougon*. Vol. 1, Gallimard Jeunesse, 2005.

Abouet, Marguerite, and Clément Oubrerie. *Aya de Yopougon*. Vol. 2, Gallimard Jeunesse, 2006.

Abouet, Marguerite, and Clément Oubrerie. *Aya de Yopougon*. Vol. 3, Gallimard Jeunesse, 2007.

Abouet, Marguerite, and Clément Oubrerie. *Aya de Yopougon*. Vol. 4, Gallimard Jeunesse, 2008.

Beaman, Jean, and Amy Petts. "Towards a Global Theory of Colorblindness: Comparing

Carey, Ryan. "Forever an Enigma: The History and Meaning(s) of Peter Milligan's and Duncan Fegredo's Postmodern Classic." *The Comics Journal*, 8 Dec. 2021, www.tcj.com/forever-an-enigma-the-history-and-meanings-of-peter-milligans-and-duncan-fegredos-postmodern-classic/.

Chapman, Herrick, and Laura L. Frader, editors. *Race in France: Interdisciplinary Perspectives on the Politics of Difference*. Berghahn Books, 2004.

Colorblind Racial Ideology in France and the United States." *Sociology Compass*, vol. 14, no. 4, 2020, pp. 1–11.

Dony, Christophe. "The Rewriting Ethos of the Vertigo Imprint: Critical Perspectives on Memory-Making and Canon Formation in the American Comics Field." *Comicalités, Études de culture graphique*, 2014

Edimo, Christophe, and Simon-Pierre Mbumbo. *Malamine, un Africain à Paris*. Les Enfants Rouges, 2009.

Fanon, Frantz. *Black Skin, White Masks*. Translated by Richard Philcox, Grove Press, 2008.

Fausset, Richard, et al. "8 Dead in Atlanta Spa Shootings, With Fears of Anti-Asian Bias." *The New York Times*, 26 Mar. 2021, www.nytimes.com/live/2021/03/17/us/shooting-atlanta-acworth.

Fegredo, Duncan. "Secret Origins or a Brief History of Style." *Enigma: The Definitive Edition*, by Peter Milligan, Duncan Fegredo, and Sherilyn Van Valkenburgh, Berger Books, 2021, pp. 214–60.

Keaton, Trica Danielle, T. Denean Sharpley-Whiting, and Tyler Stovall, editors. *Black France / France Noire: The History and Politics of Blackness*. Duke UP, 2012.

Licari-Guillaume, Isabelle. "Relocating/Dislocating the Center in Milligan and Fegredo's Enigma." *Leaves*, vol. 6, 2018, pp. 46–60.

Licari-Guillaume, Isabelle. *Vertigo Comics: British Creators, US Editors, and the Marking of a Transformational Imprint*, Routledge, 2023.

Maramba, Dina C., and Rick Bonus, editors. *The "Other" Students: Filipino Americans, Education, and Power*. Information Age Publishing, 2013.

Marker, Emily. "Obscuring Race: Franco-African Conversations about Colonial Reform and Racism after World War II and the Making of Colorblind France, 1945–1950." *French Politics, Culture & Society*, vol. 33, no. 3, 2015, pp. 1–23.

Milligan, Peter. "Introduction: A Straight Man Walks into a Gay Bar . . ." *Enigma: The Definitive Edition*, by Peter Milligan, Duncan Fegredo, and Sherilyn Van Valkenburgh, Berger Books, 2021, pp. 4–5.

Milligan, Peter, Duncan Fegredo, and Sherilyn Van Valkenburgh. *Enigma*. DC Comics, 1995.

Pahé. *La vie de Pahé: Bitam*. Editions Paquet, 2006.

Pahé. *La vie de Pahé: Paname*. Editions Paquet, 2008.

Rock, Craig, Grace Yeh, et al. *Routes and Roots: Cultivating Filipino American History on the Central Coast*. South County Historical Society, 17 Mar. 2010,

Ross, Kristin. *Fast Cars, Clean Bodies: Decolonization and the Reordering of French Society*. MIT Press, 1996.

Round, Julia. "'Is This a Book?' DC Vertigo and the Redefinition of Comics in the 1990s." *The Rise of the American Comics Artist: Creators and Contexts*, edited by Paul Williams and James Lyons, UP of Mississippi, 2010, pp. 14–30.

Shepard, Todd. *The Invention of Decolonization: The Algerian War and the Remaking of France*. Cornell UP, 2006.

Tamayo Lott, Juanita. "Demographic Changes Transforming the Filipino American Community." *Filipino Americans: Transformation and Identity*, edited by Maria P. P. Root, Sage Publications, 1997, pp. 11–20.

Trouillot, Michel-Rolph. *Silencing the Past: Power and the Production of History*. Beacon Press, 1995.

PART 2

TRANSFORMATIONS

5

THE MARVELOUS MUTANT GAZE

On Seeing and Being Bluer[1]

Anna F. Peppard

I was twelve years old the first time a comic book inspired me to touch myself. I don't remember the issue number, writer, or artist, and haven't been able to track it down. But I clearly remember the scene. Peter Parker had a bad dream. When he woke up, he shot upright in bed, shirtless, sweaty, and visibly breathless. Then he touched his bare, sweaty chest, hand resting on his smooth, taut pecs for a single panel that was so much more than that during that formative first encounter, lengthier and dense with meanings my adult self is still struggling to untangle. Before I touched myself, I touched the comic, running my fingers over the absent texture of the lines on the page that both created Peter and caressed him. Then, at last, I touched myself, but not between my legs. Instead, I touched my chest, imagining it was Peter's chest, imagining my chest was Peter's, imagining myself touching Peter, imagining being Peter. My hands may have wandered elsewhere after that, I can't precisely recall. But I'll never forget the erotic charge of that moment, in which I realized I didn't have to choose between having the boy or being him. This genre, which is so suffused with body doublings, transformations, and spectacles, combined with this marvelous medium, in which every sweaty spectacle exists as a frozen moment in time that lets you look however you want to, facilitated fluidities I already felt but made them realer—more visible, urgent, and touchable.

This complex confluence of desires isn't unique to superhero comics. Queer fantasies that vacillate between having, being, and becoming the object of one's desire can be found in any medium or genre, depending on who's looking and how. Yet comics might be especially suited to this type of subjective multiplicity. Scott McCloud's seminal theories of "closure" (63) and "amplification through simplification" (30) describe comics as a medium that thrives off participatory investment, soliciting readers to inhabit universalized faces and bodies and palpate fragments to satisfying states of completion. Darieck Scott and Ramzi Fawaz more explicitly argue, "There's something queer about comics" (197). For Scott and Fawaz, this extends from comics' tendency to embrace outsider protagonists as well as comics' formal properties, wherein "the literal intersection of lines, images, and bodies" might signal both an openness to intersectional analysis and opportunities to "creatively materialize and literalize seemingly formless experiences of nonnormative erotic desire, pleasure, and intimacy" (199). If there's any truth to any of these theories of reading comics, within this medium of expression, objectification might be a loyal albeit promiscuous bedfellow of identification, these supposedly antithetical states of being and seeing caught in a sensuous if sometimes uncomfortable tryst.

I'm certainly trying to seduce you into seeing comics like I do and getting excited by the view. But don't get so glazed you gloss over the word "uncomfortable." The ways comics make us look often excite me; sometimes they also upset me. Take my other most enduring memory of encountering comics in my youth: at a friend's X-Men themed Pizza Hut birthday party when I was nine years old. I vividly remember how the boys started snickering about boobies and how it quickly became clear us girls weren't in on the joke. Worse than that, we became the object of the joke, because after pointing at Storm and Jean Grey's thong-clad butts and large, perfectly separated, impossibly firm breasts, the boys pointed at us, the plastic, fantastic exaggerations on the collector cups and placemats inspiring and sanctioning fleshy, mundane objectification and exclusion in the booths beyond the page. And yet, as an adult comics scholar, I find myself wondering whether any of those boys toyed, then or later, with the idea of being any of those mutant women who, for all their objectification, are nonetheless complex objects, simultaneously serving male privilege and capable of reducing anyone to ash or drooling incompetence with a thought or flick of the wrist. While the vast majority of superhero comics reflect a male gaze, because both comics and superheroes are always transforming and multiplying, the bodies at play are always also simplified and amplified in ways that make them have-able in ways that make them be-able. This isn't true of every image, gaze, or moment of looking; a lot depends on a lot of things. But the tension between objectification and identification never expires. It's always simmering, tempting queerer pleasures.

Can I prove this? Not really. Since I'm talking about subjective effects, I can only hope to show you, using images that personally excite me. So that's what the rest of this chapter will do. I want to show you what I see when I look at certain images of certain comic book superheroes, and why what I see matters—to me, and to you, assuming you're a person who cares how comics work, and if you're reading this book, you probably are. We can't properly appreciate the complexity of looking at comics or superheroes—and what that complexity might offer larger discourses around identification, objectification, and the gaze—without making marginalized gazes visible. Where superhero comics are concerned, most gazes are marginalized. Much to my chagrin and thoroughly at odds with my personal experience within fandom communities filled with women and queer folks, too many fans, critics, and scholars continue to assume superhero comics only appeal to a narrow subset of cis, straight men and boys (Peppard, "'This Female Fights Back!'" 108–9). And on those rare occasions when marginalized gazes do become visible, they're often accused of misinterpretation and misappropriation, of "liking the wrong things and liking them in the wrong ways" (Busse 74). One way to write from a position of marginalization involves making your own desires visible and hoping the reader is touched by their urgency. In service of this, I'll be turning my sensual scholarly gaze toward a different wall-crawler whose association with deviant desires is both subversive and canonical, consistently emphasized across the character's forty-five-year history though occasionally failed by conservatizing retcons. Grab your popcorn and step right up for a singularly seductive sermon on the death-defying, boundary-busting, heart-heartening importance of the multitudinously marvelous mutant who's part man, part monster, all sexy—Kurt Wagner, the amazing Nightcrawler.

Ways of Seeing (Mutants)

If you're only familiar with the X-Men's resident blue-furred, fork-tailed teleporter from popular adaptations like *X-Men: The Animated Series* (1992–97) or the film *X2* (2003), you might be surprised to learn he's one of the most sex-positive male superheroes in the history of comics. Those animated and live-action portrayals are dominated by Catholic guilt, but in comics, Kurt's Catholicism came later, introduced eight years after the character's 1975 debut[2] as part of the "All-New, All Different" X-Men in

Giant-Size X-Men #1. And beyond one brief storyline that was later retconned as brainwashing by an antimutant cult (comics, everybody!),[3] Kurt's Catholicism has rarely impacted his sex-positivity. He's always up for a jaunt or a dip or a swashbuckling swing from the rafters with an alien princess or a bad-girl bounty hunter or any girl he meets on any deserted island or in any alternate dimension and, on occasion, folks who aren't girls, like the gender-ambiguous gargoyle who's seduced by his charms and seduces him in turn amid a raging inferno in *Excalibur* #6 (1989). In reams of fan fiction and fan art[4] and on Esad Ribić's infamous cover of *Wolverine*, vol. 3, #6 (2003), spotlighting Nightcrawler's naked backside as he poses like Michelangelo's David, it also includes his best buddy, Logan.[5] Within official comics as well as the hearts and minds of many fans, Kurt consistently defies expectations regarding religious characters, male characters, and monstrous characters. And he does it by being sexy. Which is exactly why he's sexy. That's certainly the case in one of my favorite pages from any comic: a scene from *Uncanny X-Men* #168 (1983), written by Chris Claremont and penciled by Paul Smith, in which Nightcrawler gives his girlfriend the perfect Christmas gift—himself.

It would be facetious to say this scene changed my life, but in a way it did, because so much of my professional and fannish lives revolve around comics, specifically superhero comics, and even more specifically, ways of seeing superhero comics as more than the sum of their on- and off-panel parts. I won't say I always fall for the monster, but I'm always chasing difference. Generically smooth, triangular, symmetrical, heavily muscled male bodies are fine if that's what you're into. Personally, I prefer men and mutants who look uniquely like themselves. But looking different isn't enough. The movie version of Nightcrawler left me cold. The twenty-year-old girl who encountered that guy in *X2* (2003) liked his powers but was disturbed by his intense Catholic repression; a man who cuts dozens of scars into his own skin in response to perceived sins needs help, not kisses. In contrast, the comics version of Kurt Wagner I encountered as a graduate student in my mid-twenties both looked and *was* different. After reading and academically analyzing so many superhero stories in which men become monsters and forever melodramatically mourn their transformations into those more spectacular albeit admittedly persecuted shapes, encountering a Marvel monster who didn't want to be normal was both a revelation and a relief. From that first flush of recognition, our relationship proceeded like a courtship. With each new adventure, our shared history

Figure 5.1. Chris Claremont and Paul Smith, *Uncanny X-Men* #168, Marvel Comics, April 1983.

grew and deepened, transforming a crush into full-blown passion. Soon, when I wasn't watching Kurt's beautifully different body weave across the page, I was bringing Pygmalion passion to daydreaming about him. And of course, I dreamed of having and being. I imagined the calming sureness of holding his unique hand and holding with his unique hand. I stared up at skyscrapers and across lonely fields and precisely pictured the contraction and release and pulse-pounding, fearful joy of teleporting, on my own and secured in the sinewy arms and sensual coils of my beloved's arms and tail. I felt the friction of fur on skin and the warmth that came with it, of feeling a human animal and feeling like a human animal, otherwise known as feeling fully human. Yet while I was immediately drawn to the comic book version of Nightcrawler, *Uncanny X-Men* #168 was the first time I truly believed my love might be reciprocal—that Kurt Wagner's delectable, dexterous difference might be deliberately drawn *for* me.

I'm eager to get to more academically informed gushing about the greatness of this scene, but first, I need to address another elephant in the room. Kurt's girlfriend, a flight attendant/sorceress named Amanda Sefton, isn't just his girlfriend. She's also his foster sister, Jimaine Szardos. Kurt doesn't know this when he first starts dating Jimaine as an adult; Jimaine uses magic to disguise herself as Amanda for reasons related to her mother's murderous grudge against Kurt for his perceived role in the death of her biological son (comics, everybody! again). Yet once Kurt does learn the truth, in *Uncanny X-Men Annual* #4 (1980), he's not dissuaded. Instead he seems delighted, and he and Amanda will continue to hook up for much of the next thirty-two years. The intent behind this storytelling choice has never been clear. If it's a kink, it's underplayed, the canonical story reducing it to little more than an odd plot detail. Maybe the relationship was meant to explore taboos, or perhaps Kurt and Amanda, raised in a German circus by a sorceress, are less tethered to traditional American notions of family. This story beat may also reference fairytale tropes involving disguises, class politics, and fantasies of upward mobility, Kurt playing the penniless adopted orphan whose happy ending includes becoming betrothed to the beautiful princess played by Amanda. In any case, because the storyworld leaves these complexities unexamined, I'm going to stick with discussing those things I am sure of, like the fact *Uncanny X-Men* #168 presents a joyful erotic exchange between consenting adults. It also deliberately foregrounds a female gaze and Kurt's willingness to play to it in ways that were revolutionary and remain remarkable.

Kurt's pose in this scene is a reference to *Cosmopolitan* magazine's first male centerfold from 1972, featuring Burt Reynolds reclining naked on a bearskin rug, a cigarillo stashed between the white teeth of his similarly playful smile as a single hand discretely covers his genitals. The Reynolds centerfold appeared at the behest of legendary *Cosmo* editor Helen Gurley Brown, author the 1962 bestseller *Sex and the Single Girl*, who wanted to prove women had the same "visual appetites" as men ("A Look Back"). In an article on Reynolds's star text, Jacob Smith recounts, "This photo spread was, in the words of a contemporary *Los Angeles Times* article, 'the chatter of 1972,' and made Reynolds a household word: 'Possibly never has a photo inspired so many lines or headlines. Copies, if you can find them, are selling for $15 a piece. A host of jokes and imitators (including the underground paper Rolling Stone, with a photo of teen-age idol David Cassidy in the buff) have resulted'" (26). Not coincidentally, *Playgirl*, the first mainstream American pornographic magazine targeted at women, debuted the following year. Among the many men to imitate the Reynolds pose was Stan Lee, who interestingly copied it the same year Nightcrawler did, in a promotional photo that, at the time, went unreleased. The original photo didn't become widely available until Marvel historian Sean Howe shared it online in 2012 (Gallaher).

Lots has changed since 1972, but lots also hasn't. The parody of the Burt Reynolds centerfold used to market the first *Deadpool* film in 2016 (Lincoln), or the overt eroticism of Colossus's choice of formalwear for the 2021 Hellfire Gala event (Gelman),[6] which adorns the character's exposed chest with gold chains and a Chippendales collar and includes a generous bulge creasing the crotch of his skintight black pants, are memorable in part because where male superheroes are concerned, these images remain unusual. Recent controversy surrounding Batman's penis appearing in a comic book aimed at adults (Peppard, "Introduction," 9–11) supports the continued relevance of Laura Mulvey's famous contention that "the male figure cannot bear the burden of sexual objectification" because "man is reluctant to gaze at his exhibitionist like" (12). Moreover, the corporate decision to nix a reference to Batman performing oral sex on Catwoman in the animated series *Harley Quinn* (2019–present) (Otterson), a show similarly aimed at adults, speaks to continued discomfort with the idea of male superheroes having real or rich sexual lives, particularly, it seems, when that richness involves catering to female pleasure. Yet forty years ago, Kurt Wagner was totally cool with being consumed by women. Which is not to suggest the appeal of Kurt or Burt is limited to women. While both Nightcrawler posing for Amanda and Reynolds posing for *Cosmo* foreground a heterosexual female gaze, as the considerable gay male audience for *Playgirl* can attest (Rowe), anyone of any gender or sexual orientation who wants to look is welcome to. Arguably, the Nightcrawler scene is especially disruptive of gender and sexual binaries. Jacobs argues that within the context of the Reynolds centerfold, "*Cosmo* was not so much challenging the *Playboy* ethic as trying to reproduce it for female consumers" (26). In contrast, the *Uncanny X-Men* #168 pinup of Nightcrawler unconventionally eroticizes an unconventional male body within a space that typically assumes a straight male reader. As such, this scene incorporates gender play that goes beyond a simple role reversal to suggest other (queerer) webs of desire and affiliation. Amanda's initial confusion and shock might anticipate and mirror the reaction of certain readers, watching their supposed ego ideal become a connotatively feminized erotic ideal. Whether and to what degree individual readers might continue following Amanda into her subsequent expression of carnal desire undoubtedly varies. But the invitation is there.

Still, because Kurt isn't naked, his pose could be considered tamer. Claremont and Smith negotiate this by doubling down on the theme of consumption. The most potent phallic symbols in this scene are also liquid consumables. This includes the champagne bottle and Kurt's prehensile tail curled around a glass of champagne, both of which are angled toward Amanda. They're also angled toward the reader, since we're sharing Amanda's perspective gazing at Kurt. The liquidity of this phallic symbolism is interesting for a variety of reasons, not least of which is the implication that Kurt's three-and-a-half-foot tail both thrusts and squeezes, evoking exotic penetrative possibilities as well as softer, more sensual ones. Kurt's softness is also contextual; regular readers will know his body is coated in soft fur that later comics compare to the texture of velvet.[7] Nightcrawler might feel like a real animal; he might also feel like a stuffed animal. This possibility is evoked by Kurt's replication of himself in a toy of himself, the "BAMF doll" notably positioned in front of his genitals. This suggests Kurt is a toy and so is his cock, and specifically, a cute and comforting toy. The large present framing the panel ties a nice bow around everything, which is given an additional flourish by Amanda's exclamation of "Yum!" In a thread for the @ClaremontRun Twitter account, J. Andrew Deman describes this as "a perfect encapsulation of the consumption metaphor," wherein Amanda and the reader are invited to drink champagne with Kurt/drink Kurt and unwrap Kurt's gift/unwrap Kurt. More bluntly, Amanda is unashamedly hungry to devour and/or play with Kurt.

There's humor here, but the sexiness isn't a joke. Stylistically, Smith's bodies are composed of smooth lines and soft curves reminiscent of romance comics. Where Nightcrawler is concerned, this represents a striking difference from previous portrayals. Before Smith, *Uncanny X-Men* was regularly penciled by Dave Cockrum and John Byrne. While his style evolves over time, Cockrum's early depictions of Nightcrawler tend to emphasize his monstrousness, elongating his limbs and enlarging his pointed ears. Byrne, for his part, tends to emphasize the character's animality, frequently drawing him crouching and crawling. Smith, however, draws an eminently huggable Nightcrawler, maintaining his monstrousness and masculinity while cultivating cuddliness and suggestively feminine sensualities. Moreover, the following issue makes good on the promise of unwrapping Kurt by displaying his implicitly naked body in appealing contexts of romance and action: in a hot tub with Amanda and teleporting around the city to save Angel's lady friend Candy Southern, whom Kurt subsequently drops in the tub with the still-naked Amanda, teasing a three-way sexual encounter.

Arguably, though, the most important difference between this Nightcrawler scene and the Reynolds centerfold isn't the contrast of Kurt's spandex with Burt's buffness, but rather the fact that Kurt's a mutant, and specifically, a mutant marked by monstrousness. He's got blue fur, pointed ears, fangs, a forked tail, glowing yellow eyes, three-fingered hands and two-toed feet—your standard demon package, similar to the ones that menaced so many maidens and gentlewomen (and sometimes gentlemen) in Medieval and Renaissance art. Nightcrawler is a sexy monster. And that matters. In Western culture, anything that's not the stereotypical desires of cisgendered, straight, white, able-bodied men has often been characterized as monstrous. Other desires have been persecuted, pathologized, or simply ignored by those wielding the most cultural capital. Yet *Uncanny X-Men* #168 offers us a sexy mutant demon we're not only allowed but encouraged to consume, happily and without guilt, because he's welcoming our gazes and because the exchange of looks doesn't neglect subjectivity; while objectification is often thought to diminish agency, Kurt's sexiness extends from and deepens his character. *Uncanny X-Men* #168 flips the script on a whole bunch of bigoted, prudish ideas about who gets to be sexy and does so within a genre that's better known for replicating those ideas. It also connects Nightcrawler's liberated sexuality to his defining rejection of the expectations a judgmental society heaps upon his connotatively monstrous body.

Deman agrees that Nightcrawler is "[portrayed] as gender deviant by the standards of his time, medium, and genre" (123), and similarly attributes a portion of this deviance to Claremont and Co.'s mobilization of Kurt's self-acceptance as a heroic rejection of bigotry. According to Claremont, "The original concept of Nightcrawler was that he was an angry, bitter, tormented soul. You know, 'I'm trapped in the body of a monster.' Well, Dave [Cockrum] and I both felt we'd seen that movie before" (quoted in Deman 115). Elaborating on this quote, Deman argues, "Claremont's account for the origins of Nightcrawler . . . speak to this impulse to depict a mutant for whom self-acceptance is a given. Nightcrawler's character arc throughout the Claremont run is thus more focused on his pursuit of social acceptance" (116). A representative example of this characterization is the story "The Big Dare," written by Claremont and penciled by John Bolton, appearing in *Classic X-Men* #4 (1986). In this flashback to Kurt's early days with the X-Men, Wolverine challenges his friend and teammate to walk down a public street as himself, without the protective veil of the "image inducer" (Claremont and Bolton 5) that lets him disguise himself as human. Kurt denies being ashamed, insisting the image inducer is simply practical. But, using some interestingly queer-coded adjectives, Wolverine insists mutants will never be accepted unless they "stand straight up an' tell the flaming world" (7). Kurt eventually accepts the dare and confronts a mix of positive and negative reactions, culminating in a near-fight with some bigoted young men in a hot rod. In response to the challenge "You know what you look like, Kraut—?" Kurt replies, "Ja, isn't it wonderful?" (11). This further provokes the bigots, but that both is and isn't the point. What makes Kurt threatening to bigots is the same thing that makes him powerfully heroic to other outsiders: his refusal to be ashamed of his difference.

But while Deman takes Claremont at his word regarding his intentions for Kurt's characterization, I've long wondered whether feedback from female fans played a role in transforming Nightcrawler from the angry misanthrope of his earliest appearances to the flirtatious romantic he quickly became, climaxing in Kurt aping Burt and rippling outward thereafter. The letter column of *X-Men* #96 (1975), the third issue with the All-New, All-Different team, includes a letter from future Marvel writer and editor Mary Jo Duffy that apparently describes Nightcrawler as "cute."

I say "apparently" because the section that discusses Nightcrawler is cut for space but addressed in the printed response to the letter, presumably written by editor Marv Wolfman: "We must tell you that a certain Kurt Nagner [*sic*], residing in Westchester, takes exception to being called . . . 'cute.' Nightcrawler may be many things . . . but *cute*???" (emphasis in original). While obviously comedic, this editorial response is also dismissive, mocking Duffy's gaze. And readers didn't stand for it. In the letter column of *X-Men* #100 (1976), a fan identified as Ann Nichols revisits the issue of Kurt's cuteness while referencing the image inducer. "Why can't Nightcrawler be cute?" wonders Nichols. "He's cuter as himself than in that disguise. (Well, if you object to 'cute,' will you accept 'attractive'?)" In *X-Men* #103 (1977), Michele Crossgrove agrees: "As for Nightcrawler being cute . . . why, I knew that right from the start. Much cuter than that silly disguise, anyway!" I'm not done, and neither were the ladies thirsty for Mr. Wagner. In *X-Men* #105 (1977), Sophie Davenport declares, "Kurt is simply delightful; what more can I say? He looks like something Ray Harryhausen made come to life, but he's actually so boyish and exuberant and unaffected that I think I'm in love with him." In *X-Men* #117 (1978), Suzan Kizzar writes, "My favorite is Nightcrawler; he's so dreamy and super-cute." And in *X-Men* #120 (1979), Lori Wildern opines, "*I* think Nightcrawler is cute, too. Or attractive, if you like. Visually stimulating? I like his personality, and his abilities" (emphasis in original). The final reference I've found to this particular debate appears in *Uncanny X-Men* #173 (1983), in which Susan Murrie writes, "Nightcrawler is anxious over whether or not the New Mutants will accept him. Personally, I think Kurt's cute."

As any fandom scholar worth their salt knows, letter columns don't constitute valid surveys of anything. Published fan letters are selected by editors for a combination of deeply subjective and market-driven reasons. On occasion, they're even faked by the creators of the comics (Stein 50). Yet I remain fascinated by the prominence of these (seemingly) female voices speaking back to (seemingly) dismissive male writers and editors in speaking up for Nightcrawler, while really speaking up for each other and their shared desire for a furry blue demon-elf who's persecuted for his appearance but chooses to love and share himself anyway. It's also interesting that the debate about Kurt's charms seems to end in 1983, the same year he struck the Reynolds pose and effectively settled it. Or at least, should have settled it. Too many popular and scholarly histories of comics continue to critique marginalization while neglecting moments like these, in which marginalized readers did assert their gazes and achieve a modicum of visibility, even influencing representation within otherwise exclusionary genres.

In the interests of revealing further feminist foundations for my favorite fuzzy elf: Duffy's contributions to the history of sexy Nightcrawler don't stop at her seemingly incendiary fan letter. She would later write two official stories starring the character. The first, "Show Me the Way to Go Home," cowritten by Bob Layton and penciled by Dave Cockrum, appears in *Bizarre Adventures* #27 (1981). In this story, Nightcrawler's teleportation powers combine with those of the villainous Vanisher to send the pair on an interdimensional adventure. On his initial jaunt, Kurt lands in a heap at the feet of a cadre of criminally curvaceous alien women, denizens of an all-female society eager to make Kurt their king (and use him to help perpetuate the species). Given Duffy's fannish story, the first thing the women say about Kurt shouldn't surprise: "You know he's really cute!" (Layton and Cockrum 48). This story's interdimensional plot device would later become the basis for the first *Nightcrawler* miniseries (1985), written and drawn by Cockrum. And Cockrum's miniseries would in turn become a kind of urtext for the character, with many subsequent Nightcrawler stories calling back to it ("Kurt Wagner"). I'm not suggesting Duffy is the real author of my preferred version of Kurt Wagner; serialized superhero comics are always collaborative, as even this brief history illuminates. But I am suggesting there's a compelling argument to be made that when Amanda says "Yum!" in *Uncanny X-Men* #168, she's meant to serve as a surrogate for real female gazes Claremont and Co. were intimately aware of, and that Kurt's sexiness is shaped, in part, in response to those gazes. I also want to once again underscore the complexity of these gazes by taking a closer look at Duffy's other Nightcrawler story, *The Saga of Crystar, Crystal Warrior* #6 (1984), penciled by Ricardo Villamonte.

Kurt guest stars in this comic book series tied to an obscure toy line seemingly for no other reason than Duffy wanted to write him. The story is told from Kurt's perspective, decentering the supposed protagonists of the series. And, relevant to topic at hand, it's quite explicitly a sex farce. The comic opens with several pages of Kurt dodging obstacles in the X-Men's Danger Room, including a two-page, largely wordless spread in which he contorts himself into a variety of acrobatic (or kama sutric) poses while dodging a small purple projectile that bears a striking resemblance to a dildo. The sequence concludes with Kurt using his prehensile tail to tease the eager dildo into going kaboom (or more accurately, "SKRA-BOOM").

An offscreen voice compliments Kurt's "panache," and in the next scene, Kurt keeps aspiring to that adjective, swapping his superheroic spandex for a tux complete with corsage to spend date night with Amanda. The couple embraces inside a big pink heart accented by a smaller, pinker heart symbolizing the sound and sentiment of their smooch. But Amanda barely has time to put her flowers in a vase or fix her beau a drink before Kurt makes the mistake of teleporting inside a room suffused with "transdimensional magic," accidentally BAMFing himself on a one-way journey to the realm of Crystalium. In Crystalium, Kurt is narratively misidentified but symbolically correctly identified as a "chaos demon." He subsequently attracts the attention of both a seemingly naked bad red lady who runs a lustful finger down his bicep and overtly admires his backside ("Do they all have tails like yours, where you come from?"), and a good blue lady in a chainmail bikini who makes a loaded overture after Kurt rescues her from the baddies.

It's tempting to read these red and blue ladies as embodying a virgin/whore dichotomy, but befitting its nature as sex farce, this tale isn't so simple. The blue lady, Ika, may be good but isn't virginal. When Kurt observes, "I didn't know anyone here would even **know** about Earth . . ." (emphasis in original), Ika replies, "Oh I know lots. You have no idea what an education it can be, having a powerful enchanter as a parent . . ." As the enchanter's daughter seems to enchant our fuzzy friend, their differently blue faces become silhouettes against the full moon. "If you'd stay a little while longer," says Ika, "I could show you **how** really grateful I am . . ." (emphasis in original) The victorious hero being rewarded with a princess is a trope as old as time. But it's twisted here by Ika's agency and Kurt's always-evident monstrousness; when their faces fade to black, Kurt's large, pointed ears remain visible, marking his difference from the square-jawed, pink-skinned barbarian who usually gets the girl in sword-and-sorcery settings.

The trope is further twisted by Kurt's subsequent return to his home dimension and Amanda's reaction to his adventure. Unlike Kurt, Amanda has heard of Crystalium. She's also heard of Ika; she immediately recognizes Kurt's souvenir jewels as the kind worn by the enchanter's daughter. But Amanda isn't troubled by her boyfriend's possible infidelity. Though Amanda teases Kurt about the encounter, her expression is playful and eager before becoming arch in the final panel, where she awaits Kurt's explanation with a cocked eyebrow, thinking, "Knowing you, I bet it'll be a beauty. . . ." While most of the story privileges Kurt's perspective, this final panel privileges Amanda's gaze, which becomes a surrogate reader gaze through the

Figure 5.2. Mary Jo Duffy and Ricardo Villamonte, *Saga of Crystar, Crystal Warrior* #6, Marvel Comics, July 1984.

promise of Kurt retelling the story to Amanda and her eager anticipation of that retelling. From one perspective, Amanda is enabling a stereotypical masculine fantasy by sanctioning Kurt's playboy adventures. But there's also a way of reading Amanda as a woman much like me, or Jo Duffy, or any of the women who wrote fan letters in response to Duffy's, who love and desire Nightcrawler in part because doing so feels rebellious—because it defies a male editor's incredulous refusal to see what we see, which is Kurt's similar (and sexy) defiance of restrictive cultural norms. In other words, there's a way of reading Amanda's knowing expression as a wink at female readers who might want to both have Kurt and live vicariously through him, enjoying the freedom he enjoys: to be both monstrous and beautiful, monogamous and polyamorous, heroic and huggable.

Female (Mutant) Masculinity

I'm trying to find my way back to that tryst between identification and objectification, and I think I've finally found the right portal, into a fantasy that's occupied many of mine. *Excalibur* #43 (1991), written and penciled by Alan Davis, opens with a largely wordless three-page dream sequence in which a blonde lady who looks a little like me transforms into a woman who looks a lot like Nightcrawler.

I want to focus on the visualization of this transformation, but my reading requires a bit of narrative context. The blonde lady is Meggan, an "empathic metamorph" with sometimes-unpredictable emotion-based shapeshifting powers who's in a sometimes-troubled relationship with Captain Britain/Brian Braddock. For much of the first forty issues of *Excalibur*, Kurt, Meggan, and Brian form a love triangle that's open to many interpretations. Kurt, a visibly different mutant raised by a poor Romani circus family in rural Germany, can be read as an exotic interloper juxtaposed with the idealized Aryan masculinity of the blond, muscular, aristocratic national hero Captain Britain. However, the narrative doesn't idealize Brian, instead depicting him as a pompous, insecure man with anger issues, suicidal ideations, and a drinking problem, who often chafes against the demands of his station, including his role as Meggan's boyfriend; in several early *Excalibur* issues, Brian appears to be having an affair with an old flame. While Kurt often struggles with self-doubt, he's also depicted as more compassionate, secure in his identity, and a better leader. In addition, he often receives Meggan's emotional confessions about both her relationship with Brian and her own insecurities, as in *Excalibur* #3 (1989), wherein he holds a crying Meggan in the rain and tells her, "If there's one thing I—above all others—know . . . it's that a person cannot be judged by their looks . . . only their heart and soul. And yours, dear Meggan, are as lovely as the sunrise. If some people are too blind to see that . . . it's **their** shame. **Their** loss" (emphasis and ellipses in original). In other words, Kurt is often framed as a more attractive romantic partner, despite his supposedly monstrous appearance, which is notably tamed by Davis's art. Although Davis's version of Nightcrawler maintains the character's unique physicality, he also makes him ideally lithe and graceful and definitely very male; unlike many of his contemporaries, Davis often gives male superheroes noticeable bulges, with a particular penchant for displaying said bulges in soft, clingy loungewear.

Meggan's superpowers further complicate the love triangle. Meggan can't always control her body's responses to the desires of others. For instance, in *Excalibur* #6 (1989), she instinctively shapeshifts to embody the desires of a crew of randy sailors, expressing both pleasure in that embodiment and distress at her seeming submissiveness. She also shapeshifts in response to both Brian's desires and Kurt's, as illustrated by a scene from *Excalibur* #4 (1989), written by Claremont and penciled by Davis. The scene begins with Kurt and Meggan engaging in flirtatious acrobatic daredevilry and concludes with both characters falling from the rafters of Kurt's personal jungle gym to land in a messy pile, Meggan falling on top of Kurt. There, as Kurt is drawn to Meggan, Meggan is drawn to Kurt. Over the course of four moment-to-moment panels, Meggan transforms into a feminine version of Nightcrawler, complete with indigo skin, pointed ears, glowing yellow eyes, and an unruly tower of curly indigo hair. At the climax of Meggan's transformation, the characters (nearly) kiss. As I've discussed elsewhere, Meggan's messy powers and Kurt's instigation of the encounter can raise uncomfortable questions about consent ("Blue Becomings"). And Meggan and Kurt both ostensibly regret their dalliance with infidelity. But neither character forgets it. Meggan becomes blue several more times over the next several dozen issues, and in *Excalibur* #43 (1991), written and penciled by Davis, Kurt does something I've done many times—he restages and amplifies *Excalibur* #4's transformative seduction in a dream that feels real when he dreams it, because of how Davis draws it and because I've dreamed it, too.

The title page splash of *Excalibur* #43 shows Kurt and Meggan's parallel bodies soaring through the air amid a dizzying labyrinth of silver metal bars, the same gym showcased in *Excalibur* #4. The callback is underscored by the characters' outfits; Meggan is wearing the same string bikini she was wearing in the earlier issue, and Kurt is wearing the same tight white pants and equally revealing tank top. Through their outfits and poses, Kurt's and Meggan's bodies are displayed and idealized in a manner typical of superhero comics: Kurt is an ideally masculine collection of hard, powerful curves, while Meggan is fit but also fabulously curvaceous, with a small waist and generous, gravity-defying breasts that somehow stay steadfastly affixed to the minimal fabric of her bathing suit. Yet both characters also bear signs of monstrousness, Kurt through his usual blueness, tail, and claw-like hands and feet, Meggan through a mane of golden hair that becomes a fiery energy trail extending past her feet and the edge of the frame. In addition, the parallelism of Kurt and Meggan's poses both highlights their gender dimorphism and invites comparison. The longer I look at this page, the less I notice the ways Kurt and Meggan are different, seeing, instead, all the obvious ways they're similar. Both stomachs bear evidence of firm abs; both chests are shaded with voluptuous volume; both sets of legs have shapely thighs that taper into delicate ankles; both heads are adorned with salon-quality waves; both faces are lit by blindingly white smiles. Their bodies are also upside down and innocent of gravity. In other words, they're both inverted and impossible and thus, ripe for rereading.

A sense of topsy-turvy surreality is exaggerated on the next page, a wordless sequence in which Kurt and Meggan perform an aerial routine. But Kurt doesn't throw and catch his female partner, as a male trapeze artist customarily would. Instead, these partners perform in tandem, Meggan perfectly copying Kurt's skillful journey through the jungle gym. This mimicry becomes additionally literal as Meggan begins to transform, becoming, by the end of the page and the routine, exactly as blue as Kurt. I'm saying Meggan mimics Kurt because he's the one who starts off blue and because he's consistently in the foreground. In addition, the following page reveals the sequence is Kurt's dream, not Meggan's. But there's still that topsy turviness to contend with, which is signaled, in part, by the irregular shape of the panels and how the bodies are cropped within them. On the *Oh Gosh, Oh Golly, Oh Wow! Podcast*, cohosted by yours truly, Christopher Maverick observes that throughout this page, Kurt and Meggan are consistently cropped in defiance of the photographic rule of thirds; bodies are cut off at their knees and elbows in ways that frustrate the easy aestheticization that the rule of thirds is meant to facilitate. This disruptive framing creates

Figure 5.3. Alan Davis, *Excalibur* #43, Marvel Comics, February 1991.

a sense of unease that evokes the moral quandary of the dream within the narrative. Meggan insists she's monogamously devoted to Brian, but that doesn't stop suspicion around Kurt's desire for Meggan or Meggan's desire for Kurt. Later in the issue, Brian, in a fit of jealous rage, instigates a fight in which he breaks Kurt's leg, symbolically emasculating him. But Davis's visual rule-breaking does more than forecast broken legs and symbolic penises. And Kurt's desires are deviant in ways that go beyond the threat he poses to the sanctity of an Aryan power couple. This dream can be about both sex and gender, and desires that are deviant because they're diverse.

The unease generated by Davis's defiance of the rule of thirds is both exaggerated and subverted by his manipulation of space and time, which encourages a sense of contemplative, subjective timelessness. Barbara

Postema argues that wordless comics often "draw attention to the active processes involved in reading and interpretation" (320). This invitation to self-reflexivity is sweetened by Davis's composition, wherein the interweaving bars of the jungle gym extend and connect across and beyond the borders of the five panels that (don't) contain them. This technique has a long history in comics. In *Little Nemo in Slumberland* (1905–1927), Winsor McKay often uses it much the same way Davis does in *Excalibur* #43: to indicate a series of movements within and across a grand space. But in McKay's strips as in Davis's comic, there's a dreaminess to this technique which speaks to the inherent dreaminess of comics. Within comics in general and the *Excalibur* #43 dream sequence in particular, time is not linear and space is not succinct. Jared Gardner argues that because past and present are always simultaneously visible on a comics page, "the comics form retains that which cannot be reconciled to linear narrative—the excess that refuses cause-and-effect argument, the trace which threatens to unsettle the present's narrative of its own part and thereby of itself. The comics form is forever troubled by that which cannot be reconciled, synthesized, unified, contained within the frame; but it is in being so troubled that the form defines itself" (177). Gardner is, in essence, offering a further complexification of McCloud's theory of closure, whereby readers exercise considerable agency in deciding how to fill in the gaps between panels. But in Gardner's formulation, the gap is never fully filled, indeed cannot be fully filled, because it's always graphically evident; readers can't unsee the fragmentation of the story. What this actually does is debatable. Some readers are clearly more troubled and/or excited by the possibilities of the gap than others, for whom it's simply the accepted grammar of comics. In addition, the trace and its trouble are more visible on some pages than others.

Within the example at hand: Davis's emphasis on the subjectiveness of time, sequence, and signification in the *Excalibur* #43 dream sequence can be further magnified by the ways the X-Men's persecuted mutant superbodies similarly defy easy categorization. In Scott Bukatman's influential formulation, whereas Golden Age superheroes tend to signal phallic impenetrability, "Mutant superheroes are not invulnerable; not only are they distinguished by (a frequently maudlin) emotionalism, but their first and most dangerous enemies are their own bodies" (66). Nightcrawler's monstrous difference always bears the trace of this trouble. As a shapeshifter, Meggan can hide her difference, but in *Excalibur* #4 and *Excalibur* #43, she chooses, briefly, not to. Yet in both examples, the categorical instability introduced by Meggan's shapeshifting isn't treated as monstrous. Instead, it's treated as desirable. This isn't just a dream; it's a fantasy. Bukatman argues, "Identity is the obsessional center of superhero comics, as revealed by endless processes of self-transformation and the problematic perceptions of others" (54). I'm with him on this one, but not when he reads this obsession as a reflection of bodily disgust: "The bodily torment of the mutant superhero expresses a desire, a need, to transcend the confines of the body, to exist as pure spirit" (71). In contrast, Scott and Fawaz, while emphasizing the queer potential of comics, find solace in the manifestation of bodily difference within a form where "anything that can be drawn can be believed" (201). Which might include a woman becoming more desirable by transforming into a golden-eyed, blue-furred monster.

Do I wish the *Excalibur* #43 dream sequence properly reflected Meggan's desires alongside Kurt's? Part of me definitely does. But there's more to be said about the deviance of Kurt's desires. It's notable that despite the boundlessness of dreams, Kurt doesn't imagine himself becoming any less different than he's always been. It's also notable that he desires Meggan most when she's less normative; his fantasy is not an escape from difference, but rather a fall into more difference. It's also, however, a fantasy of sameness, since Meggan copies Kurt's difference. In this, Meggan's transformation might manifest Kurt's ego, or a darkly Freudian aspect of his desire; the blue, golden-eyed Meggan unavoidably resembles the natural form of Kurt's biological mother, Mystique, who is also, like Meggan, a shapeshifter.[8] But Meggan's transformation can also be read as a powerful fantasy of acceptance. In Kurt's dream, this empathic metamorph, who spent years resembling a werewolf before learning to present herself as an impossibly beautiful blonde, decides, instead, to adopt Kurt's connotatively monstrous appearance and embrace a different kind of desire. This gesture would be meaningful to anyone but is doubtless more meaningful to a man who's faced a lifetime of persecution for being one of a kind. Alternatively, or additionally, building on the contrast and comparison of the opening splash, Meggan's incorporation of Kurt's monstrous difference encourages us to see this difference as not only acceptable or merely attractive, but specifically beautiful, in a specifically feminine way. To put it simply, just as Meggan is monstrous like Kurt, Kurt is beautiful like Meggan. As such, this scene suggests Kurt's gender deviance, or perhaps gender fluidity, or perhaps his desire for one or both. Or perhaps he wants to be who Meggan becomes. In response to the *Oh Gosh, Oh Golly, Oh Wow! Podcast* episode about this comic, Twitter user @GentlyPress wrote a thread interpreting Kurt as transfeminine, with Meggan representing his transition goals. I find this a compelling reading, especially in the final panel of the wordless aerial sequence, in which Kurt finally surrenders the foreground. In this wide panel, Kurt and the fully transformed Meggan are pictured in profile, at equal heights, mirrors of each other against an empty, pale green background pregnant with possibility.

Of course, this is also a sex dream; the pregnant pause leads to a passionate embrace on the following page. @GentlyPress reads the sexualization of Kurt's transformative fantasy as another "extremely trans experience: the 'do I want to fuck her or BE her?' feeling. In fact, sexual attraction can often obfuscate gender dysphoria and delay a trans person's gender realization this way." This is good and true, in general and because @GentlyPress believes it. But my own emotional and erotic investment in this scene is less tethered to a particular goal. For me, this scene conjures Frederik Byrn Køhlert's description of comics reading: "Because comics rely on both highly personal hand-drawn aesthetics and a serially networked approach to narrative, the form can challenge conventional representational schemes in a complex dance of appropriation and resignification that is always open to the creation of new meanings. Further, the multimodal hybridity of the comics form—consisting, as it does, of multiple overlapping, interdependent, and often competing verbal and visual codes—creates a distinctly unstable and decentered reading experience" (4). And this description of comics reading as multiple, messy, deviant, and decentered in turn conjures my own version of the desire to have as well as be. I don't want to be a man, super or otherwise. But I want the freedom some comic book supermen have to resignify objectification by multiplying and diversifying what gender might do or mean. Because Nightcrawler's dream is a dream, and because this dream occurs within a comic book about marvelously malleable mutant superheroes, and because the marvelously malleable mutant superhero dreaming the dream has elements of gender fluidity and a long history of incarnating the complex desires of female fans, Kurt Wagner gets to live the dream I dreamed at twelve and keep dreaming at forty: he doesn't need to choose between having and being. Kurt gets to be both desiring and desirable and indeed desirable through his desires. In this, Nightcrawler is someone/something I want and someone/something I want to be, a way I want to want and a way I want to be wanted.

Unfortunately, Meggan isn't afforded the same freedom. In the end, it's only Kurt who dreams of beautiful transformations, while Meggan chooses to remain a stereotypically beautiful blonde with her stereotypically beautiful blond boyfriend who later becomes her stereotypically beautiful blond husband and the stereotypically beautiful blond father of her stereotypically beautiful blonde daughter. But the first two pages of *Excalibur* #43 at least tease reciprocities that keep me dreaming. And the comics form lets me linger there, since comics, like Kurt and Meggan's timeless journey through the jungle gym, chart winding courses to their climaxes. According to Postema,

> Sequences in comics signify in a process of reading back and forth. As one reads forwards, details in previous panels become more important (again) or come to signify in different ways. Retroactive resignification may take place based on the reading of more recent panels; but on the other hand, reconsidering previous panels may also then lead to a reevaluation of action in the present panel. Consequently, the creation of action in a comic is an intricate and continuous negotiation and (re)consideration of various panels at the same time, based on visual information that panels, as signifying syntagms, provide. (66)

I know this reading of how we read comics is true because I've done it, with many comics over many years and every time I read *Excalibur* #43. The first time, as a twenty-something grad student already head-over-heels for Nightcrawler, it took my breath away and made me angry the way puberty does, inspiring too many emotions my ostensibly mature self didn't know how to name or channel. Now, over a decade later, I've got more names and channels. But my sexiest transformation sees me caring less about fidelity, both to some parts of some plots and to the notion that there's any right way to read a comic. The me I am now sees Kurt's very male body and Meggan's very female body collide in a fervent kiss and shamelessly retreats to the pregnant pause before the climax, where, for one eternal moment, everything felt possible.

Conclusion

I'm tempted to conclude this essay in a utopian fashion, invoking queer temporality to justify my continued identification with male superheroes and continued disidentification with female ones, despite (mostly) describing myself as a woman and (usually) dressing the part. But maybe I'm cuter without that disguise. The truth is, I identify with the same male superheroes I eroticize because, too much of the time, I don't feel like I have a choice. This is evident in my feelings about a character who is, for most intents and purposes, a female version of Nightcrawler: Talia Josephine Wagner, a.k.a. Nocturne, the alternate universe daughter of Kurt Wagner and Wanda Maximoff/the Scarlet Witch.

Nocturne first appears in *X-Men: Millennial Visions* (2000). She subsequently stars in the series *Exiles* (2001–2008), featuring a group of young, dimension-hopping heroes before making more sporadic appearances, including a recurring role in the Claremont-penned *New Excalibur* (2006–2007). I love TJ, and how could I not? She's the ultra sex-positive, body-positive, adventure-loving, rock band-fronting daughter of two of my favorite superheroes and looks a lot like Meggan when Meggan's doing Kurt. But I've never properly wanted to have her or be her. On the contrary, I generally recoil at the thought. I like Kurt's tight pants and pinup postures in part because on a male body, that flamboyance feels rebellious. In contrast, TJ's hyperfeminine reembodiment of Nightcrawler, with her perpetually scarlet lips, impossibly tiny waist, and perfectly separated, always-perky breasts, can cast me back into the bad parts of puberty, when I lived in terror of the obligations of womanhood. Earlier I said I don't want to be a man. But I've never really wanted to be a woman, either. I've always just wanted to be me. Which means being a boyish girl, or maybe a girlish boy. Whatever that means, but it makes sense to me.

My favorite scene in my favorite TJ story, "Nocturne's Tale" from *Exiles* #41–42 (2004), written and penciled by her creator, Jim Calafiore, magnifies my messy feelings. Midway through *Exiles* #41, Kurt supervises TJ in a training session. TJ's wearing Kurt's classic costume, except the white gloves are longer and the white boots become thigh-highs to better showcase her shapely legs. But TJ's not excessively objectified, at least not reductively. Her sexiness is athletic, joyful, and shameless, evoking but exaggerating the stuff I love about Kurt. And yet, nothing TJ does is good enough for her father. Kurt harshly criticizes his daughter for not taking things more seriously or following his instructions, causing TJ to retaliate with a typical teenage complaint: "I'll never be you, so stop trying to **make** me you! And you're not going to **change** me by constantly yelling, and lecturing, and reprimanding! It just **hurts**! When do I get to be **me**?!" (emphasis in original).

When I read this admittedly generic exchange, it's more and different than that. It's not just TJ talking to Kurt. It's also me talking to me about

Figure 5.4. Jim Calafiore, "Nocturne's Tale," *Exiles* #41, Marvel Comics, January 2004.

the ways my younger self sometimes thought I could escape misogyny by copying it. I wish teenage me had had the strength TJ does here, to embrace my boyishness without devaluing my femininity. In the end, I can't be Nightcrawler any more than TJ can. Not because he's a man or because he's not real, but because, like TJ, I need to be me. Which isn't Kurt Wagner or Talia Josephine Wagner, but does remind me of the latter at the conclusion of this scene, when she walks out on Kurt, flatfooted and unfetishized, to be her own version of her hero and mine.

Now I'm worried I've veered too far into dystopia, so let me weave back to the tryst that started this tale. I can't tell you how to read superhero comics or why you should. I can't even really tell you how I read them. I can only offer a fleeting glimpse of those feelings I've found ways to express. This includes a dream about more ways to talk about superheroes, which this chapter has tried to make real. For better or worse, superhero comics are always beautiful monstrosities, the best ones transforming endlessly in the eye of the beholder and, in certain sparkling moments, transforming us in turn. How they transform us both is and isn't our choice. But we can choose to chronicle our choices in the interests of making more.

Notes

1. Parts of this chapter are reworked from previous web-based essays and writeups, including: "Nightcrawler Is a Sex-Positive Superhero. Here's How—And Why It Matters"; "Blue Becomings: Revisiting *Excalibur* #4"; and "The Multiverse According to ComicsXF!"

2. Nightcrawler's Catholicism was introduced through a scene of the character praying in *Uncanny X-Men* #165 (1983).

3. For a fuller picture of the canonical history of Nightcrawler's sexuality and how it has interacted with his Catholicism, see "Nightcrawler Is a Sex-Positive Superhero."

4. For more on the history, context, and symbolism of Kurt/Logan slash, see Christopher Michael Roman's book *Queering Wolverine*.

5. According to comics critic Brian Cronin, Ribić consciously styled this cover after pulp erotica and was surprised editors didn't reject it.

6. The yearly Hellfire Gala event involves Marvel's mutants hosting a party on their island nation of Krakoa, for which each character receives a new one-off costume combining high-fashion formalwear with elements of the character's usual superhero costume or colors. The Gala has been an opportunity for artists and fans to experiment with new (and often queerer) forms of eroticism, particularly where male superheroes are concerned. However, as documented by Gelman, fans singled out Colossus's costume as being particularly erotically charged.

7. In *Excalibur* #44 (1991), a woman asks to stroke Nightcrawler's fur and marvels, "My, my, blue velvet." The miniseries *X-Calibre* (1995) includes a similar scene. The character Silver Sable also describes Nightcrawler's fur as resembling the texture of velvet in *Uncanny Spider-Man* #2 and 3 (2023).

8. While Mystique wasn't canonically confirmed as Nightcrawler's biological mother until *X-Men Unlimited* #4 (1994), earlier issues, including *Uncanny X-Men* #142 (1981), strongly hinted at the connection. Because Claremont wrote both *Uncanny* #142 and *Excalibur* #4, there's reason to suspect he was aware of the Freudian implications of Meggan resembling Mystique.

Works Cited

Bukatman, Scott. *Matters of Gravity: Special Effects and Supermen in the 20th Century.* Duke UP, 2003.

Busse, Kristina. "Geek Hierarchies, Boundary Policing, and the Gendering of the Good Fan." *Participations: Journal of Audience and Reception Studies*, vol. 10, no. 1, 2013, pp. 73–91.

Calafiore, Jim (writer and artist). *Exiles*, vol. 1, no. 41, Marvel, 2004.

Claremont, Chris (writer), and John Bolton (artist). "The Dare." *Classic X-Men*, no. 4, Marvel, 1986.

Claremont, Chris (writer), and John Byrne (artist). *X-Men*, vol. 1, no. 117, Marvel, 1978.

Claremont, Chris (writer), and John Byrne (artist). *X-Men*, vol., no. 120, Marvel, 1979.

Claremont, Chris (writer), and John Byrne (artist). *Uncanny X-Men*, vol. 1, no. 142, Marvel, 1981.

Claremont, Chris (writer), and Dave Cockrum (artist). *X-Men*, vol., no. 100, Marvel, 1976.

Claremont, Chris (writer), and Dave Cockrum (artist). *X-Men*, vol. 1, no. 105, Marvel, 1977.

Claremont, Chris, and Bill Mantlo (writers) and Dave Cockrum and William Robert Brown (artists). *X-Men*, vol. 1, no. 103, Marvel, 1977.

Claremont, Chris (writer), and Alan Davis (artist). *Excalibur*, vol. 1, no. 4, Marvel, 1989.

Claremont, Chris (writer), and Paul Smith (artist). *Uncanny X-Men*, vol. 1, no. 165, Marvel, 1983.

Claremont, Chris (writer), and Paul Smith (artist). *Uncanny X-Men*, vol. 1, no. 168, Marvel, 1983.

Claremont, Chris (writer), and Paul Smith (artist). *Uncanny X-Men*, vol. 1, no. 173, Marvel, 1983.

Claremont, Chris, and Bill Mantlo (writers) and Dave Cockrum (artist). *X-Men*, vol. 1, no. 96, Marvel, 1975.

Claremont, Chris (writer), and John Romita Jr. (artist). *Uncanny X-Men Annual*, vol. 1, no. 4, Marvel, 1980.

@ClaremontRun. "In UXM #168, Nightcrawler is presented (and presents himself) as an object of sexual display." Twitter, 5 Aug. 2022, 7:53 a.m., twitter.com/ClaremontRun/status/1290979215161135104?s=20.

Cronin, Brian. "Comic Legends: The Racy Wolverine Cover That Got Past Marvel Editorial." *ComicBookResources.com*, 30 Dec. 2017, www.cbr.com/wolverine-racy-cover-marvel-editorial/.

Davis, Alan (writer and artist). *Excalibur*, vol. 1, no. 43, Marvel, 1991.

Davis, Alan (writer and artist). *Excalibur*, vol. 1, no. 44, Marvel, 1991.

Deman, Andrew J. *The Claremont Run: Subverting Gender in the X-Men*. U of Texas P, forthcoming.
Duffy, Mary Jo (writer), and Ricardo Villamonte (artist). *Saga of Crystar, Crystal Warrior*, vol. 1, no. 6, Marvel, 1984.
Duffy, Mary Jo, and Bob Layton (writer) and Dave Cockrum (artist). "Show Me the Way to Go Home." *Bizarre Adventures*, vol., 1, no. 27, Marvel, 1981.
The Editors. "A Look Back at Burt Reynolds' Iconic Nude Photoshoot in *Cosmopolitan*." *Cosmopolitan.com*, 7 Sept. 2018, www.cosmopolitan.com/entertainment/news/a48108/burt-reynolds-cosmo-classic/.
Ellis, Warren (writer) and Ken Lashley, Roger Cruz, Renato Arlem, Charles Mota, and Eddie Wagner (artists). *X-Calibre*, nos. 1–4, Marvel, 1995.
Gallaher, Valerie. "The One Where Stan Lee Became a Centerfold." *MTV.com*, 23 Aug. 2012, www.mtv.com/news/7unysy/stan-lee-centerfold.
Gardner, Jared. *Projections: Comics and the History of Twenty-First-Century Storytelling*. Stanford UP, 2012.
Gelman, Samuel. "X-Men's Colossus Redesign Has Twitter Thirsty for the Marvel Mutant." *CBR.com*, 28 Apr. 2021, www.cbr.com/x-men-colossus-hellfire-gala-trending-topic/.
@GentlyPress. "Catching up on @GoshGollyWow episodes and was really struck by Nightcrawler's portrayal in this issue." Twitter, 15 Mar. 2022, 9:06 p.m., twitter.com/GentlyPress/status/1503900366596816896?s=20
Køhlert, Frederik Byrn. *Serial Selves: Identity and Representation in Autobiographical Comics*. Rutgers UP, 2019.
Lincoln, Ross A. "Ryan Reynolds Reveals Deadpool Costume with Burt Reynolds Parody." *Deadline.com*, 27 Mar. 2015, deadline.com/2015/03/ryan-reynolds-deadpool-costume-burt-reynolds-1201400013/
Lobdell, Scott (writer), and Richard Bennett (artist). *X-Men Unlimited*, vol. 1, no. 4, Marvel, 1994.
McCloud, Scott. *Understanding Comics: The Invisible Art*. Harper Perennial, 1994.
Mulvey, Laura. "Visual Pleasure and Narrative Cinema. *Screen*, vol. 16, no. 3, 1975, pp. 6–18.
Otterson, Joe. "How 'WandaVision,' 'The Umbrella Academy,' 'Harley Quinn' Subvert the Superhero Genre." *Variety.com*, 14 June 2021, variety.com/2021/tv/features/subverting-superhero-tv-wandavision-harley-quinn-umbrella-academy-1234992069/.
Postema, Barbara. "Following the Pictures: Wordless Comics for Children." *Journal of Graphic Novels and Comics*, vol. 10, no. 3, 2024, pp. 311–22.
Postema, Barbara. *Narrative Structure in Comics: Making Sense of Fragments*. RIT Press, 2013.
Peppard, Anna. "Blue Becomings: Revisiting *Excalibur* #4." *TheMiddleSpaces.com*, 11 May 2021, themiddlespaces.com/2021/05/11/excalibur-4/.
Peppard, Anna. "Kurt Wagner, Nightcrawler—Primer." *ComicsXF*, 8 Apr. 2022, www.comicsxf.com/2022/04/08/kurt-wagner-nightcrawler/.
Peppard, Anna. "Nightcrawler Is a Sex-Positive Superhero. Here's How—And Why It Matters." WomenWriteAboutComics.com, 29 Apr. 2022, womenwriteaboutcomics.com/2022/04/patreon-exclusive-nightcrawler-is-a-sex-positive-superhero-heres-how-and-why-it-matters/.

Peppard, Anna F. "'The Female Fights Back!': A Feminist History of Marvel Comics." *Make Ours Marvel: Media Convergence and a Comics Universe*, edited by Matt Yockey, U of Texas P, 2017, pp. 105–37.
Peppard, Anna F. "Introduction: Presence and Absence in Theory and Practice: Locating Supersex." *Supersex: Sexuality, Fantasy, and the Superhero*, edited by Anna F. Peppard, U of Texas P, 2020, pp. 1–30.
Peppard, Anna, et al. "The Multiverse According to ComicsXF!" *ComicsXF*, 5 May 2022, www.comicsxf.com/2022/05/05/the-multiverse-according-to-comicsxf/.
Peppard, Anna, Christopher Maverick, and J. Andrew Deman, hosts. "Excalibur #43: 'Home Comforts.'" *The Oh Gosh, Oh Golly, Oh Wow! Podcast*, episode 45, 8 Jan. 2002, goshgollywow.com/2022/01/08/202/.
Roman, Christopher Michael. *Queering Wolverine in Comics and Fanfiction: A Fastball Special*. Routledge, 2023.
Rowe, Michael. "Great Scott: After Years of Struggling with His Sexuality, *Playgirl* Centerfold Scott Merritt Is Coming All the Way Out. To His Surprise, So Is *Playgirl*." *The Advocate*, no. 895, 19 Aug. 2003, archived at the Wayback Machine, 2 June 2006.
Scott, Darieck, and Ramzi Fawaz. "Introduction: Queer about Comics." *American Literature*, vol. 90, no. 2, 2018, pp. 197–219.
Smith, Jacob. "Showing Off: Laughter and Excessive Disclosure in Burt Reynolds' Star Image." *Film Criticism*, vol. 30, no. 1, 2005, pp. 21–40.
Spurrier, Si (writer), and Javier Pina (artist). *Uncanny Spider-Man*, nos. 2–3. Marvel, 2023.
Stein, Daniel. *Authorizing Superhero Comics: On the Evolution of a Popular Serial Genre*. Ohio State UP, 2021.

6

"My Other Life"

Queering Genres in Search of Bisexual Female Superheroes

Samantha Langsdale

I have never really considered myself to be a late bloomer, although I have always progressed through various life stages in my own time. Sure, certain aspects of who I am now seemed slow in manifesting, but the more I think about it, the more I realize that these things were always there, I just didn't know how important they were, or how to talk about them. The two that concern me here are my love for comics and my bisexuality.[1] Like most comics scholars, I could tell an origin story about becoming a fan that begins with my older brother and culminates with me as a scholar, but frankly, that would be disingenuous. I did indeed inherit my older brother's Spider-Man comics and accompanying 45 rpm vinyl records, but I don't recall these treasures being any more meaningful to me than his donated Star Wars action figures or my collection of My Little Ponies. They were all equally a part of my landscape of play. Nevertheless, because Spider-Man was a resident of my childhood imagination, it makes sense that I found my way back to comics and comics media in more personal ways later in life.

Specifically, blockbuster superhero films of the 1990s and early 2000s drew me in and led me to seek out more comics. I no longer wanted to engage with superhero fantasies via my brother's tastes; now I wanted to see *myself* in the stories I read. Falling in love with Jean Grey of the X-Men not only helped pave a unique path for me as a fan, but it also jumpstarted my scholarly career. Similar to other feminist media scholars, I began writing as both a fan and a critic of representations of women in mainstream superhero comics. Yes, it's exciting to see oneself as the protagonist of a story about fighting for justice and to be encouraged to imagine having the power to win that fight. But it is also disheartening when those opportunities are markedly rare, or when they are couched in visual rhetoric that maintains patriarchal ideals. Although I didn't start publishing these insights until well after I finished my PhD (creating a substantial lapse between my Spider-Man days and my debut as a comics scholar), I can say that superhero comics are an important part of who I am.

In some ways, my understanding of my sexuality runs parallel to my relationship to superhero comics: I have always had feelings and experiences that exceed heteronormative definitions of female sexuality, but I didn't know they were indicative of anything in particular until early adulthood. Throughout my adolescence, I had very little awareness of sexual identities beyond heterosexual and homosexual, and because there were long phases where I would classify myself as aggressively the former, I assumed the latter had nothing to do with me. It was not until undergraduate and graduate school that I was introduced to different ways of thinking about gender, sex, and sexuality. My feminist education taught me that like other aspects of our identities, sexuality is fluid, dynamic, and often so much more complex than social norms would have us believe. University-level gender studies helped me to understand that my experiences of physical and emotional intimacy with women were not glitches or flukes, but rather real expressions of the expansiveness of my desires. Even if I did not openly adopt the term until my early thirties, I now know that bisexuality has always been and continues to be a central aspect of my identity.

At this point you might be wondering what all this has to do with cartoonist Terry Moore's long-running independent comic *Strangers in Paradise*. The short answer is that it was the convergence of these two parts of myself that brought me to the Terryverse.[2] As I mentioned previously, I reentered comics fandom wanting stories that spoke to my own lived experiences. Unfortunately, the superhero genre has a long androcentric history. In fact, even cursory surveys of the representation of women and girls in superhero comics point to overwhelming trends of underrepresentation and marginalization, oversexualization and objectification, and the near ubiquity of whiteness, cisnormativity, heterosexuality, and able-bodiedness (Peppard; De Dauw 1–15).

Statistics reflecting the current state of affairs are hardly better. According to scholar Carolyn Cocca, "Female characters starred in about 15% of superhero comics in 2020, with about the same percentage being written or drawn by a female creator. In 2015 it was about 12%, in 2010 about 6%, and in 2000 about 5%. Women star in about 16% of superhero TV shows on air or in development, and in about 18% of films scheduled for release or in development." As Cocca notes, "given that women are 50% of the population, these proportions are quite low" (7). Representations of queer characters have often been just as disappointing. Esther De Dauw writes that while female characters did enjoy some increase in numbers over the years, "only a few superheroes came out as gay, and, at the time of writing [2021], gay superheroes remain low in number" (12). In short, the superhero titles I had to choose from to find stories about compelling bisexual female characters were slim pickings, so I went elsewhere.

What I found delighted and surprised me. Moore's *Strangers in Paradise* (hereafter SiP) focuses on the complicated relationships between its three main protagonists, Francine Peters, Katina Choovanski (a.k.a. Katchoo), and David Qin, as they come to terms with their pasts, their feelings for each other, and the uncertainty of the future. A genre-bending book, it is as much slice-of-life as it is romance, dramedy, thriller, and crime comic. SiP is also a title that floats around comics studies in a similar way to Los Brothers Hernandez *Love and Rockets*. Everyone has read them; everybody knows why they are considered foundational in some way. This kind of status made me assume that SiP would be altogether different from the superhero comics I had read and analyzed thus far. Even within comics studies there is a tendency to treat superhero comics as one-dimensional and unserious. When I arrived on the comics studies scene, for instance, people were generally welcoming, but I also got my fair share of annoyed sighs when I mentioned being interested in superheroes. So if everyone had read SiP, even the no-more-superheroes contingent, I figured it had to be the good stuff. Knowing that SiP is primarily about women's lives and relationships only added to my assumption that this was not like all the other (superhero) comics.

I was both right and wrong. *Strangers in Paradise* is indeed the good stuff, but part of what makes it great is its tendency to celebrate bisexual female characters through the rhetoric of the superhero genre. Although not ostensibly about superheroes (i.e., characters with extraordinary powers who are trying to save the world), SiP nevertheless cultivates a focus on themes such as bravery, love, and sacrifice. There is action, drama, suspense, and even alter egos. The bad guys are really bad, and the good guys are loveably flawed. The cast of SiP may not be trying to save the world, but they are trying to make their world a better place. Unlike many mainstream superhero comics, however, Moore eschews hypersexualizing, victimizing, objectifying, or marginalizing his female characters. Instead, they are depicted as women whose sexualities are just one part of their identities; they fight for themselves and each other; they are wholly human; and the women of SiP are the stars of the show. Moore also successfully avoids heteronormative tendencies to either erase bisexuality or to frame it as monstrous and deviant.

As an independent comic almost entirely focused on queer women, *Strangers in Paradise* can be identified as a queer counterpublic, that is, to cite the definition provided in this collection's introduction, "a self-consciously marginal discourse space capable of generating all kinds of fantasies about 'deviant' bodies and identities." But is it also a *superhero* story? I argue that Moore's willful use of visual and narrative elements common to the superhero genre in his composition of SiP does indeed demonstrate the instability and mutability of superheroes. And perhaps more importantly, as *Origin Stories* editors Michael Kobre and Peter Nagy suggest of the other superhero comics analyzed in this book, SiP enables fans like me to become initiated "into non-normative counterpublics" in which readers outside the cultural mainstream can find reflections of queer identities and experiences (4). True, SiP cannot be conventionally labeled a superhero comic, but in exploring and celebrating bisexuality as an inextricable aspect of powerful super women, Moore has given me the heroes I have longed to see.

Situating SiP's Superheroism

One of the ways fans and scholars typically identify a superhero comic is by its publisher. As the oldest and most prolific publishers of superhero comics, DC and Marvel are widely considered the paragons of the genre. They have each grown into multibillion-dollar transmedia franchises, becoming almost synonymous with the very idea of superheroes. Terry Moore's career has very little to do with either of the Big Two. Over the last thirty years Moore has drawn a handful of covers for both Marvel and DC and authored several issues of various titles for each, but by and large, the work for which he is most renowned has been published under his own Abstract Studio imprint. Read enough interviews with Moore during which he is asked about Batman, and you might get the impression that he doesn't even like superheroes (e.g., Loss). However, like the rest of us, Moore simply loves some characters (Supergirl) far more than others, and much of his disgust with characters like Batman (Moore refers to him as "Batcrap") is an expression of his aversion to the genre's troubling tendency to spotlight misogyny, hyper-individualism, patriarchy, sensationalist violence, and so on.

What I loved about SiP the first time I read it was the feeling I got that Moore had taken his favorite superhero stories and stripped away all the toxic elements of the genre. For me, it became clear that if Batman represents everything Moore hates about superheroes, SiP is everything he loves and wanted to see more of. This interpretation is certainly subjective, but I am also confident that it arises from Moore's signification of the superhero genre through particular "visual and verbal cues." Frederick Luis Aldama argues that this kind of reading is indicative of the co-creative nature of comics.

> When we open a comic and begin to read and view its pages, we *co-create*. The authors and artists select in *and* out details (writing and visuals) that at once hit our perception system *and* guide our imagination to thrill in their filling in of gaps; our emotions and thoughts fill in and complete drawn figures, gestures, dialogue, and character interaction, for instance. When we fill in the gaps, we co-create and we make the story our own. We don't change the story; we follow the carefully selected visual and verbal cues that make up the blueprint to *co-create* the story. We become chiasmic transformers, all while not changing the DNA of the story itself. (91)

In other words, there is no doubt that my perspective as a bisexual feminist scholar of superhero comics impacts the ways I fill in the gaps and co-create SiP as I read, but my insistence that Moore's comic bears the mark of the superhero genre is not entirely subjective. As I will demonstrate, superheroes are in the DNA of SiP, which can be seen in various visual and verbal cues in Moore's work. Because discussing all nineteen books in the SiP series is beyond the scope of this chapter, I will focus the remainder of my discussion on the eighth book, *My Other Life*,[3] where these cues are particularly visible.

Two aspects of SiP that resonate with superhero comics are its setting and the rules that govern the Terryverse. Like Spider-Man or Daredevil comics, SiP is primarily set in a real US city, in this case Houston, Texas. According to Jason Bainbridge, using a real US city as a backdrop is a hallmark of Marvel comics, which rely on a type of realism that sutures "the Marvel Universe to the real world, providing a material context for" its superheroes (172). This strategy allows Marvel to give their characters more depth (Spider-Man is both a superhero and a New Yorker), to connect them to lived communities, and to ground them in relatable ways. SiP's three main protagonists, Francine, Katchoo, and David, share an apartment together in Houston, and while *My Other Life* takes them across the country, early scenes and flashbacks make it clear that their community, and the roots of their relationship, are in Houston. For knowledgeable readers, this setting acts as one way into Katchoo, Francine, and David's world. As Bainbridge asserts, the use of a city as a setting makes the universe in question "*legible* for the reader by offering both connectivity (a city-based community) and an element of realism" because these are real places (168). For example, the eighth book opens with the three friends taking a road trip to a beach. This sequence not only shows us that they drove to the beach from Houston, but also that it's possible to see dolphins swimming in the water. For a Texan like myself, I am able to connect with David, Francine, and Katchoo by filling in the gaps and imagining that they are in South Padre Island. As part of the co-creative process, the setting of SiP invites me into the book in a similar way a New Yorker might connect to Spider-Man as he battles rush hour in Manhattan.

City settings are also foundational parts of building a shared universe in superhero comics. By locating several different characters in the same city, or at least allowing them to pass through, publishers like Marvel were able to establish a universe "predicated on connectivity and social networks" (Bainbridge 169). Moore similarly takes advantage of recognizable locations like Houston, New York City, and Hawaii to engender crossovers between his various casts of characters and, to borrow Bainbridge's words, create "the idea of a cohesive whole, a community of characters and titles that could collectively be thought of as" a universe. In Moore's case, this is the Terryverse. Such a cohesive universe also provides the context for creators to establish rules for their imagined worlds. Interestingly, for superhero comics, the use of real city places usually indicates that the surrounding universe should be imagined much like our own. Sam Cowling and Ley Cray write that "despite the presence of fantastic powers, technology, aliens, magic, and other oddities in superhero comics, there is a prevailing trend within superhero comics: they are (characteristically) set in the present in a storyworld that departs from actuality only minimally and in ways that primarily accommodate the existence of superheroes" (171). The Terryverse too is set in a contemporary age, and although it also incorporates "fantastic powers, technology, aliens, magic, and other oddities," it generally resembles our universe in all other ways. In *My Other Life*, for example, we see depictions of psychic visions, displays of extraordinary strength, miraculous survivals, and the presence of spirits or guardian angels all while the narrative centers on very real human problems that unfold in very real places.

In fact, the sequence in *My Other Life* where readers witness extraordinary strength (a point to which I will return) serves as just one of several examples throughout the book where Moore employs motifs common in superhero comics. The first is a dream sequence that opens the second issue in the book. Francine dreams that she is about to get married. The first three panels are close-ups of her face with caption boxes that narrate her thoughts about having waited her whole life for the big day. The subsequent panels pan out and reveal that rather than reflecting quietly in a dressing room, Francine has instead climbed out onto the window ledge of a high-rise brick building. As various relatives and guests plead for Francine to come back in, she becomes increasingly flustered and eventually loses her balance. In the dream, her father catches her by the ankle and holds her as she dangles out the window over the traffic below. Just at that moment, Katchoo appears in a lower window and offers to pull Francine to safety: "Take my hand," Katchoo says. "I'm **afraid!** What if you **drop** me?" screams Francine. "What if I save you?" Katchoo retorts. While various other elements of this dream indicate that it is meant to be read as surreal or absurd (the groom is a Disneyfied duck, Francine dangles with her dress tumbling up around her shoulders), this interaction between Katchoo and Francine resonates strongly with superhero comics. There is no small number of heroes who have either talked worried civilians down from ledges or saved them from precarious perches not of their choosing. Superman, Spider-Man, and that guy who dresses like a nocturnal animal who shall not be named have all saved people from themselves or the horrifying heights at which they find themselves. At this point in SiP, Katchoo has made it abundantly clear that she is in love with Francine, and while Francine is sure that she loves Katchoo as a best friend, her conservative Christian upbringing and low self-esteem cause her to struggle to know what she feels beyond that. Like a superhero with an outstretched hand, Katchoo offers Francine a way out of the danger she finds herself in. It frightens Francine, even though maintaining a (hetero) normative path also makes her feel as though she is dangling from a high-rise window with her knickers showing. Moore couches this conversation in a dream because whether Katchoo could literally save Francine from a window ledge is not the point (she probably could); rather, it is Katchoo's love and confidence that could help save Francine from a life she doesn't truly want.

This reading is substantiated by the fact that it is the second dream sequence in which Francine envisions Katchoo as a superhero capable of saving her from being trapped in the wrong life. The first occurred in book four of SiP, *Love Me Tender*, and was part of the only issue in the entire series where Moore invited another artist to draw pages. That artist was none other than Jim Lee, one of the most renowned contemporary superhero comics creators, cofounder of Image Comics, and currently the chief creative officer of DC Comics. In Moore and Lee's dream sequence, Francine imagines herself and David in monochrome as old-fashioned print journalists. Francine has a secret superhero alter ego, the Purple Phantasm, but we soon learn that she's not especially adept at saving the day. As she stands apologizing to a shop keeper for her botched attempt at fighting crime, a portal opens and futuristic villains in full color (another rarity in SiP pages) burst through, pursued by a roguish, gun-slinging, blonde hero. Francine's hero persona can hardly understand the dream version of Katchoo, as the blonde heroine's contemporary references and sarcastic humor leave the Purple Phantasm flummoxed and confused. As the superhero version of Katchoo prepares to leap out of the scene, Francine's alter ego screams, "Take me with you! **Don't leave me here!**" Lee's characteristic art gives Francine's dream a larger-than-life feel that exaggerates Francine's feelings of her own ineptitude while also lionizing Katchoo. Francine's monochrome coloring and inability to understand contemporary cultural references signal that she is stuck in an old-fashioned mindset, however desperately she may want that to change. Like the window ledge dream above, Moore and Lee's superhero dream aligns love, self-knowledge, bravery, and salvation with Katchoo. Because it is Francine who has these dreams, there is an implication that she does indeed desire Katchoo; they are, after all, fantasies. But the dreams also implicate Francine's inaction; like Spider-Man offering to swing Mary Jane through Manhattan, Katchoo's invitations are only part of the equation. Moore cuts both of Francine's superhero dreams short, cuing the reader to understand that dreaming is not enough. Francine must take Katchoo's outstretched hand; she must step out of dichotomous, "black and white" thinking for her desires to truly take flight.

That is not to say that Katchoo only performs superheroics in Francine's dreams. As mentioned previously, SiP emulates superhero comics by incorporating the fantastic into an otherwise realistic universe, and Katchoo's bravery often exceeds what is humanly possible. At the end of the second issue in *My Other Life*, Katchoo and David travel to New York City on an airplane that begins experiencing mechanical failure. Katchoo understands from the captain's announcements and the performance of the plane that they will crash. The third issue opens in a field alight with flames, black smoke filling the sky. Moore's intricate inks blend the mangled wreckage, raging flames, and billowing smoke in terrifying ways that consume each page and confuse the eye. Multipage panels and insets show Katchoo from various angles as she kneels in the wreckage where her seat would have been, her clothes ripped from her partially burned body, and her eyes filled with reflections of flame. As she comes to consciousness, she sees the spirit of her deceased former lover Emma walking toward her through the fire. Emma offers her hand to Katchoo, but as the weight of this gesture begins to sink in—a woman Katchoo loved and lost beckons her toward death—Katchoo says David's name in a weak and questioning voice. Emma looks through the flames toward the wrecked plane. Katchoo frantically scans for signs of David, alternately calling for him and looking to Emma for guidance. Although Katchoo has long been in love with Francine, she is also in love with David, and the presence of her lost love Emma reminds her of what she stands to lose again. Katchoo spots David unconscious, bleeding, and wedged into his seat. She desperately claws at twisted metal to free him, and as the flames and explosions intensify, so too do her anger and determination. Growling "RRRGH! ARGGG . . . !" as she rips away the impossibly large debris that traps David, Katchoo lets out one final scream as she frees him and hoists him over her shoulder. Emma disappears from the page as Katchoo stumbles away from the wreckage just before the plane erupts in a full-page blast, "KWA-BAUOM!" Nearby farmers run to the explosion to look for survivors and find Katchoo cradling a badly injured and still unconscious David in her arms.

Although the conclusion of this scene is decidedly more dire, I argue that it nevertheless recalls Stan Lee and Steve Ditko's much-loved sequence in issue 33 from *The Amazing Spider-Man*. Beginning two issues prior, Spider-Man, a.k.a. Peter Parker, has been battling one of his most formidable foes, Dr. Octopus, for access to a serum that could save his Aunt May from a fatal illness. The fight leaves Spider-Man badly injured and trapped beneath tons of fallen steel while the serum lies just feet away. He struggles to maintain consciousness as his strength fails underneath the weight of the steel and water falls all around him. As he tries to rouse himself, visions of

Figure 6.1. Terry Moore, *Strangers in Paradise: My Other Life*, Abstract Studio, July 2000.

Figure 6.2. Stan Lee and Steve Ditko, *The Amazing Spider-Man* #33, Marvel Comics, February 1966.

his Aunt May (the loved one he is trying to save) and Uncle Ben (the loved one he lost) float in the foreground of the panel. Eventually, Spider-Man realizes that he can't give up, regardless of his own injuries and the seeming impossibility of the task. Two pages of struggle finally lead to a splash page on which Spider-Man frees himself with one last effort. He grabs the serum just before the structural integrity of the room gives way and is then swept away by a wall of water. The issue concludes in the hospital where Aunt May, who has been unconscious, awakens slightly at Peter's presence. May and Peter hold hands briefly before Peter leaves the hospital for some much-needed rest.

While the circumstances that land them in these life-threatening situations differ, the parallels between Katchoo and Spider-Man's battles to overcome death cannot be ignored. Both are physically battered and in grave danger. Where the threat of rushing water worsens Spider-Man's situation, the threat of flames exacerbates Katchoo's. Both characters see visions of lost loved ones, which spurs each of them on to save those whose lives are now in their hands. Panic, exhaustion, intense pain, and fear eventually give way to determination and an extraordinary show of strength. In the panels where Spider-Man finally frees himself, and Katchoo finally frees David, Moore and Ditko draw their characters in dynamic action poses that accentuate their musculature and give the impression of rapid motion. Once Katchoo and Spider-Man have performed their herculean tasks and grabbed what they need (David in one instance, the serum in the other), each hero is swept away by the respective element that threatened their lives. Similar to the conclusion of *The Amazing Spider-Man* #33, *My Other Life* ends with David lying unconscious in the hospital. Katchoo comes to visit, and despite his grave condition—he is wrapped entirely in bandages and on a respirator—David rouses slightly at the sound of Katchoo's voice and squeezes her hand before she departs.

The first time I read this sequence I *felt* its impact more than I understood it. As I witnessed Katchoo rise from the flames and tear David from his seat, I recognized in myself the same level of excitement I got from reading superhero comics, and yet, SiP affected me so much more. Feminist scholars like Cocca critique the superhero genre's tendency to indulge in fantasies of strength as a substitute for collective political action. And while I agree entirely that "a punch to one white man's jaw from a glowing female fist doesn't dismantle multiple and overlapping systems of inequalities" (Cocca 88), as a bisexual woman embedded in systems designed specifically to work against my liberation, I still occasionally dream of being powerful enough to overcome all odds. Seeing Katchoo refuse death and summon extraordinary strength ignited my senses; I *know* the ferocity of that kind of love. Who wouldn't want to believe that they could summon that love to save a life? Later, after I reread this sequence (again and again) and identified its resonances with Spider-Man, I began to understand why it was so meaningful to me. Here was the first hero I had ever met, the one who brought me into the genre, but now she was like me. Katchoo is my favorite SiP character, and while it feels like she has abilities that exceed what is humanly possible, Moore does not imbue her with magic, mutation, or superpowers induced by spider. So why would he choose to compose a sequence that resonates with one of the most recreated scenes in Spider-Man's history? Because it is about love. Sure, Spider-Man survives being crushed by an entire steel structure because of his superpowers, but that's not what gives him the *will* to escape. Peter's love for his family and his desperate desire to protect the people around him from harm were what freed him; these are the elements that truly make him Spider-Man, and Moore's emulation of these aspects underscore what he values most about superhero stories. That he chooses to embody these traits in Katchoo, a queer woman, demonstrates both the protean qualities of the superhero genre and the ways SiP is distinct from it.

Distinguishing SiP's Superheroism

At the beginning of this chapter I reflected on my early assumptions about SiP and my insecurities about the quality of superhero comics. Reading and loving SiP helped me to address both. As I hope to have shown, although SiP may be conventionally labeled as distinct from superhero comics, the queerness of the genre has allowed Moore to incorporate certain of its aspects in the building blocks with which he constructed the series. Being able to recognize SiP's superhero DNA helped me shrug off reductive ideas about the one-dimensionality of superhero comics. Nevertheless, as I also mentioned previously, there are aspects of mainstream superhero comics that I still find troubling from the perspective of a feminist scholar, namely the under- and misrepresentation of women and the persistence of cisheteronormative patriarchal ideals. In this respect, I argue that SiP is quite different from many mainstream superhero comics.

Like the majority of creators at Marvel and DC responsible for bringing female characters to life, Moore is a straight white man. I suggest that what sets him apart from many of his counterparts at the Big Two is his feminist will to style. According to historian Estelle Freedman, feminism is "a belief that women and men are inherently of equal worth. Because most societies privilege men as a group, social movements are necessary to achieve equality between women and men, with the understanding that gender always intersects with other social hierarchies" (22). Whether or not Moore would call himself a feminist, I am applying the term to his creative ethos for two primary reasons: first, the sheer number of female characters in SiP (to say nothing of their complexity and dynamism) acts as a corrective to the disproportionate privileging of male characters across US media.

Second, at a creator spotlight panel at the 2022 International Comic-Con in San Diego, Moore discussed his inspirations behind making SiP a woman-centered queer comic. He admitted that as a younger man, he was fairly oblivious to patriarchy and its effects. At some point in the late 1980s and early '90s, the increasing number of women working as stand-up comedians caught his attention. Through their acerbic wit Moore learned the importance of listening to women and the need to view the world through the lens of their experiences. He also discussed his cousin, whom he loved and with whom he was close. The pain and suffering his cousin endured as a young gay man in the southern US had a profound impact on Moore. He became determined to tell stories like his cousin's, but also to create worlds where queer people like his cousin could find love and flourish. These motivations are part of what Aldama calls a creator's "will to style." He writes that "the will to style is shorthand for identifying the responsibility of the creator (or creators) in understanding well the building blocks of reality that they are reconstructing as well as the degree of presence of a willful use of skills and technical devices to give shape to the making of" pop culture phenomena (4). Therefore, following this definition, Moore's will to style may also be characterized as feminist because of the sense of responsibility he feels to understand well the building blocks of queer women's lives in his reconstruction of reality. The same cannot be said of the majority of mainstream superhero creators, particularly with respect to representations of bisexual female characters.

A Google search for "bisexual superheroes" returns a wealth of listicles arranged to highlight characters whom audiences probably did not know were bisexual (Wyatt, Gupta, Colby). This illegibility arises partly from dichotomous tendencies within the superhero genre and partly from problems created by heteronormative standards of representation more broadly. Jeffrey A. Brown writes that "what the superheroes repeatedly enact for readers is a symbolic policing of the borders between key cultural concepts—good and evil, right and wrong, us and them. Intertwined with these abstract concepts are corporeal boundaries between male and female, mind and body, self and other" (137). The attempt to secure boundaries and adhere to binary classifications also extends to sexualities. As discussed previously, most superheroes are heterosexual, but even beyond that there is a tendency to maintain what scholar Maria San Filippo calls "*compulsory monosexuality*, that is, the positioning of *either* heterosexuality *or* homosexuality as the two options for a socially recognised sexuality that is perceived as mature and sustainable" (71). When a superhero like X-Men's Mystique shapeshifts and takes on a gender different from her own, for example, whatever romantic or intimate encounters she may have in her alternative form were, for a long time, explained as a necessary byproduct of her powers rather than evidence of the fluidity of sexual desire. A reader may not know Mystique is a bisexual simply because, for much of her history, her nonbinary sexual identity only appeared as a narrative device.

Bisexuality is also made illegible by wider cultural trends. For instance, as San Filippo argues, "Bisexuality, unlike heterosexuality and homosexuality, seems to rely on a temporal component for its actualisation; at any given moment a bisexual person or character might appear monosexual depending on his/her present gender-of-object choice, thus contributing to bisexual (in)visibility" (71). As Ramzi Fawaz and Darieck Scott note, because comics are a sequential medium that repeats, proliferates, and expands across countless iterations, pointing to an original or authentic version of a character or story is almost impossible. This endless set of possibilities queers comics and allows for difference to manifest (202–3). Paradoxically, however, the iterative quality of comics may also serve to erase bisexuality. If, as San Filippo asserts, the visibility of bisexual identity is contingent on an expanse of time, rather than on any given moment, then the tendency for superhero comics to reboot with each creative team may serve to subsume bisexuality within heterosexuality or homosexuality. There may be no way to argue that a character is *only* heterosexual or *only* homosexual because of their capacity to appear as both across various iterations of a superhero title, but it is also difficult to insist that they are bisexual unless creators and readers are willing and able to take *every* iteration of the character into account. Finally, popular representations of bisexuality have historically framed bisexuals as untrustworthy, deceitful, immature, temporarily gay or straight, hedonistic, oversexualized, and promiscuous (Klesse; San Filippo). Again, one might recall the ways Mystique has been characterized as a femme fatale, a villain, a traitor, and a monstrous mother (Murray).

Moore not only avoids these problems in SiP, he also actively addresses them. All the main female characters in SiP are queer, and throughout the series, readers witness them entering into relationships and having intimate experiences with people of varying genders. From a feminist perspective, the depiction of intimacy is important because, as scholar Sarah Panuska notes, even as mainstream superhero publishers have slowly increased the number of LGTBQ+ characters, "expressions of intimacy are rare" (130). The dynamism of SiP's women as sexual subjects is important because it allows Moore to explore their diverse relationships within each issue, as well as over long spans of time throughout the series. As such, one would be hard pressed to erase bisexuality from the SiP equation. Moore also manages to create intrigue and suspense around his characters without framing them as duplicitous by nature of their sexualities. The title *My Other Life*, for instance, could be read as alluding to both bisexuality and superhero-like alter egos. As mentioned previously, throughout the book Katchoo expresses her love for both Francine and David, and by the time readers get to this volume, they are already aware that Katchoo has a troubled past that she is trying to overcome. The same could be said for David, who, like Katchoo, was raised under violent circumstances and who begins a new life in an attempt to atone for his wrongs and become the kind of person he wants to be. Katchoo and David are never characterized as having troubled pasts *because* of their sexual identities. Moore never intimates that these characters seek out other lives because they are untrustworthy by nature, but rather, because they have suffered from toxic upbringings.

Refreshingly, Moore also confronts these kinds of biases head on. Rather than ignore how biphobia might affect his characters, and thus present a somewhat disingenuous rendition of queer life, Moore includes a scene in *My Other Life* that acts as another point of access for readers like me. Although only Katchoo and David wound up on the plane to New York, the second issue of the book makes it clear that Francine was intended to join them. Rather than come to terms with her own internalized homophobia and her jealousy of Katchoo's relationship with David, Francine simply tries to say that she doesn't feel right joining the pair on the trip. The argument

Figure 6.3. Terry Moore, *Strangers in Paradise: My Other Life*, Abstract Studio, July 2000.

that unfolds between Francine and Katchoo reveals Francine's inability to conceive of bisexual desire as authentic and sustainable. Resonant with many biphobic sentiments, Francine tries to frame Katchoo's feelings for David as confused, and she tries to insist that Katchoo must choose between herself and David (and thus by extension, between loving a woman and a man). Even though both Francine and Katchoo shout at each other and end up in tears, it is only Katchoo who can clearly articulate what love means: someone who will support her, accept her unconditionally, sacrifice when needed, and most importantly, someone who knows that they love her back.

Moore makes clear the kind of biphobia a character like Katchoo would experience by virtue of Francine's accusations. Powerfully, Moore also undercuts the validity of Francine's words by revealing that it is she who is confused about herself and about love. This kind of scene sets SiP apart from many superhero comics because, as Panuska argues, "a willingness to accurately reference and reflect real-life LGBTQ community and culture" is just as important as "making LGBTQ sexuality *visible*" (131, emphasis in original). It also acts as confirmation of Moore's feminist will to style. For me personally, this scene helped to cement everything I had learned about myself up to the point that I picked up SiP. At that stage, I had the feminist vocabulary to discuss gender and sexuality, but I had only just begun to use it to describe myself. I won't say that Katchoo, Francine, and David's interactions were *the* deciding factor in my identifying publicly as bisexual, but they mattered. Why couldn't I feel desire for both my own gender and for other genders? Why shouldn't I be able to embrace that as an integral part of who I am? Katchoo's reaction to Francine helped me to affirm that our society is often unreasonable in its demands on people's desires—be it for love or comic books—and that I didn't have to choose between narrowly defined categories.

The original *Strangers in Paradise* series concluded in 2007. Thankfully, Moore brought the crew back for a shorter series celebrating the comic's twenty-five-year anniversary, *Strangers in Paradise XXV*, and several of the characters have appeared in other of Moore's books. Moore also regularly posts sketches of his characters on social media, many of which focus on Katchoo and Francine. Not infrequently, Moore draws the two women cosplaying as superheroes. My favorite sketch recreates the upside-down kiss from Sam Raimi's 2002 *Spider-Man* film, only in Moore's drawing Katchoo hangs in the web-slinger's place as Francine leans in for the kiss. This kind of sketch shows the women getting fully into character, but others feature Katchoo, Francine, or both complaining about the impractical nature of the costumes designed for female superheroes. These sketches perfectly demonstrate the mutability of superheroes as well as Moore's playful yet unique engagement with the genre. His use of certain aspects of superhero comics, like a recognizable yet fantastic world or death-defying rescues, underscores the elasticity of the genre. Further, because Moore employs superhero motifs to celebrate a cast of mostly queer women, he proves that there is nothing about the superhero genre that makes its history of patriarchy, cisheteronormativity, androcentrism, and white supremacy inevitable. As an independent comic, *Strangers in Paradise* can certainly be counted as a queer counterpublic; one that I argue has superheroes embedded in its DNA. By building on and exceeding the conventions of mainstream superhero comics, Moore can explore and celebrate the lives of bisexual women in ways that inspire readers like me to imagine that we could be heroes.

Notes

1. According to Christian Klesse, "Bisexuality has been evoked as the proper name for a desire that does not limit itself to the eroticization of one gender; or it has been described as desire that does not discriminate in terms of either gender or the morphology of the sexed body" (230). My own understanding of the term suggests that as a bisexual, I experience desire toward and may have intimate experiences with people of my gender and people of other genders.

2. Terry Moore has cartooned numerous books, which, in addition to SiP, include *SIP Kids*, *Echo*, *Rachel Rising*, *Motor Girl*, *Strangers in Paradise XXV*, *Serial*, *Five Years*, and *Ever*. While they all have their own casts of characters and unique storylines, it is clear that they are all part of the same world. Most of Moore's characters also make appearances in storylines not originally their own. Moore's name for this shared fictional world is the Terryverse.

3. SiP was originally published as ninety individual issues. It was compiled into nineteen trade paperbacks (of which *My Other Life* is one), as well as three hardback omnibus volumes and six pocketbook collections. Moore is also currently working on new hardback omnibus editions.

Works Cited

Aldama, Frederick Luis. *Latinx Superheroes in Mainstream Comics*. U of Arizona P, 2017.

Bainbridge, Jason. "'I Am New York'—Spider-Man, New York City and the Marvel Universe." *Comics and the City: Urban Space in Print, Picture and Sequence*, edited by Jörn Ahrens and Arno Meteling, Continuum, 2010, pp. 163–79.

Brown, Jeffrey A. *Beyond Bombshells: The New Action Heroine in Popular Culture*. UP of Mississippi, 2015.

Cocca, Carolyn. *Wonder Woman and Captain Marvel: Militarism and Feminism in Comics and Film*. Routledge, 2021.

Colby. "10 DC Characters You Didn't Know Were Bi." *CBR*, www.cbr.com/dc-characters-bisexual/.

Cowling, Sam, and Wesley Cray. *Philosophy of Comics: An Introduction*. Bloomsbury Academic, 2022.

De Dauw, Esther. *Hot Pants and Spandex Suits: Gender Representation in American Superhero Comic Books*. Rutgers UP, 2021.

Fawaz, Ramzi, and Dariek Scott. "Introduction: Queer about Comics." *American Literature*, vol. 90, no. 2, June 2018, pp. 197–219.

Freedman, Elizabeth. *No Turning Back: The History of Feminism and the Future of Women*. Ballantine, 2003.

Gupta, Manas Sen. "10 LGBTQ+ Superheroes You Probably Didn't Know About." *Lifestyle Asia*, www.lifestyleasia.com/bk/entertainment/lgbtq-superheroes-comic-books-you-didnt-know/.

Klesse, Christian. "Shady Characters, Untrustworthy Partners, and Promiscuous Sluts: Creating Bisexual Intimacies in the Face of Heteronormativity and Biphobia." *Journal of Bisexuality*, vol. 11, nos. 2–3, 2011, pp. 227–44.

Lee, Stan (w), and Steve Ditko (p, i). *The Amazing Spider-Man*, no. 33. Marvel Comics, 1966.

Loss, Robert. "Afflicting the Comfortable: An Interview with Terry Moore." *PopMatters*, www.popmatters.com/143876-afflicting-the-comfortable-an-interview-with-terry-moore-2495999448.html.

Moore, Terry. *Strangers in Paradise*. Abstract Studio, 1993.

Moore, Terry. *Strangers in Paradise: Love Me Tender*. Abstract Studio, 1997.

Moore, Terry. *Strangers in Paradise: My Other Life*. Abstract Studio, 2000.

Moore, Terry. *Echo*. Abstract Studio, 2008.

Moore, Terry. *Rachel Rising*. Abstract Studio, 2011.

Moore, Terry. *Motor Girl*. Abstract Studio, 2016.

Moore, Terry. *Strangers in Paradise XXV*. Abstract Studio, 2018.

Moore, Terry. *Five Years*. Abstract Studio, 2019.

Moore, Terry. *Ever*. Abstract Studio, 2020.

Moore, Terry. *Serial*. Abstract Studio, 2021.

Murray, Ross. "The Feminine Mystique: Feminism, Sexuality, Motherhood." *Journal of Graphic Novels and Comics*, vol. 2, no. 1, 2011, pp. 55–66.

Panuska, Sarah. "'Super-Gay' Gay Comix: Tracing the Underground Origins and Cultural Resonances of LGBTQ Superheroes." *Supersex: Sexuality, Fantasy, and the Superhero*, edited by Anna F. Peppard. U of Texas P, 2020, pp. 129–50.

Peppard, Anna. "'This Female Fights Back!': A Feminist History of Marvel Comics." *Make Ours Marvel: Media Convergence and a Comics Universe*, edited by Matt Yockey. U of Texas P, 2017, pp. 105–37.

San Filippo, Maria. "The Politics of Fluidity: Representing Bisexualities in Twenty-First Century Screen Media." *The Routledge Companion to Media, Sex, and Sexuality*, edited by Clarissa Smith, Routledge, 2017, pp. 70–80.

Spider-Man. Directed by Sam Raimi, Sony Pictures, 2002.

Wyatt, Liz. "10 Bi Superheroes Marvel & DC Fans Forget Exist." *Screen Rant*, screenrant.com/marvel-dc-comics-bisexual-superheroes-fans-forgot/.

7

BITTEN BY THE BUG OF WOMEN'S FASHION

Superman's Pal Jimmy Olsen as Transvestite Fantasy Fiction

Peter Nagy

> Superheroism is a kind of transvestism; our superdrag serves at once to obscure the exterior self that no longer defines us while betraying, with half-unconscious panache, the truth of the story we carry in our hearts, the story of our transformation, of our story's recommencement, of our rebirth into the world of adventure, of story itself.
>
> —**Michael Chabon,** "Secret Skin"

Picture the following scenario: Sensing someone in danger with his super hearing, Clark Kent, the clumsy, hapless *Daily Planet* reporter, ducks into a phone booth or empty alleyway and begins his transformation. Removing his glasses and tie, Kent rips open his collared shirt in that most iconic image of heroic metamorphosis. But then something unexpected happens. Underneath the shirt he reveals not the familiar red S logo emblazoned on blue spandex, but rather, traditional women's clothing—perhaps a colored brassiere, or a corset. Swiftly swapping out his sports jacket and khaki pants for a wig, skirt, nylon stockings, and heels, Clark Kent comes out dressed not as a super-man, but as a woman. Her name is Clara Katherine, or maybe Claire Kensington. Walking the streets of Metropolis with a small purse over her shoulder, she catches the eyes of some men—and even some women. But no one suspects her alter ego. Underneath the average man, we discover, is not the hardest of hardened masculinities, a man of steel. Quite the opposite. It is a much more mutable, irreverent secret identity:

a man-turned-woman, a man who takes pleasure in dressing and being seen as a woman, and who, in doing so, transgresses the very permeable boundaries of normative masculinity.

Of course, this never happens in Superman comics. At least not explicitly, as far as I know. But something like it does occur more than once in a solo title featuring Superman's sidekick, the *Daily Planet* photographer Jimmy Olsen. Beginning in the late 1950s, Olsen starred in his own adventures in a series called *Superman's Pal Jimmy Olsen*, which was under the editorship of Mort Weisinger, who creatively steered Superman through the late fifties and sixties and introduced a variety of innovations, such as the bottle city of Kandor, the idea of the yellow sun as the source of Superman's power, and several new kinds of kryptonite. Weisinger created the Olsen comics and another spinoff title, *Superman's Girlfriend, Lois Lane*, as a way to expand Superman's world with a cast of supporting characters that came to be known as the Superman family. Like the Batman family (Robin, Batwoman, and Batgirl), the Superman family, which later included figures such as Supergirl and Superman's dog, Krypto, reflected DC's effort, in the late fifties, to provide a heteronormative corrective to the perception that comics were perverse, a view popularized by Fredric Wertham's *Seduction of the Innocent*, which inspired public hearings about the perceived depravity of comics and the subsequent creation of the Comics Code Authority, the self-regulatory rating system adopted by many comics publishers as a means to appease public demands for censorship.

But in the sixties, Superman and his family grew to resemble something quite different from what DC initially intended. As Matt Yockey notes in "Superman Family Values," the Superman family ultimately subverted as much as it reinforced the notion of the traditional nuclear family. It comprised not only Superman's blood relatives but also a range of uncanny figures from the expanded comic universe whose exotic differences contrasted with classic Superman's powerful white nationalist body. These figures included Bizarro (a monstrous inversion of Superman), Mxyzptlk (a magical alien from another world), and Chameleon Boy (a colored shapeshifter from the future) among others. In this way, the Superman family represented a "dialectic between the familiar and the strange," between the heteronormative and that which lay clearly outside the "boundaries of the heteronormative family" (58).

Weisinger's transformation of Superman into the paterfamilias of a bizarre family was part of his larger assault on some of the more normative aspects of the character. As several biographical accounts suggest, Weisinger had a rather emotionally complicated relationship with superheroes. On the one hand, he was proud of his work on Superman. But on the other, he was ashamed of what he did for a living. Being a comics editor was emasculating. It meant sacrificing his creative autonomy and his lofty literary ambitions to work in an industry stigmatized as child's play. As a result of this ambivalence, Weisinger, as he confessed to learning in therapy, developed a "psychological rivalry" with Superman, who was the face of the comics profession and the fictional embodiment of the masculine authority he felt lacking in himself (Crippen 226). This rivalry manifested itself in the quasi-Oedipal war that Weisinger waged on the character during his editorship, as he produced comic after comic that systematically "humiliated" and subverted Superman as a patriarchal symbol (229). These "destroy-the-icon" issues, as they came to be known, displayed a weakened, subdued, and sometimes infantilized Superman, effectively tarnishing him as an icon of fatherly authority (230).[1]

If Weisinger's work on Superman was his dirty little secret—what was, at once, a hidden source of pleasure and shame—one can hardly guess how he felt about *Superman's Pal Jimmy Olsen*, a series that, at times, openly and unapologetically risked the very kind of emasculation with which Weisinger struggled. Why Weisinger greenlighted some of the title's more extreme stories, those that would, at least on the surface, call his masculinity into question, is entirely a matter of speculation. But perhaps it is not too much of a stretch to imagine that, like other men whose ambivalence toward normative manhood expresses itself in unpredictable (and sometimes decidedly antinormative) ways, on some level Weisinger, whose manhood was so embattled and precarious that he needed to dominate a fictional character to prove himself, wanted to explore what being a man would look like without the imposition of patriarchal masculinity. Apparently, what it looked like was Jimmy Olsen, the symbolic son of Superman.

In the absence of a traditional father figure, and in keeping with the youth culture of his day, Jimmy was free, in the pages of *Superman's Pal Jimmy Olsen*, to experiment with his body and identity.[2] As a result, the Olsen comics read like an acid trip. Straight out of the silver-age emphasis, in the nuclear era, on the plasticity and adaptability of the human form, in almost every issue Jimmy Olsen underwent some kind of fantastical metamorphosis, either through his nifty disguise kit or by means of exposure to supernatural forces—aliens, magic lamps, chemicals, and other various predictable comic tropes.[3] Sometimes these transformations looked like conventional masculine fantasies, as Jimmy turned into a rock star, international spy, or some other desirable figure. But quite often they were wildly imaginative, playful spins on the concept of heroic transformation that pushed the superhero genre firmly into the terrain of the nonhuman and issued a radical challenge to traditional notions of male embodiment and identity. At various points, Jimmy morphed into, among other things, a wolfman, a robot, a Martian, a skyscraper, a circus clown, and a ventriloquist dummy.

Undoubtedly, these transformations were safer to try out on Jimmy, who was not restricted to Superman's brand of hegemonic white masculinity and who was, as a sidekick, more apt to have his conventionality called into question.[4] But regardless, by extending "male" into the terrain of the fantastical, by stretching that category to accommodate a range of bodies and identities, Jimmy's bizarre and theatrical makeovers worked to destabilize the rigid phallic ideal typically embodied by the male superhero. Echoing the "multiplicity" that Anna F. Peppard identifies in her work on the television show *Lois & Clark*, Jimmy's malleability "demystifies" masculinity by showing that it "*can* be played with" (232). It attests to a "genericness" that shows "Masculinity might be no more than a fetish, a disguise or costume that a man (or, perhaps, the right woman) can put on or take off as they need to or want to" (235). As man who traded in his secret identity for decidedly nonphallic costumes, for uncanny iterations of the heroic self that Yockey sees as characteristic of the sixties Superman family, Jimmy shattered masculinity into a kaleidoscope of possible configurations.

In what were arguably the most shocking of all these configurations, Jimmy occasionally transformed into a woman. Commonly referred to as the Olsen transvestite stories, three comics in the series—*Superman's Pal Jimmy Olsen* #44 (1960), #67 (1963), and #84 (1965)—featured Jimmy, in his most blatant subversion of the phallic ideal, crossdressing and disguising himself as a woman for various reasons.[5] These moments of gender fluidity were ambiguous. On the one hand, they were clearly transphobic spoofs meant to comically subvert a man's desire and ability to pass as a woman. But on the other, they seemed to insist that such identifications persist in the face of suppression.

In what follows, I attempt through a mixture of analysis and personal reflection to answer some questions about Jimmy's transformation into a woman. I'm interested in how the images of Jimmy in women's clothes challenge the phallic ideal typically associated with male superheroes. In "Superheroes, Pornography, and Phallic Masculinity," Jeffrey A. Brown argues that the conventional male superhero's costume functions to preserve the phallic ideal—the mythology of male size, potency, and invulnerability—by accentuating and making a spectacle of the hero's powerful body. It "serves as a literal veil for the secret identity and the penis," for the "inherent weakness" of the man underneath the spandex (252–53). If that is the case, does Jimmy Olsen's drag lift the veil of conventional costumes? Does it bring to the surface the soft interior the male super body typically disavows? What does it mean that the Jimmy Olsen transvestite comics make a spectacle not of a phallic male body but an effeminate one? I'm also interested in how men, such as myself, who have a more tenuous relationship to phallic masculinity, work through gendered fantasies and anxieties in their encounters with images of male fluidity. What does it mean for such men to encounter images of feminized masculinity, even as those images are, as I will show with respect to the Jimmy Olsen comics, ambiguously or ambivalently presented? In what ways do such images make accessible to men the desires, forms of embodiment, and styles of self-fashioning that exceed the rigidity of the phallic ideal? To what extent do they open and/or foreclose a more multiplicative, kaleidoscopic masculinity?

Catching the Bug

I don't remember the exact moment I first encountered the Jimmy Olsen comics. Or whether it even happened the way it plays out in my memory. But when I was a kid, I was introduced to superheroes by my favorite uncle, a child-like man in his early twenties who was the youngest of three boys in a family of six children growing up in a townhouse in Queens. He lived in the basement among his toys, glass figurines, science fiction posters, and the hundreds of comics he kept in towers of long cardboard cartons in the laundry room. At some point, somewhere in those towers, on a comic cover with the words "Jimmy Olsen" printed in oversized purple lettering, I remember looking at a pastiche of panels displaying a freckled man dressed in various disguises. This, I would later learn, was the cover of issue #95 of *Superman's Pal Jimmy Olsen*, a giant-sized collection of back issues that featured Jimmy on the cover and that included the first Olsen transvestite story, #44. In one panel, this man (Jimmy) wore a cowboy hat and counted dollar bills, a southern tycoon of sorts. In another, he was bald and brandishing a gun while wearing a tuxedo. But only one image,

Figure 7.1. Otto Binder and Curt Swan, *Superman's Pal Jimmy Olsen* #95, DC Comics, September 1966, cover.

in the lower left-hand corner, really caught me. In this one, he had large arms, but the rest of him was small. He was wearing white undergarments, boxer shorts, I think, and a tank top. He was putting on lipstick in front of a mirror and wearing a red wig and pink stockings. A slight bend in the waist accentuated his petiteness. It looked like he was showing off his delicate legs and dainty rear end. A long green dress with black polka dots hung in the corner of his dressing room.

Something about the image thrilled me. Already at the age of five or six I had looked through my fair share of comics. I was familiar with the swift costume changes that turned Clark Kent into Superman, Peter Parker into

Spider-Man, and Barry Allen into Flash. But there was something captivating about the meticulousness of Jimmy's transformation. It was like he was more excited about the costume than his reason for wearing it. I remember panels showing Jimmy pulling the green dress out of his disguise trunk, instantly recognizing that it needed to be ironed, and then spending an entire scene smoothing out the wrinkles. This threw me because I was accustomed to every comics panel being filled with action and suspense. I didn't remember Batman ever posing in front of a mirror before leaving the Batcave, or Flash taking the time to smooth out what should have been the very wrinkled spandex suit concealed in his compression ring. A whole panel spent on ironing a cute dress? Revisiting the comic now I think I understand part of what struck me about Jimmy and the piece of myself I saw in him: his sheer enthusiasm for women's clothes. As he works the iron, he's already dressed in stockings and heels. I guess he just couldn't wait to get started.

Something else struck me too. I knew what I held in my hand was a Superman comic. After all, it was titled "*Superman*'s Pal." It defined its titular character through Supes, who, in one panel, appeared on the cover alongside Jimmy—to boost sales, probably. But the funny thing is that there wasn't much Superman in the comic itself. Just as he was lost in the pastiche of costumed Jimmies on the cover, so too was Superman, who made only occasional appearances, all but eclipsed in the stories. Before I knew anything about Weisinger and his rivalry, I had the feeling that Superman, in his boring three-color spandex, couldn't compete with Olsen. Jimmy, in all his marvelous multiplicity, was the star. I remember yearning for the beautiful variation of his clothes. His pink bathrobe, blue dress, green dress, and even the rather skimpy skirt he wears at one point. I was in awe of his drag. He disappeared into being a woman so completely. It's like his body was ready for it. I envied his long, smooth-looking legs that flowed into those heels. He was very, very leggy. One panel showed him kicking his smooth legs high into the air along with a line of chorus girls from whom he was hardly distinguishable.

I believe there was something about the gorgeous image of Jimmy dressed as a woman that got inside me when I was young, something that spoke to, or perhaps instilled, impulses I was hardly aware I possessed. As Michael Kobre and I discuss in the introduction to this collection, in "Queer about Comics," Ramzi Fawaz and Darieck Scott offer a theoretical framework for understanding this kind of identification. Drawing on Michael Warner, they suggest that superhero comics function as a queer counterpublic, a

Figure 7.2. Otto Binder and Curt Swan, *Superman's Pal Jimmy Olsen* #44, DC Comics, April 1960.

self-consciously marginalized discourse space that challenges "normative social relations" and courts various social outsiders, including outsiders to gender and sexual normality (200). As a queer counterpublic, comics provide such outsiders with avenues for self-recognition, as they, with respect to gender and sexual outcasts, mirror various desires, identifications, and forms of embodiment that are generally excluded in the dominant culture. One's recognition of one's own difference through comics and one's entry into the counterpublic can happen at any time, even before (as Scott's first encounter with queerness through the image of the Wonder Woman villain Nubia suggests) one has the awareness or language to name their queer attachments. In his memoir, *Sense of Wonder*, Bill Schelly's memories of his first encounters with comics provide an illustration of this process. Schelly describes how the narrative and visual elements he took in as a young fan, such as the tropes of secrecy in *Superboy* and the bulging crotches in

Spider-Man, amounted to an education in homosexual desire that shaped him as a gay man. Before he was even conscious of homosexuality or could name the male body as an object of desire, Schelly felt something in these comics that spoke to him. They opened him to desires to which he, growing up in 1960s suburbia, might not otherwise have been exposed.

As for me, I didn't know at the time I first saw the Olsen comics that I, like Weisinger's experimental son, Jimmy Olsen, was compelled to break the shackles of patriarchal norms, to identify with women, and even, on occasion, to dress like them. I'm not really sure how to connect the dots, but as a child and then as a young man (or "man") I was shaped by what initially felt like competing attachments but now, looking back through the lens of comics history and queer theory, fit together quite nicely. A part of me loved conventional male superheroes. As a short, scrawny, thin-skinned boy, I thirsted for the power fantasies many of them represented. Sometimes I'd pretend I was Batman. Growing up, my brother and I would dress up in PJs and chase coat-hanger-and-yarn batarangs over the backs of couches. Or I'd pretend I was the Thing or Hulk, and I'd smash and clobber invisible enemies with pillows I'd stuff into oversized shirts. But other times I channeled my inner Jimmy, whether I knew it or not. A few years after I initially pondered Jimmy's legs, when I was seven or eight, I cross-dressed for the first time. One afternoon my older sister, who I followed around for years and who had taught me to play with girls at recess and to love so-called girly things like New Kids on the Block (my favorite was the nerdy Jonathan), made me into a girl. Grabbing what she found in her closet, she dressed me up in a skirt, clip on earrings, a headband, and all the blush and eyeshadow possibilities from a child's makeup kit. I remember loving my reflection in the mirror. There was no sense of shock. I was at home in women's clothing. It was just so much more imaginative and detailed, so much more alive, than men's clothing. She then pranced me about, her pristine creation, in front of our mildly surprised mother. While I would only later learn terms like transvestite, autogynephilic, queer, gender fluid, I knew this was for me.

But it isn't all pleasure. In fact, for me, there was, and remains, a lot of shame in my desire for a feminine self-image. I remember feeling that shame keenly more times than I care to count. But one memory stands out. When I cross-dressed for the third time, in middle school, for Halloween, a young boy who, as I made my trick-or-treat rounds through our neighborhood dressed in my sister's clothes and my mother's makeup, stopped me and asked whether I was actually a boy or girl. I asked him defiantly:

"What does it look like?" "A girl!" he responded mockingly. The boys around him, and the one dad watching them, broke out in laughter. Hating myself, I retreated home. I didn't cross dress again for years.

I see this same shame in the Olsen comics. If Jimmy was free to play with feminine identification, he was also conflicted about it. One way to make sense of this ambivalence is by understanding the Olsen comics in light of what Chris Straayer dubs, in "Redressing the 'Natural,'" the "temporary transvestite" story (402). In this kind of story, a character, typically a man, is compelled to cross-dress by outside circumstances and, as a woman, flirts with the possibility of homosexual romance until s/he is unmasked as a heterosexual man at the end of the story. By ultimately assuring the impermanence of character's transvestitism and the indelibility of his "real" sex, these kinds of stories provide a transphobic relief of sorts, giving audiences (presumably straight, cisgender audiences) the safe thrill of momentary exposure to fluid displays of gender and desire (402).

The Olsen comics echo the temporary transvestite stories in two ways. First, in these comics, Jimmy typically is compelled to pass as a woman for external reasons. In the original transvestite story, issue #44, the motivation is straightforward. Using the name Julie Ogden, Olsen goes undercover as a woman and wears a polka dotted green dress, makeup, and red wig (all of which he, curiously enough, happens to have on hand) to get the inside scoop on Monte McGraw, a mobster suspected of a jewel robbery who is looking for chorus girls for a musical he's putting on as a front for his crimes. In the second transvestite story, issue #67, the outside motivation for cross dressing is slightly more complex. In what appears to be a response to its historical moment, the comic depicts Jimmy dressing in women's clothing in order to, paradoxically, secure his masculinity against the growing presence of women in conventionally male jobs. When Jimmy realizes that Lucy Lane (Lois Lane's niece and his main romantic interest throughout the *Superman's Pal* series) makes more money than he does, he feels unmanned and so asks his boss, Perry White, the chief editor at the *Daily Planet*, for a raise. When White refuses, Jimmy quits and tries to land a job at the rival paper, the *Globe*, only to learn, in an experience of further emasculation, that they have already hired a female reporter. That's when Jimmy concocts the plan to disguise himself as "Leslie Lowe, Girl Reporter!" to get his old job back (Dorfman and Swan 1). "If everybody is hiring girls, maybe that's the way I'll get my job back!" he says. "Perry will need someone to replace me! I'll fool him into hiring me as a girl reporter" (4). Two panels show

Jimmy putting on a green dress, high heels, a pearl necklace, and a red wig, and then passing seamlessly in public, in front of men who catcall him. The last of the comics, issue #84, similarly presents an external motivation for Jimmy's transvestitism. But here the plot device is especially flimsy. In this comic, the president of the all-male Jimmy Olsen fan club (apparently he has one) leaves and Jimmy must choose the next leader. He decides that to do this fairly, he must infiltrate the clubhouse disguised as a woman, to secretly gauge the leadership qualities of the members. Wearing a purple dress and red wig, Olsen shows up at the club and works to gain membership in it by proving that s/he can be one of the boys.

In addition to presenting practical reasons for his transvestitism, the Olsen comics further mirror the temporary transvestite tale by reinforcing notions of natural sexual difference and heteronormativity despite their playful depictions of gender and sexual fluidity. That is, even as Jimmy passes as a woman and flirts with homosexual attraction, the comedic situations he finds himself in at various points insist that he is fundamentally male and straight. In issue #44, for instance, as part of the musical, Jimmy must dress up in a baseball uniform and pretend to play ball. The layers of gender fluidity (Jimmy dresses as a man as he's dressed as a woman) call attention to the performativity of gender, suggesting that perceived sexual difference is a matter of costume and conduct. But this performativity is quickly undercut by Jimmy's "natural" male athleticism when he forgets to "throw like a girl," shocking the director of the musical and almost blowing his cover (quotations mine). In another scenario, Jimmy, living with McGraw's girlfriend Maisie, accidentally burns dinner and replaces it with what turns out to be dog food, illustrating his laughable ineptitude at doing "women's work" (quotations mine). And in perhaps the most memorable moment, Jimmy, in order avoid a good-night kiss with McGraw, who finds him more attractive than his own girlfriend, substitutes himself with Maisie's pet chimpanzee. McGraw, eyes shut, kisses the chimp thinking it's Julie. Here the comic undercuts the sexual fluidity it flirts with—the possibility of a (homo)sexual encounter between a straight man and a man dressed as a woman. Such scenes, which are repeated in issue #67, when Jimmy narrowly avoids being exposed by hiding himself in a bubble bath, and in issue #84, when he is the only fan club member not afraid of the snakes and frogs he's forced to collect, represent the notion of a man passing as a woman as a joke—as a laughably tenuous spectacle that fundamental sexual difference always threatens to disrupt. Taken this way, the

Olsen comics belong in the same vein as comedy films (*Some Like It Hot*, *Tootsie*, *Mrs. Doubtfire*, *Sorority Boys*, to name just a handful) in which men temporarily disguise themselves as women for outside reasons.[6]

Yet something as complex and unpredictable as queer desires and identifications cannot be neatly swept away. And sometimes they persevere, despite our best effort to suppress them. Forgetting the transphobic laughter of my youth, in college I rediscovered my love of crossdressing. One night I fell asleep in a friend's dorm. As a joke, she put lipstick and eyeliner on me. I pretended to be grossed out, but I walked back to my dorm without washing. On a trip to Paris I wore nail polish, eyeliner, and eyeshadow. I remember young French girls giggling at me in the airport. I smiled back at them. On another occasion I cross-dressed for sociology class as part of an assignment to break social norms. I walked into a local comic shop wearing full face makeup. The shop owner stared at me as he rung up my *Flash* comics.

It's apparent to me that on some level Weisinger wanted Jimmy to persist, just as I did. For while the Olsen comics exhibit some of the characteristics of temporary transvestite tales, they are also remarkably resistant to the form's insistence on essential sexual differences. For one, the comics refuse the final emphasis on heteronormativity characteristic of such tales, which typically resolve their depiction of gender and sexual fluidity by ultimately exposing the MTF transformation of the protagonist as a mere ruse. In direct contrast to this, at least two of the issues conclude with an ambiguous, if not outright queer, final image. At the end of issue #44 Jimmy's cover is blown when McGraw notices his Adam's apple: "I get it! You posed as a dame to get the goods on me! You played me for a sap! Okay! This is your last impersonation!" (Bernstein and Swan 9). The exposure momentarily subverts the comic's exploration of gender fluidity by emphasizing the inescapability of anatomical sexual difference. But the story doesn't end there. The final panel shows Jimmy at work at the *Daily Planet*, typing up the McGraw story. Inexplicably he's still in the green dress he wore as Julie Ogden, sans the red wig. In the image, several male colleagues hover over him. "Hey, cutie! How about a date?" one says. "What's your name, baby?" another says. "Beat it, you guys. I saw her first," the last declares. The tone of the men isn't clear. Are they sincerely hitting on Jimmy? Are they being sarcastic? A winking Jimmy says, "Sorry, gents! I'm a changed 'girl'! From now on, I'm Mr. Jimmy Olsen" (9).

This is, I think, meant to be funny. In one sense, it is, like the narrative cues indicating Jimmy's fundamental manhood, a wink to the reader that

Figure 7.3. Otto Binder and Curt Swan, *Superman's Pal Jimmy Olsen* #44, DC Comics, April 1960.

confirms his transformation back into his true, male self. Yet the image is also unmistakably queer. It shows a man in a green dress being hit on by other men. In this context, Jimmy's transformation takes on a different meaning. He has "changed" into a man who still wears a dress and who has become an object of male sexual attraction (9). This is a Jimmy who retains the gender and sexual fluidity he has enacted throughout the story. Simply put, Jimmy still wants, in some sense, to be a "girl" (9). After all, he had time to change before going into work, no? Why not show up in trousers and dress shirt, what the men who hit on him are clearly wearing? Simply put, there's no story-driven reason for him to be wearing the dress. Thus, for all its insistence on his external reasons for cross-dressing, the comic also suggests that Jimmy wants to dress as a woman simply because he enjoys it.

I get this. As someone who frequently looked for excuses to cross dress, I understand Jimmy's pretext for putting on women's clothing. Early on I learned that Halloween was a great opportunity for transformation. The first time I put on women's clothing without my sister's help was in elementary school, when I dressed in her clothes and put on my mother's makeup (blush and mascara as I remember) for the Brookside Elementary

Halloween parade. I recall that when we pulled into the bus off area, a young girl sitting on the bus next to us noticed my blush and mascara. Her eyes lit up in amused surprise. We were both excited for my dress.

We see such pretexts being exposed for what they are throughout the Olsen transvestite stories. Issue #67 presents a scenario like that in #44. At first, the comic seems to remasculinize Jimmy. At the end, after Jimmy gets the raise he wanted, he asks his girlfriend Lucy Lane to celebrate it over a steak dinner, in an attempt to correct his initial emasculation. But the comic subverts this convention. Lucy Lane refuses Jimmy and accuses him of cheating on her after spotting, in his car, the pearl necklace and green purse he wore as Leslie Lowe. After having his romantic triumph spoiled by his feminine alter ego, Jimmy returns home and puts on a bubble bath for himself. The last panel shows him immersed in suds, playfully blowing bubbles in a provocative, stereotypically feminine manner. "Well, anyway," Jimmy thinks to himself, "I learned one thing from masquerading as a girl . . . I like bubble baths!" (Dorfman and Swan 9). This is, on the surface, a lighthearted conclusion that pokes fun at the whole scenario of passing as a woman. Jimmy learns to like something self-indulgent, sensuous, that is usually associated with a woman. But taken another way, we can see the comic invested in indicating that there's actually something more profoundly transformative going on. There's something permanently feminizing about the experience of passing as a woman. The experience has, in a sense, queered Jimmy by leaving intact a trace of the feminine persona. While this is clearly meant to be comical, there is also the sense that the comic is purposely refusing to remasculinize Jimmy. It does not provide him the fulfillment of "being the man" by taking out Lucy Lane (quotations mine). Rather than undoing his initial feeling of emasculation, Jimmy indulges in the feminization that initially threatens him.

As these final panels suggest, the Olsen comics are a much more porous container for gender and sexual fluidity than temporary transvestite stories. And in contrast to those stories, which, as Straayer argues, yield subversive meanings only insofar as viewers resist their heteronormative thrust, the Olsen stories actively solicit the queer imagination through ambiguous images and plot points. Take, for example, the convention of the male transvestite's external motivation. If, in the comics, Jimmy wears women's clothing as a practical disguise, he also does it, unmistakably, as an act of pleasure. Not only does he always seem quick and eager to cross-dress, he is also very knowledgeable about how to dress like a woman, and he pays

Figure 7.4. Edmond Hamilton and John Forte, *Superman's Pal Jimmy Olsen* #67, DC Comics, March 1963.

meticulous attention to detail as he puts on women's clothes. In issue #67, for instance, as Jimmy transforms himself into Leslie Lowe, he says to himself in the mirror, "I used rouge over my face to cover my freckles and this desire me lipstick will make me look like a doll, even if I do say so myself!" (4). There is, here, enthusiasm in becoming a woman (something he inexplicably needs no help doing) and autogynephilic pleasure at seeing one's feminine self-image. Jimmy wants not just to look like a woman, but an attractive one. His "desire me lipstick" is hot—and he knows it (4).

Other similar moments sprinkled throughout the comics further show Jimmy's pleasure in being a woman. When, in issue #84, the male fan club attempts to exclude Jimmy-as-Jacky by saying that members have to wear bowties, and that, as a woman, she couldn't possibly do so without a collared shirt. Jimmy/Jacky lifts her skirt and shows some leg, revealing that she's wearing a bowtie garter. This is an interesting scene. Aren't there other ways to resolve this plot point? Why include this panel? Couldn't Jimmy have worn the garter on his arm or some other less erotic body part? To the queer reader, the implications are clear: Jimmy wants to show leg. After all, he shaved.

I'm moved by the persistence of Jimmy's feminine identifications, by the large and small ways he takes pleasure in embodying normative womanhood, in showing off his smooth legs and the hottest shade of lipstick. I love his indifference to being a proper heterosexual male, the attention he receives from men, and the way in which he'd rather indulge himself in a bubble bath than pursue Lucy Lane. I also love the way in which he walks around fearlessly in women's clothes. While I'm sure it was beyond the scope of the comic to engage with the very real issue of transphobic violence, there's something about the cool confidence with which Jimmy carries himself in a dress that suggests he's unafraid. Looking at the comics now, I see Jimmy as the embodiment of queer masculinity that's relatively immune to the demands of the patriarchal manhood Mort Weisinger associated with Superman and that he wanted to stamp out, if only because he was envious of the fatherly icon. Jimmy does not cave to the pressures of needing to prove his masculinity or his heterosexuality. He gets to live out a desire to dress and be seen as a woman and to playfully flirt with men despite the pressures of heteronormativity.

In this way, the Olsen comics function, for me, as a kind of wish fulfillment, one that is markedly different from the power fantasies typically associated with superhero comics. Their capacity to fulfill queer desires that are difficult to enact in a trans- and homophobic society leads me to believe that they might have a different historical root than we've assumed. In my mind, the transvestic images in the Olsen comics echo those in transvestite fantasy fiction, a subgenre of stories about crossdressing that emerged alongside modern transvestite communities. Grant Morrison, in *Supergods*, was the first to make this connection: "The transvestite Olsen stories seem deeply rooted in the underground world of mimeographed porn mags and the bondage comics of Eric Stanton, whose studio also employed a certain Joe Shuster, Superman creator. The language used recalls stories like *Panty Raid* (discussed at length by Robert J. Stoller, M.D., in his 1985 book *Observing the Erotic Imagination*) and other 1950s transgender tales in which hunky young jocks got more than they bargained for when a trip to the sorority house turned into a forced initiation into the pleasures of female underwear and makeup" (66). Morrison's references, here, to popular spoofs of male transvestitism, and to Stoller, a psychoanalyst who reads transvestite stories like *Panty Raid* as proof that men cross dress as a defensive response to emasculation, effectively places the Olsen comics within the once common understanding of transvestitism as a farce or pathology.[7] But, as Morrison also recognizes, what separates the Olsen comics from these stereotypical crossdressing stories and reductive psychological interpretations of transvestitism is their clear lack of a defensive posture. As he puts it, "The difference being that Olsen was fully in control of his transformations and could hardly wait more than a couple of pages to get them underway" (66).

Given Jimmy's unbridled enthusiasm to cross dress and, as I have suggested, the persistence of his feminine persona, I want to argue that a more precise cultural touchstone for the comics are the crossdressing fantasies that came directly out of the transvestite societies rather than those, like *Panty Raid*, that were written for a mainstream (cisgender, straight) audience. It is no coincidence that the Olsen series emerged alongside the modern transvestite movement. In the sixties, around the same time that Jimmy was strutting around in heels and pearls in the pages of comics, Virginia Prince emerged as an icon of organized transvestitism in the US. After her desire to cross-dress (I will use female pronouns to refer to Prince for the years she assumed a feminine persona) led to a public divorce that made newspaper headlines, Prince gained a national following among (mainly male) transvestites and became the representative of transvestite communities where she lived in LA and across the country. As part of the movement, Prince founded several transvestite-specific periodicals, including *Transvestia*, *Femme Mirror*, and *Clip Sheet*, in which members of the transvestite community published and exchanged a variety of letters and articles about cross dressing (Bullough and Bullough 284).[8]

Named Chevalier Publications after the famous historical transvestite figure Chevalier d'Eon, these magazines (like publications associated with other transvestite societies across the world, such as Britain's *Beaumont Bulletin* and Australia's *Feminique*) amounted to a minority literary subculture. Most importantly, for our purposes, these magazines published transvestite fantasy stories created by members of the community. Like superhero comics, these stories represented a form of wish fulfillment. Sent in by the magazines' largely male readership, they depicted coming-out fantasies in which male protagonists with a secret desire to cross-dress transformed themselves into women and then passed in front of loved ones and the broader public. These fantasies echo comics in several interesting ways. Like comics, they were seen as perverse, obscene, and in need of censorship, which the Postmaster General's Office happily provided at one point. But more importantly, the transvestite stories, like the Olsen tales, presented a variety of realistic and unrealistic circumstances (such as secret missions or kidnappers) as the external compulsion behind male cross-dressing. As Biegel and Feldman have argued, this was a convention meant to relieve the transvestite writer and reader of the shame surrounding the desire to cross dress. It enabled the male transvestite to imagine scenarios in which he had no choice but to wear women's clothes.[9]

Understood in light of transvestite fantasy fiction, the Olsen stories take on new meaning. Jimmy's outside reasons for cross dressing (to get the scoop on a mobster, to reclaim his job, to infiltrate his fan club) need not be seen as a heterosexual safety net that subverts gender fluidity, à la the temporary transvestite tale. Rather, they can be thought of as a mechanism that enables Jimmy, and the queer readers like me who identify with him, to explore the desire to appear and be seen as a woman without fear or guilt. Interestingly, the transvestite fantasies also dabble in the same kind of surrealistic plot devices common not just in the Olsen comics but in the superhero genre more broadly. As Harry Brierley puts it, "Almost without exception stories in these magazines elaborate on the fantasy of how a boy becomes a beautiful girl and magic, supernatural, or even science fictional themes appear. . . . The stories are always of a fairy-tale quality even if they do not resort to magic mirrors and mysterious potions. There is invariably the theme of the miracle of a strongly male hero emerging instantaneously as a beautiful woman. It is rare indeed for stories to be based on the real-life efforts of the transvestite to acquire the skills to 'pass'" (132). A man miraculously and instantaneously transformed into a different physical state through science or magic who then passes in public and even in front of those who know him best. Sound familiar? Transvestite literature's theme of sudden, astonishing change in appearance and identity can be understood as a parallel to the swift makeovers characteristic of DC superheroes like Batman or Superman. Here, too, transformation represents male wish fulfillment. But one that subverts rather than consolidates patriarchal masculinity. As the Jimmy Olsen comics make plain, it satisfies a wish to become a beautiful woman. Thus, rather than gamma or cosmic rays, mutant genetics, or a radioactive spider bite, it is Jimmy's desire for feminine identification that is the agent of his transformation. He is, we might say, bitten by the bug of women's fashion.[10]

Comics History, Queer History

Given their apparent responsiveness to contemporary transvestite fantasies, the Olsen comics, I want to argue, exemplify the "mutually constitutive" relationship between queer history and queer comics that Ramzi Fawaz and Darieck Scott theorize (199). In this light, Jimmy Olsen's crossdressing adventures represent the superhero genre's response to the history of transvestitism, specifically to an emergent community of gender outsiders, some of whom who were, through trans magazines, circulating their own fantasies about ostracization and metamorphosis. Just as transvestite fantasy fiction helped to foster a minority community through stories that addressed and linked together gender outcasts, the Olsen comics can be understood as a medium for queer identification and self-recognition that helped link together those on the fringes of gender normality, especially men who take pleasure in dressing and being seen as women.

While there is, as far as I know, no direct evidence that links the Olsen stories to the transvestite fantasy narratives that came out of Chevalier Publications, online archives of fantasy and sci-fi transgender/crossdressing fiction, the modern successor to those narratives, illustrate the strong ties between the genres.[11] For instance, on the website *fictionmania*, which collects over forty thousand trans stories published by anonymous authors, one finds gender transformation stories that explicitly focus on superheroes, stories that draw out queer subtexts from classic storylines or reimagine seemingly cis/straight characters as trans. Supporting my argument that Jimmy Olsen resonates with genderqueer fans, one author, BobH, provides his own spinoffs on the silver-age Olsen crossdressing stories. Manipulating scans of original panels, he creates new trans comics out of old cis ones. In one instance, he recreates the cover of giant-size issue #95 but replaces the images of Olsen dressed in various masculine disguises with more images of Jimmy crossdressing. The subtitle reads "Jimmy Olsen's Female Masquerades," and an accompanying story pokes fun at the flimsy circumstances for Jimmy's feminine impersonations. In another, BobH recreates a storyline from Jimmy Olsen #74 in which, for plot-related reasons, Olsen disguises himself as a tall, brawny, dark-haired upper-class man while his blonde-haired love interest, Lucy Lane, disguises herself as a redheaded debutante. In the original story, Olsen and Lane, who do not recognize each other, find themselves attracted to each other despite their disguises, attesting to the transcendent power of heterosexual attraction. But in BobH's rewrite, it is Olsen who transforms into a woman and Lane who turns into a man. And they do so for no reason other than to fulfill a longing to cross-dress and to explore same-sex desire—in Olsen's case, to Lucy in drag, and in Lane's, Jimmy as a woman.

The significance of the Jimmy crossdressing stories hasn't been lost on comics writers and artists either. In *Supergods*, Grant Morrison, one of the

Figure 7.5. BobH, "The Confessions of Jimmy Olsen"

most celebrated comics writers of his generation, remembers the Olsen comics as his gateway into more fluid identifications.[12]

> Artist Curt Swan drew the cub reporter as outrageously attractive in his makeup and a red wig. In heels and stockings, Olsen looked like he'd wandered in off a Pussycat Dolls video shoot. And there were a few gloriously disorienting panels where, sans wig, he was seen talking to Superman while still casually dressed in a pink dressing down, fluffy slippers, and movie star makeup. And yet, if it was okay for Olsen, wasn't it okay? I grew up with this idea of the disguise kit and the performance, the idea of both body and identity as canvas.

> When I adopted as a youthful role model the shapeshifting, bisexual assassin Jerry Cornelius from Michael Moorcock's novels, I was following in the footsteps of Jimmy Olsen. (66)

I, too, followed in the footsteps of Jimmy Olsen. Revisiting the transvestite stories now, as a queer scholar in my thirties, I'm reminded of Michael Chabon's poetic description, in "Secret Skin," of the superhero as a queer figure, a transvestite whose "superdrag" represents "the story we carry in our hearts, the story of our transformation." The story of my own transformation is hardly heroic. It is not a triumphant coming-out narrative. The transformation itself was not sudden or miraculous. There was no fortunate accident with gamma or cosmic rays. It is, as I imagine to be true for other genderqueer, fluid, or transvestic men (and women), rather oscillatory. It's an open-ended process of self-understanding and self-fashioning. And as I hope the personal asides make clear, this story (and I do carry it in my heart) is inseparable from my first encounter with the Olsen transvestite stories, which have been calling out to me my whole life. Through Jimmy, I entered the queer counterpublic of superhero comics at a formative age, well before I became aware of the historical context of the Olsen comics or had the conceptual language—words such as gender-queer, gender fluid, or transvestite—to understand what kinds of identifications and attachments the images of Jimmy in drag engendered in me. Olsen was, for me, a source of trans fantasy that initiated a lifelong process of coming-into-being as a genderqueer person. As I hope I've demonstrated, superhero comics, particularly those with gender-fluid imagery and queer narrative elements, function not just as mirrors for gender and sexual outsider-ness, but as a symbolic network through which we outcasts, particularly those of us who fall through the cracks of the gender binary, constitutes ourselves as such.

Notes

1. For examples of Weisinger's emasculating Superman stories and for a wider discussion of his effort to humiliate Superman, see Tom Crippen's interview with him in "Mort Weisinger Talking at Parties." For more about Weisinger's feelings about Superman and working in comics, see Gerard Jones's *Men of Tomorrow* and Weisinger's 1975 interview with Guy H. Lillian III. In the interview Weisinger confesses, "When people asked me what I did for a living, I would suppress the fact that I was editing *Superman*. I'd tell people that I wrote for *Collier's* or *The Saturday Evening Post, True* magazine . . . where I had published articles."

2. The father-son dynamic between Superman and Jimmy was something that Weisinger actively poked fun at. The cover of *Superman's Pal Jimmy Olsen* #30, for instance, shows Superman punishing an apologetic Jimmy (in this issue, the adopted son of Superman) for getting him a crappy Father's Day gift, a robe that he destroys with his heat vision.

3. For a fuller list of Jimmy's multiple disguises, see "Episode 26—Jimmy Olsen" in the podcast *Three Panel Contrast*.

4. See Joseph Brennan's "I Think That's My Favorite Weapon in the Whole Batcave." Brennan explores how superhero porn parodies amplify the stereotype of the young sidekick as a sexual bottom.

5. Jimmy Olsen was not the first crossdressing male superhero. That honor goes to Richard Stanton, a Golden Age DC hero, featured in *Crack Comics*, who disguised himself as elderly woman Madame Fatal to get the upper hand on unsuspecting criminals.

6. For observations about gender fluidity and transvestitism in fan culture, see Anne Kustritz's "Meet Stephanie Rogers, Captain America."

7. Stoller offers a reading of "Panty Raid" as an example of transvestite fantasy literature. He interprets the story as a dramatization of the psychosexual roots of transvestitism, what he sees, drawing on Freud's understanding of fetishism as a defense mechanism, as a pathology rooted in the heterosexual male subject's need to overcome the so-called trauma of his mother dressing him as a girl at a young age (which was in vogue in the early twentieth century) by, paradoxically enough, crossdressing and thus exercising agency over that early experience of emasculation.

8. For an overview of Virginia Prince and the history of organized transvestitism, see Vern L. and Bonnie Bullough's *Cross Dressing, Sex, and Gender*. See also Susan Stryker's *Transgender History*.

9. For an additional early analysis of transvestite literature, see Neil Buhrich and Neil McConaghy's "Transvestite Fiction." For historical context and overview of studies of transvestite fantasy literature, see Vern L. and Bonnie Bullough's *Cross Dressing, Sex, and Gender*, which includes summaries of the findings by the analysts referenced in the essay. For a psychoanalytic reading of a single transvestite fantasy story, see Robert J. Stoller's *Observing the Erotic Imagination*.

10. The theme of miraculous alteration that the Olsen comics share with transvestite fantasy fiction can also be understood, alternately, as a representation of the kind of hybridity that Ramzi Fawaz sees, in *The New Mutants*, as characteristic of the postwar superhero, which was defined by "constant transition and change" as opposed to the static, unchanging bodies and identities of classic superheroes (22). According to Fawaz, in the 1960s atomic-age anxieties about the impact of technological advancement on bodies and identities spurred comic book writers to imagine mutants who were born through modern pseudoscientific accidents that had radically destabilizing effects on the human form and who were often, as a result, hybrid subjects that—like the Fantastic Four, Hulk, or Spider-Man—represented a miraculous fusion of the human and nonhuman. Understood in this context, Jimmy's transvestitism represents the embodiment of radical alterity, an effect of his encounter with Otherness, in this case the opposite gender.

11. Given their propinquity, it's probable that the writers and artists behind *Superman's Pal Jimmy Olsen*, and maybe even Mort Weisinger himself, were shaped by the modern transvestite community and its influence on cultural understandings of gender and sexuality. It is also possible that this went both ways. The superhero-like conventions

of transvestite fantasy fiction, such as miraculous physical transformation and the idea of secret identity, suggest that the authors of those stories might have been just as easily shaped by comics. After all, it's no small coincidence that transvestite fiction was produced largely by men who, very much like comic fans, felt different and ostracized, and who desired to find other outcasts like themselves. Might they have enjoyed dual membership in comic fan communities as well as transvestite societies?

12. I wish there were more anecdotal evidence like Morrison's from fans of the Olsen comics, but I've found none yet. As is the tradition with serial comics, a section of the Jimmy Olsen series, called "Jimmy Olsen's Pen-Pal's," was devoted to fan mail. In these letters, fans excitedly weigh in on everything from Jimmy Olsen's various transformations to his romantic failures. But as far as I can tell, no reader ever responded to him transforming into a woman. Though perhaps the silence itself is telling. It could mean that even for those who identified with Jimmy, or who simply wanted to discuss his crossdressing, there was a desire to remain closeted about it. Or it could also mean there was hesitance or fear of discussing the image of Jimmy as a woman—that for all their excitement over Jimmy as a werewolf, robot, or ventriloquist dummy, fans didn't know what to do when he put on a dress.

Works Cited

Beigel, Hugo B., and Robert Feldman. "The Male Transvestite's Motivation in Fiction, Research and Reality." *Advances in Sex Research*, Harper and Row, 1963, pp. 198–212.

Bernstein, Robert (writer), and Curt Swan (artist). "Miss Jimmy Olsen!" *Superman's Pal Jimmy Olsen*, no. 44, DC Comics, 1960.

Binder, Otto (writer), and George Papp (artist). "Jimmy Olsen's Female Fan!" *Superman's Pal Jimmy Olsen*, no. 84, DC Comics, 1965.

BobH, "The Confessions of Jimmy Olsen." www.fictionmania.tv/stories/readhtmlstory.html?storyID=14206567171091392759

Brennan, Joseph. "I Think That's My Favorite Weapon in the Whole Batcave: Interrogating the Subversions of Men.com's Gay Superhero Porn Parodies." *Supersex: Sexuality, Fantasy, and the Superhero*, edited by Anna F. Peppard, U of Texas P, 2020, pp. 265–90.

Brierley, Harry. *Transvestism: A Handbook with Case Studies for Psychologists, Psychiatrists and Counsellors*. Pergamon Press, 1979.

Brown, Jeffrey A. "The Visible and the Invisible: Superheroes, Pornography, and Phallic Masculinity." *Supersex: Sexuality, Fantasy, and the Superhero*, edited by Anna F. Peppard, U of Texas P, 2020, pp. 245–64.

Buhrich, Neil, and Neil McConaghy. "Transvestite Fiction." *The Journal of Nervous and Mental Disease*, vol. 163, no. 6, 1976, pp. 420–27.

Bullough, Vern L., and Bonnie Bullough. *Cross Dressing, Sex, and Gender*. U of Pennsylvania P, 1993.

Chabon, Michael. "Secret Skin." *The New Yorker*, 3 Mar. 2008, www.newyorker.com/magazine/2008/03/10/secret-skin

Crippen, Tom. "Mort Weisinger Talking at Parties." *The Comics Journal*, vol. 302, 2013, pp. 223–35.

Dorfman, Leo (writer), and Curt Swan (artist). "Leslie Lowe, Girl Reporter!" *Superman's Pal Jimmy Olsen*, no. 67, DC Comics, 1963.

Fawaz, Ramzi. *The New Mutants: Superheroes and the Radical Imagination of American Comics*. NYU Press, 2016.
Fawaz, Ramzi, and Darieck Scott. "Introduction: Queer about Comics." *American Literature*, vol. 90, no. 2, June 2018, pp. 197–219.
Jones, Gerard. *Men of Tomorrow: Geeks, Gangsters, and the Birth of the Comic Book*. Basic Books, 2004.
Kustritz, Anne. "Meet Stephanie Rogers, Captain America.: Genderbending the Body Politic in Fan Art, Fiction, and Cosplay." *Supersex: Sexuality, Fantasy, and the Superhero*, edited by Anna F. Peppard, U of Texas P, 2020, pp. 317–40.
Lillian III, Guy H. "Mort Weisinger: The Man Who Wouldn't Be Superman." *The Amazing World of DC Comics*, no. 7, July 1975, theages.superman.nu/Creators/weisinger_interview.php. Accessed July 14, 2020.
Morrison, Grant. *Supergods: What Masked Vigilantes, Miraculous Mutants, and a Sun God from Smallville Can Teach Us About Being Human*. Random House, 2012.
Peppard, Anna F. "No One's Going to Be Looking at Your Face": The Female Gaze and the New (Super)Man in *Lois & Clark: The New Adventures of Superman*. *Supersex: Sexuality, Fantasy, and the Superhero*, edited by Anna F. Peppard, U of Texas P, 2020, pp. 221–44.
Peppard, Anna F., Andrew Deman, and Michael Hancock "Episode 26—Jimmy Olsen." *Three Panel Contrast*, Apple Podcasts, podcasts.apple.com/us/podcast/three-panel-contrast/id1438637823.
Schelly, Bill. *Sense of Wonder: My Life in Comic Fandom—The Whole Story*. North Atlantic Books, 2018.
Stoller, Robert J. *Observing the Erotic Imagination*. Yale UP, 1985.
Straayer, Chris. "Redressing the 'Natural': The Temporary Transvestite Film." *Film Genre Reader IV*, edited by Barry Keith Grant, U of Texas P, 2012, pp.484–509.
Stryker, Susan. *Transgender History*. Seal Press, 2008.
Warner, Michael. *Publics and Counterpublics*. Zone Books, 2005.

PART 3

MASKS

8

Sound of Her Wings

Feminist Counterpublics and the Gender of Death in *The Sandman*

Alison Wellford

As a kid in the 1980s and '90s, I remember scanning the comic book aisles for women superheroes to look up to. I only found near-softcore porn on the pages: Black Canary in fishnet stockings and bustier, Catwoman in skintight latex, blonde bombshell Supergirl poised as if to leap off the page to ravish the reader. This trend in comics began as early as the forties with Good Girl Art, comics that depicted "good-looking girls" such as Betty Page lookalike Phantom Lady, inspired by pin-up models and drawn as diversions for servicemen in World War II. By the nineties, comics were full of Bad Girl Art supervillains: sex-drenched, violent femme fatales in stilettoes who were even wilder and more dangerous than their predecessors, such as the revival seventies comic *Vampirella*.

These hypersexualized superheroines never appealed to me as a girl. Women superheroes were drawn by men for male readers—cartoon versions of *Playboy* models. But then, one day, a friend from school loaned me a pile of comics and magazines, where I first found *The Sandman*. I had little interest in Dream, the comic's brooding protagonist, nor its creator, Neil Gaiman—decades later, his abuse casting a shadow over everything. I only remember the breakout character Death's iconic gothic figure pressed into the paper grain and the kinship I felt. Death revolutionized the woman superhero. And at the time, for me, she changed everything.

Death made her debut in vol. 2, #8 of Neil Gaiman's *The Sandman* series in 1989 and in 2022, episode 6 of the Netflix series, played by Kirby

Figure 8.1. Kurt Busiek and Louis Small Jr., *Vampirella*, vol. 2, #2, Harris Comics, March 1992, cover.

Howell-Baptiste. Originally drawn by Mike Dringenberg and modeled on goth fashion designer Cinnamon Hadley, Death the superheroine resembled a real-life woman with spiky black hair wearing a simple black tank top and jeans. That in itself was pretty radical in the eighties.

Death revolutionized the woman superhero by representing a femininity that didn't need to prove itself to be powerful. She's Death, after all, the character who will survive existence itself. "When the last living thing dies, my job will be finished. I'll put the chairs on the tables, turn out the lights and lock the universe behind when I leave," she says in the series "Dream Country" (20).

Figure 8.2. Neil Gaiman and Mike Dringenberg, "The Sound of Her Wings," *The Sandman*, vol. 8, Vertigo: DC Comics, March 1997.

As one of the Endless, Death belongs to an all-powerful, immortal family of seven siblings: Death, Delirium, Desire, Despair, Destiny, Destruction, and Dream—anthropomorphizations of the natural forces and emotions in all the DC Universe. Her character continues in the tradition of superheroines with godhead origins or godlike power, such as Wonder Woman, a demigod born of Queen Hippolyta of the Amazons and Zeus. However, unlike conventional superheroines, Death wears no mask, no cape, and most distinctively, no corset or skintight bodysuit. Her strength doesn't rely on her erotic potential. She's beyond that.

Death paved the way for less sexualized superheroines in comics who came later, like Marvel's Jessica Jones, and importantly, she opened the doors to women readers of superhero comic books, often first-time readers, including me.

You see, Death had a secret power that I wanted for myself. As the embodiment of the last hurrah, the final word, no one could harm her even if they tried. Death was untouchable. And as a kid, I wanted more than anything to be like her.

In 1987, I was eleven and in love with my Jordache jeans and T-shirt, with its turquoise logo of a wild horse imprinted on the front. I traced the loose and feral lines over and over in my notebooks. I often pretended I was that wild horse, throwing off my shirt and running alone through the fields behind our farmhouse in Virginia.

But I was shy and polite around company. The first time I remember meeting my father's tennis partner from Florida, I quietly sat on the arm of the living room sofa, braided my long hair, and read *Sweet Valley High*. I didn't know how my father knew him or how they had met, nor did I care enough to ask. He wasn't much taller than me, seemed overly nice, and stared at me at length, a greedy smile on his lips. It was the first time anyone had looked at me that way, as if he were devouring me with his eyes. I couldn't comprehend why my father's friend, nearly a forty-year-old man, would find a kid so interesting or what his gaze meant.

"Do you like art?" he asked me one time while I was doodling in a notebook. He showed me a painting he had recently finished. It was a portrait of our house, an old tenant farmhouse, not one I thought beautiful or worthy of a painting.

I must have said yes or shown polite enthusiasm for his artwork, because I remember his next words clearly, how he had tried to manufacture connection.

"We have a lot in common," he said. "We like the same things." His face betrayed a pleasure I didn't understand or share.

He started coming over more often. He sat perched on the edge of his chair, his hands on his knees. I remember he wore a big metallic watch that looked expensive and old, inherited rather than earned. The wristband was too large, and it hung loose on his wrist. While he stared at me for long stretches of time, he'd shake his wrist and rattle it, reminding me of the sound a rattlesnake makes before striking.

When my parents left the room to grab a beer or to feed the dogs, he'd move to the sofa, to get closer to me. I remember he smelled of mothballs, must. He had a drunk look on his face when he slipped me gifts in small boxes: an ugly black and white photo of him wearing thick black spectacles as a boy, a game of jacks I would never play, notes written in spooky, scrawling handwriting that I couldn't decipher. I thought so little of his gifts, I never shared them with my parents. I piled the boxes beside my dresser and didn't look at them again.

One late spring afternoon when my parents had taken my brother to tee-ball practice, the phone rang. They had just installed a handheld phone in my bedroom, and I was excited to hear from a school friend. I jumped off the bed, my toes digging into my thick pink carpet. My pink curtains flowed in the wind. Out the window, newly planted corn stretched to the horizon; we lived miles from anything.

It was my father's friend on the line.

"Pack your things. We're going to Florida. Hurry up," he said, his voice anxious. He must have been watching the house for weeks, as my parents rarely left me alone. "I'll take better care of you than your parents do."

I don't remember what I said in return. I knew immediately I was in danger, suddenly the victim in one of the horror films everyone told me I was too young to watch. My heart pounded so hard in my chest I thought I could feel it bouncing off my ribs. I ran downstairs to the front door as fast as my legs could carry me, slammed it, and locked it. I closed the kitchen and living room windows and frantically locked them one by one. I ran back upstairs, planting my hands on each carpeted step to go faster, and hid under the bed.

First, he knocked gently on the front door, but when I didn't answer, he banged harder. He must have started kicking the door, as the windows rattled in their frames. Our door had loose hinges, and the old farmhouse windows were poorly fitted. I knew he'd find a way in.

I was in a state of pure panic. I squeezed my eyes tight and prayed. I gripped the bed frame until my hands ached. I was too afraid to let go, even to reach for my phone to call for help. But then the banging stopped. I heard his car drive away and another pull up to the house. Slowly, I peeked out from under the bed. I don't remember what happened next, other than my mom's voice calling my name over and over, and later, my dad's rage: "I'm going to kill him."

The police didn't believe our story at first. The country sheriff thought my parents were being alarmist. During Reagan's war on drugs in the eighties, the most sought-after criminals where we lived were drug dealers, not pedophiles, not kidnappers. Child kidnapping didn't happen in our middle-of-nowhere conservative Christian town. My parents stormed out of the police station and returned with the gifts he had given me, including the love notes, the ones too illegible for me to read.

What the police found afterward would forever haunt me, which I only learned by eavesdropping on my parents later that night. The police discovered nearly a hundred dog collars in the back of his car. Someone had been hanging dogs to their death from trees in the area. They found cutouts of body parts from porn magazines pasted all over his bedroom walls and a circle of rocks he had placed in a gradient from small to large in the middle of the floor. They found that he had been harassing women convenience store workers, waiting late at night down lonely roads for them to get off work. This was insane behavior, beyond anything my young mind could imagine, and I was nearly, and still could be, his next victim.

"I'm sorry for not taking your case more seriously," the sheriff told my parents.

We filed a restraining order and tried to prosecute him for attempted kidnapping. A couple of weeks later, the police informed my parents that he had left the state. There was some relief in that, but I couldn't forget the way he had looked at me with his greedy smile. Only then did I realize its meaning.

Attempted kidnapping carries a punishment of up to ten years in prison in Virginia. But because he had fled and left state jurisdiction, the Virginia police didn't prosecute, most likely due to high extradition costs. Kidnapping is only a federal crime if the kidnapper takes the victim across state lines. As a kid, I didn't understand jurisdictional law. I only understood that there was nothing we could do to put him in jail. He fled the state, a few hours' drive away, and he was free. He had done something bad and there would be no punishment.

I became afraid to go outside alone. I never knew when he might come back or someone like him might appear. No more running through the fields shirtless behind my house. I often locked myself in my room, as many preteens and teenagers do, and turned inward.

After a while, my parents and I stopped speaking about it. I wasn't kidnapped. He never laid a hand on me. It was a happy ending, in a way. I was safe. End of story. But the attempted abduction left its mark. It exposed a vulnerability I didn't know existed: I could be preyed on at any time. My body was no longer my own, it could be stolen, and I needed to hide myself away.

Reflecting on these events now, perhaps I started to understand then what it meant to grow up in a world of gender-based violence. Perhaps I knew in my gut that this was my rite of passage into womanhood—a terrifying, precocious one— and that it was only the beginning, that like so many girls and women, my life would be marked by the transgressions of men. Little did I know then that even the writer's name on a comic book that brought me a measure of comfort from such dangers would, years later, become synonymous with predation.

Nowhere felt safe. And so, I did what any child might do. I rebelled.

Soon after the attempted kidnapping, I discovered a new world in unlikely places: music magazines and comic books. I found *Metal Edge* magazine at the drug store, advertising mail-order skull rings, goth metal T-shirts, and cassette tapes, which I painstakingly saved my allowance to buy. I fell in love with the angry voices and crunchy guitars. I bought my first make-up: Kohl black eyeliner. I cut my long hair short and draped bangs over one eye to hide my face. I started wearing only black. And when I couldn't find goth attire, I bought costume jewelry in the Halloween section of the drugstore. My parents were concerned.

There was no goth scene in my small town. My appearance was so foreign to rural Southern culture that my eighth-grade history teacher called my mother to school to ask her if I worshipped Satan. My friends distanced themselves from me. Boys at school no longer liked me. I didn't care. According to all of them, I had no reason to dress like a freak.

I wore spiked bracelets, combat boots, and black baggy T-shirts to armor myself. I unconsciously wanted to repulse people, to become a Lolita in reverse. I became goth at twelve to escape predation. I never knew when the kidnapper might come looking for me again. I couldn't articulate that then, but I understand it now. I wanted to hide in plain sight.

When I found *The Sandman* and saw Death's character for the first time in "The Sound of Her Wings," I remember being glued to the pages. I couldn't believe it—she looked a lot like me: her dark, spiky, rock-star-styled hair, her simple black clothes. In 1988, Dave McKean's iconic cover stood out from other action-packed comics with covers full of hypersexualized women, from Catwoman, to Supergirl, to issue #27 of First Comics *Whisper*, whose busty ninja heroine fearfully flees a dozen men's hands emerging from the sand, one hand gripping her dainty ankle, what seemed a frightening echo of my near abduction.

Figure 8.3. Neil Gaiman and Mike Dringenberg, "The Sound of Her Wings," *The Sandman*, vol. 8, Vertigo: DC Comics, March 1997, cover.

Death's cover was different. Two winding ivy vines framed Death's hazy, enigmatic portrait, her face turned away from the viewer. Visually similar to artist Joseph Cornell's famous assemblages of shadowboxes filled with oneiric Victorian bric-a-brac that often remind the viewer of a long-lost memory or dream, McKean's covers showcased the main character in a way that didn't rely on action-packed plot but on atmosphere and visual lyricism. As McKean said in Hy Bender's *The Sandman Companion*, his approach to the covers of the first issues of *The Sandman* meant to "symbolize the feeling of each story, rather than represent specific events from it" (40). The hazy portrait of Death in stillness showed her as mysterious, slightly out of reach, and unlike anything I had seen before on the cover of a comic.

And the more I read, the more I realized Death was unlike any other woman comic character I knew. Death was cheerful, compassionate, sweet, and feminine, which was unique, but not only that—she was omnipotent. In *The Sandman* issue #1 "Preludes & Nocturnes," Death escapes the trap set by the warlock Roderick Burgess, who kidnapped her brother Dream instead. In issue #8's "The Sound of Her Wings," she's not afraid to call out her brother Dream's flaws: "You are literally the stupidest, most self-centered appallingest excuse for an anthropomorphic personification on this or any other plane!" (11). When Death's captor leads her down a dark alley and traps her in a cellar in the solo miniseries *The High Cost of Living*, she shows pity on him; she's unfazed by the mad hermit who nicks her ankh necklace and buys a new one, the stolen one useless in the wrong hands. She's the most powerful of all her siblings, the seven Endless, and arguably the most powerful entity of all the DC universe.

Most of all, she isn't defined by male characters. Throughout *The Sandman* series, Death isn't anyone's love interest or sexualized by other characters—she has a job to do. "The Sound of Her Wings" begins with Death sitting on the steps of the Arc de Triumph in Paris in conversation with her moping brother Dream. Mike Dringenberg's illustrations give form to her free spirit. She inhabits space casually with an adolescent energy that depicts a character who prioritizes independence and comfort over posturing and posing for other characters or the reader. From frame to frame, she sits cross-legged, lies on her stomach smelling a flower, strolls by with her hands in her pockets, and leans her elbow on a balustrade before knocking Dream on the head with a piece of bread. When she deftly catches a stray soccer ball with one hand, her face is fierce, and she doesn't hesitate to call her brother an "idiot" (12). When the owner of the ball, Franklin, impressed with her catch, asks Death out for a soda, she replies, "Sure, Franklin. You'll see me again soon," which refers to his death by the end of the issue (13). She's no-nonsense because she has "work to do," which we see in the second half of the issue (14). As a psychopomp—a spirit or deity who escorts the deceased to the afterlife—she escorts an elderly Jewish man to his peaceful death. We see a close-up in black and white of her face in shadow as she breaks the news to him gently. In the next panel, Dream watches: "She draws him close. From the darkness I hear the beating of mighty wings," a motif that repeats throughout (17). We don't get to see her wings, but we can feel her compassion for the dying. "I thought he was sweet. Didn't you?" she asks her brother while walking away (17). Each death she delivers to the living she does with kindness, including the child she takes from his crib into her arms and the stand-up comic who dies on stage: "I'm sorry, Esme, your time was up. Come here, honey," she says (19).

When Dream confesses to her: "My sister. When I was captured . . . it was not ME they wanted. It was you." Death answers, "Yeah, I know," and, unfazed, follows, "C'mon, I don't want to miss the next one," that is, the next soul she must escort away (17). This isn't a superheroine as readers traditionally know it; she has depth, compassion, and nothing to prove.

Her power doesn't depend on skintight body suits, love affairs, marriages, motherhood, supreme fighting skills, weapons, or sorcery. She's not a damsel in distress, a sexy witch, a scorned femme fatale seeking revenge, a pious crone, nor a goddess worshipped by mortals. As musician Tori Amos said, "I relate to Neil's female characters because he doesn't put them on a pedestal, and he doesn't abuse them either" (Bender 233). Death represented a new kind of woman character to me: she could be herself, both feminine and independent of men's influence. And as the personification of humanity's demise, far removed from men's puny actions, she was utterly untouchable.

I had found a superheroine I could believe in. To this nearly abducted kid, she represented ultimate protection from harm. I bought an ankh necklace like hers, although I could only find a smaller version, to conjure some of her protection. Death felt like a lifeline when I needed it most.

As Lauren Berlant suggests in *The Female Complaint*, "a tiny point of identification can open up a field of fantasy and de-isolation, of vague continuity, or of ambivalence" (11). Although written and drawn by men, in an almost wholly male-dominated field, *The Sandman*'s Death heralded a new beginning for feminism in comics, and for me, in my pre-internet small town, offered a "point of identification" and the closest thing to a feminist utopia I knew as a girl.

In *Beyond Feminist Aesthetics: Feminist Literature and Social Change* in 1989, Rita Felski first introduced the notion of a "feminist counter-public sphere," which she establishes as "an oppositional discursive space within contemporary society defined in terms of a notion of gender identity perceived to unite all participants" (121). In Nancy Fraser's 1990 text, "Rethinking the Public Sphere," she argues that "members of subordinated groups—women, workers, people of color, and lesbians and gays—have repeatedly found it advantageous to constitute alternative counterpublics" (123). Nonessentialist narratives can be "lifelines" for those deprived of "public acknowledgment" (Felski, *Uses of Literature*, 43). These narratives honor marginalized communities by offering visions of hope and the possibility of new worlds. As Felski asks when thinking of the essential portability and translatability of any text, "What does this text create, build, make possible?" (Limits 182). What did *The Sandman*'s Death create, build, make possible?

Death has empowered women readers of comics, at the very least by making a space for women readers in a male-dominated, exclusionary genre focused on male power fantasies. The simple act of gendering death as an unassuming goth woman made a female power fantasy possible in comics, which, for women readers, holds many significances.

In her 2016 essay "A Young Woman Called Death," Gabrielle Bellot describes the first time she presented as female as a closeted trans woman one Halloween night when she dressed in cosplay of Death. She meditates on the gender of Death: "It is also possible I imagined Death as a woman because I had not as yet come out, and I often lived in a silent agony; death and womanhood were flips of a coin, it seemed, with life only being life if I could live as my truest self." Being seen as a "beautiful woman" dressed as Death "[began] to give me, too, life." Cosplay as Death gave her the agency to realize her trans identification.

In the 1980s and '90s, Death validated goth and post-punk women, a feminist counterpublic who styled their bodies in alternative ways often because they "refused to submit to the masterful gaze" (Hiding 28). Although Gaiman states in a tweet on October 1, 2020, that "Sandman wasn't seen as Goth when it started," *The Sandman* became "a Goth influence." But did women readers imitate Death or did Death appropriate a style of the time worn by many goth women? At least one other woman reader was happily surprised to find her own image mirrored on *The Sandman*'s pages as much as I was when I found the comic for the first time. Cosplay star Ashlynne Dae says in "Superhero Hype Cosplay: Death from the Sandman": "One day when I was fifteen, a guy asked if I was cosplaying Death. I didn't even know what cosplay was, but I did go home and look up what he was talking about. To my shock I was staring back at someone I saw myself in. I had the same black, curly, big, messy hair (I used to dye it black in those days), the same heavy eyeliner (sans swirl), and wore the same outfit: a black tank, skinny jeans and winklepicker boots, right down to the very same necklace I always wore every day for ten years, a silver ankh."

What's important about this trend? Death's appearance in *The Sandman* quickly made her a goth icon and fan-favorite character. She's "the cosplay of choice for most ComicCon goths," as *Entertainment Weekly* notes. And she's one that goth girls and women lacked. "She's an image that goths wish would be projected about us more; someone who's beautiful, intelligent, and has a great attitude," said Elizabeth McIntyre, who ran the popular goth website, Rosa Mvndi (Bender 10).

Cosplaying Death, intentionally or not, became a show of female power for women and girls who didn't want to conform to mainstream ideas about femininity and traditional female roles. Death validates goth girls. She validated me. By shoving my girly Jordaches and my frilly, pink dresses and blouses into storage bags, I was rejecting both traditional feminine beauty standards and traditional feminine roles designed for the attraction, and potential predation, of men. So when I found Death on the page, after that first shock of recognition, I felt less alone.

Casting Black actress Kirby Howell-Baptiste as Death in the Netflix series increased the intersectionality of *The Sandman*'s feminist counterpublics by being more inclusive to women viewers and readers of color. Death isn't always a pale white chick; as nonhumans, the Endless shapeshift. In issue #47, "Brief Lives," Death appears as a young Chinese woman. In issue #9, "Tales of the Sand," Dream, a Black man in ancient Africa, speaks about a Grandmother Death, a Black woman who doesn't appear on the page but clearly exists. TV fan sites like Black Girl Nerds and Netflix's Strong Black Lead show support for Kirby Howell-Baptiste's compassionate, tear-jerking performance in Netflix's episode "The Sound of Her Wings." And among the hundreds of images and videos of women cosplaying Death on TikTok and Instagram, now more than ever can you find women of color included in that group. In a 2022 interview for *Entertainment Weekly*, Kirby Howell-Baptiste said, "What I think is beautiful about [Death's] costume is how simple it is: People can literally just get a black tank top, black jeans, boots, and an ankh. I cannot wait to see people dressed as Death."

Death also appealed to and empowered women readers with its wholly unique take: the choice to gender Death as a compassionate woman not hell-bent on seducing or scaring the reader, which has little precedent in the history of Western art and literature. As Lanette Cadle says in her essay "The Power of the Perky: The Feminist Rhetoric of Death," "By taking the archetypical figure and regendering, Gaiman moves Death out of historical patriarchy into a mythos where women are just as likely to hold power, and not merely by re-inscribing old practices. This iteration of Death is new, and all woman" (49).

Very few cultures lack a death figure. In classical mythology, death gods, both male and female, most often showed great ferocity or cruelty: the Harpies ate their victims; the Furies punished mortals by driving them to madness; the Fates stole lives with a snip of a thread; Charon ferried the ghosts of the living to the underworld; Hades abducted and raped mortals; and the Keres, the winged female spirits of violent death, much like blood-thirsty buzzards, feasted on the dead's remains. A minor death god, Thanatos, the brother of Hypnos (Sleep), was portrayed at times as a merciless god and other times as a gentle, beautiful young man with wings, such as the marble sculpture of winged Thanatos from the Temple of Artemis in Ephesus. Artists and writers since the Enlightenment have appropriated Thanatos's gentler form to symbolize a kind, easy death, one divorced from the common, more gruesome representations to come out of Christian influence—the pervasive image of a skeleton or reaper with his scythe or hourglass, which has proliferated from the Middle Ages to today.

For English speakers, death is most often male, such as in Thomas Rowlandson's collected illustrations of Dance Macabre skeletons wielding spears and reapers gripping their scythes to take the lives of both the rich and poor in *The English Dance of Death*, John Keats's "easeful Death" in his poem "Ode to a Nightingale," Emily Dickinson's coachman in her poem "Because I Could Not Stop for Death," and Terry Pratchett's Death as a reaper in *The Discworld* series.

The male death figure has taken various forms throughout history, as Karl S. Guthke notes in *The Gender of Death: A Cultural History in Art and Literature*, which looks at the dominant ciphers of death as represented in the West. The male death figure is a gravedigger, a horseman of the apocalypse, a noble warrior or knight in a duel with his victim, a fiddler, a drummer, a hunter armed with bow and arrow, a king, and the Devil in various guises, including a jester donning a pointed cap (86). More often than not, the male death figure existed as grim fascination or penalty, a fearful reminder of our human frailty and failings, or even as instructional devices in *ars moriendi* literature, popular handbooks used to show good Christians how to die well.

However, "English literature has never been overly hospitable to the female death icon, nor has American literature," Guthke says (26). When they are portrayed, women as death figures are often an "object of fear, or fulfillment of erotic desire" (36).

They're horrible wizened hags with hanging breasts, such as Pesta, the Norwegian plague hag; banshees whose terrifying shrieks herald the end of a life in Irish folklore; goddesses of death and winter, such as Marzanna in Slavic mythology, whose arrival signals misfortune; skeletal saints or theological misfits like Mexico's Santa Muerte; and beautiful, eroticized femme fatales such as the faery-woman in John Keats's ballad "La Belle Dame sans Merci," who seduces a gentle, love-struck knight and robs him of his life in her elfin grotto. The seductive female death figures, who include "man-killing water-nymphs, vampires, Undines, Loreleis, Liliths, Sirens, Chimaeras, Gorgons, Amazons, and Sphinxes," bewitch men to murder them (188). Female death icons are monsters, othered, other-worldly, and demonized for their erotic powers.

Modern comics follow suit; Marvel's Death, also known as Lady Death, Mistress Death, and Dark Beauty, created by Jim Starlin, first appeared in *Captain Marvel* #26 in June 1973 as a skull-faced, "hypnotically sexy" woman with "alluring power," as Kayleigh Donaldson describes her in "The Seduction of Death [Or, OK But What if the Grim Reaper is, Like, Hot]." She's so sexy, "Thanos tries to destroy half of all living beings in the universe just to impress her," Donaldson says. This seductive grim reaper, often depicted as a buxom skeleton, sometimes a hot babe in black, is all femme fatale, an antagonist to male power.

Brian Pulido and Chaos! Comics' *Lady Death*, an iconic example of a hypersexualized Bad Girl Art femme fatale from the nineties, embraces theological tropes: death as seductress and devil. Falsely accused of witchcraft and nearly burned at the stake, Hope makes a pact with a demon and renounces her humanity to become goddess of hell, Lady Death, and a pin-up sexy one at that.

These two characters, as well as Jack Kirby's death character, Hela, foster both fear and desire in a potential viewer—Eros conflated not with gentle Thanatos but with the traditions of Christian ideology: skeleton, devil, or femme fatale.

More recently, *The Many Deaths of Laila Starr*, the 2022 collection written by Ram V and illustrated in technicolor pastels by Filipe Andrade, depicts a female death figure who takes on the mortal form of a cool, cigarette-puffing, twentysomething woman in Mumbai. Much like *The Sandman*'s Death character, she's not sexualized; she's cute, approachable, and compassionate. But Laila Starr lacks Death's invincibility; she still has a male boss to answer to (a three-headed god as CEO), not to mention suffering the weaknesses of

Figure 8.4. Brian Pulido and Steven Hughes, *Evil Ernie*, vol. 1, no. 1, Chaos! Comics, December 1991, 6.

a mortal female body who perishes in every issue and whose reincarnation remains at the mercy of the male Life character, whose sympathy for her might wane. Laila Starr struggles under male power, death as employed by the corporate patriarchy. At least she's cute.

On the creation of Death's character, Gaiman said, "If you look at the numerous anthropomorphic representations of Death over the years, you'll find that most of them are scary, humorless, implacable people who you really wouldn't want to spend time with. However, I already had a lead character, the Sandman, who was pale, tall, brooding, dark, relatively humorless, and Byronic in a late adolescent kind of way—in other words, who had all the characteristics ascribed to Death. . . . So I thought it would be fun to turn expectations upside down, and to provide some contrast as well, by making Death small, funny, cool, and nice." (Bender 239).

This is what is so interesting about *The Sandman*'s Death—she's just nice. She's not eroticized, sexualized, or demonized. She's not a seductress, monster, or theological misfit. She's nobody's bride. She's independent, invincible, and answers to no one. She's a character in her own right, not just a cipher for male fantasy or misogyny. Utterly unique, she's thanatological chic, a compassionate female Thanatos sans Eros.

Historically, female death icons seem products of "the masterful gaze" in one way or another. The erotic spectrum spans from a romantic courtship with death in Edward, Lord Herbert of Cherbury's 1655 love poem "To His Mistress for Her True Picture"—"Death, my life's Mistress and sovereign Queen / My heart doth love you best"—to the vilification of female sex workers in Félicien Rops's 1892 watercolor, "Street Corner, Four in the Morning, Human Parody," of a beautiful prostitute who removes her face to reveal the skull beneath. In *Women and Death* 3, Clare Bielby and Anna Richards say, "The alignment of women with death can be attributed to the 'unknowable' quality of each for the male sex" (1). It must be noted that men are more often than not the authors and artists of these icons.

Although created and drawn by men, *The Sandman*'s Death became a space for what Felski called "portability" and "translatability" for women readers; that is, Death made space for feminist counterpublics and resistance. With so few strong feminist icons in comics, women drew strength from Death, independent of her creators' intentions or biographies. Women claimed *The Sandman*'s Death and made her their own.

As a kid, when I looked in the mirror to adjust my eyeliner or to drape on another layer of black, I took Death's image and shaped it into what I needed most: both protection and protest.

Because there was no penalty for my near kidnapping, I started to lose the sense of my value in the world as a girl. I felt helpless; the law only served those with power. The system was rigged against someone like me. Going goth as a kid became an act of feminist resistance.

As Caitlín R. Kiernan, writer of *The Sandman*'s spin-off series "The Dreaming," said, "Goth attracts people whose sight has turned deeply inward." The inward, antisocial nature of goth culture was looked down on by nearly everyone in the 1980s and '90s as a bad fashion trend, a turning away from the mainstream to navel gaze at some internal flaw, and an inability to conform to society. For me, being goth was reactive. The system is clearly unjust if an attempted kidnapper can go free. Children have a keen sense of justice, and in a broken world, being goth seemed very sane.

An attempted crime doesn't have a single ending or outcome for the victim. It can echo out as a series of unceasing questions—what if my parents hadn't come home in time that day? What if he comes back? It can make you question the safety of the most basic things—is it safe at home, am I safe at school, am I safe now? The attempted crime robbed me of a concept of safety. Who could I trust?

I often think of a quote from Spanish writer Javier Marías, in defense of writing fiction. In his article, "Lo que no sucede y sucede," which I translate literally as "What Doesn't Happen and What Happens," Marías said (my translation), "We perhaps consist, in short, equally of what we are and what we have not been, equally of what is verifiable and quantifiable and memorable as well as what is most uncertain, undecided, and blurred; perhaps we are made in equal measure of what was and what could have been." Marías has also gone to describe in his novel *Fever and Spear* a similar kind of phenomenon that he calls "narrative horror," the fear of being defined by one's death and that how we die shapes the story of our lives.

I was haunted by "narrative horror" as a girl, for being a victim of attempted kidnapping but also not being recognized as a victim by the criminal justice system. I was haunted by "what could have been" and its many possible iterations, which I imagined vividly, and which came to me in terrible dreams of being chased and not being able to run away.

The horrific fate I narrowly escaped followed me around like a shadow: a brush with kidnapping, captivity, and much worse—death's finger on my shoulder, violence's voice in my ears—*not yet*. An attempted crime leaves its own kind of wound on the victim. The ghost of violence followed me for years.

Thinking of it now, perhaps I felt close to *The Sandman*'s Death because I had come so close to my own.

In April 2020, thirty-three years after his attempted abduction, my kidnapper called my mother looking for me. I had returned to my family farm in Virginia to quarantine during the pandemic. I heard her screaming from the other room, echoing my father's voice decades ago, "I'll kill you! I'm calling the police!"

During the early days of the pandemic, the world outside already seemed like it was falling apart. To deal with my childhood kidnapper was almost more than I could bear.

He had sent me a few emails over the years, having found my email address through searches online. One subject line had said, "YOU @ 12–13 . . . witchy phase." I never read them. He had sent me Facebook messages and friend requests, but I ignored and deleted those too. I had been living in different cities in Europe for nearly two decades. I had felt safe there, but now in Virginia, far from the cities where COVID raged, what I had thought was safety was clearly wrong.

I looked up his Facebook page. He had photos of guns in his photo gallery and a disturbing number of young girls around eleven years old under his "friends" list. He made bizarre comments on their photos: "TONGUE in de cornr of mouth..w/ red sash a-round a young neck . . . nice..!!" and "I want to see all grl fotos." And another post: "women . . . can't live w/them. . . . can't hide the mass grave, well enough. . . ." Who knows how many other girls he had attempted to kidnap?

My mother and I went to the same county police office as we had years before. They informed us that they had no record of our restraining order. No record of his attempted kidnapping. My mother and I were in shock. How was that possible? We had given them the evidence all those years ago. We had filed the papers. The police didn't know. I felt powerless; I was eleven again and there was nothing to do but lock the doors and hide under the bed.

"We'll call him and tell him to leave you alone, ma'am," the police officer said.

"Is that it?" I asked. I should've been used to injustice by that point, but somehow, I was still surprised. "He tried to kidnap me as a kid," I reminded him.

"I'm sorry, ma'am. That's all we can do," he said. "If he contacts you again, let us know."

I showed them his Facebook comments to young girls online. "And this?"

"We'll take a look," the officer said, "but he's not in state. He's out of jurisdiction. If he contacts you again, give us a call."

How do women and girls hide themselves? How do we construct safety where it doesn't exist? We develop eating disorders, anger issues, addictions, depression, anxiety, or self-annihilating habits to render ourselves invisible or untouched. But invisibility isn't a superpower, especially when it's not a choice, when it's all you feel. Maybe we find ways to armor ourselves against that, too. Maybe we seek danger, the opposite direction, and give ourselves away too easily because our value has been diminished.

In the 2014 *USA Today* article "The Ones That Get Away," reporter Brad Heath describes a man on the run from the police in Philadelphia, charged with sexually assaulting a fourteen-year-old girl. The felon escaped by taking a Greyhound bus to Florida, where the local police later arrested him for the statutory rape of two underage girls. Although he was a captured fugitive, the Philadelphia cops refused to take him back. The girl in Philadelphia testified against him in court on her fifteenth birthday, but she never saw justice for the crime committed against her. In Florida, he was free.

"Tens of thousands of wanted felons escape justice by crossing a state border," according to Heath's 2014 report. These felonies include homicide, sexual assault, and kidnapping. Police blamed the high costs of extradition and lack of manpower. Baltimore prosecutor and police records from 2011–13 show the city's refusal to extradite felons for one murder, one kidnapping, and one rape in the first degree, which involves the use of a dangerous weapon or threat of death.

I think about the victims. I think of the girl in Philadelphia and wonder how she coped. I think of the tens of thousands of unnamed victims who, like me, had their assailants get away by crossing state lines. What toll does it take on their bodies and minds? What are their forms of resistance? Injustice trauma leaves us with nothing but ashes in our mouths. We realize we can trust no one but ourselves.

After reading the *Vulture* exposé, "There Is No Safe Word," I think of the five women who have reported sexual assault and coercion by Death's cocreator, Neil Gaiman. These women include his babysitter, his tenant, and his fans—one woman he silenced with a $275,000 nondisclosure agreement, to another he offered to pay for therapy and donate to a rape crisis center. A coherent pattern emerges from multiple women's allegations: sadistic and violent acts.

Women fans on TikTok have shared videos of what they think: they're throwing his books into the trash and across rooms, flipping him off, mourning, and showing solidarity with the women who have come forward. "[Gaiman]'s dead now and I hope the victims get the justice they deserve," one woman on X said. For many fans, there's no separating the art from the artist, even if there's a team of illustrators and editors who contributed to the project.

As I watch a woman on TikTok trash a copy of the beautifully designed *Death: The Deluxe Edition*, I want to join in. I believe survivors. I mourn with fans, especially those who most needed Death and Gaiman's other dark fantasy characters to keep them afloat. In Death, I found safety from predation, a safety and trust Gaiman has shattered. Death's "portability" and "translatability" for women readers have limits.

I would never have dreamt that Death might meet her own end in my lifetime, that she would go first.

One morning when I was fourteen years old, I showed up to breakfast with a purple shirt on. My mother nearly fell off her chair. She told me years later that she kept quiet that morning, hopeful I was growing out of my goth phase.

I fully gave up my goth garb shortly after, although by that point I was irrevocably changed. I would always identify with outsiders, underdogs, and goth kids. I would forever mistrust a system that protected victimizers and not victims. That kid who ran free in the fields behind her house without a care in the world was long gone.

Today, the only goth relic that survived from childhood is my love of black. Recently I was at a writers residency where one of the residents asked if I used to be goth.

"How did you know?" I asked.

"I can always tell," he said. "I was one too. Once a goth, always a goth," he said, smiling.

But if being goth was an act of resistance, I don't know what resistance looks like for me anymore. I've thought hard lately about how to hide from my kidnapper, to go unseen again. I don't have an answer. I don't trust the legal system to protect me or my rights.

I think about *The Sandman*'s Death and what advice she might offer. Superhero stories restore order to the universe. They make good's triumph over evil feel inevitable and true, as it always should be. I fantasize about the easy clarity of the hero's journey as he defeats the villain. Unlike real life, in superhero comics, the bad guys usually pay for their crimes. The hero's mythos offers a clear, and enviable, throughline.

Death as a superheroine offers more complexity of character. The hero's journey involves some test of power and strength, moral or physical. As the master of all endings, Death, in her compassion and kindness, acknowledges that there are no easy narratives. Women need every lifeline they can get, even if that lifeline might fail them later. Unlike male power fantasies, my female power fantasy approximates something closer to perseverance and wisdom. Death helped me see things for what they are, which is its own kind of strength.

Works Cited

Bender, Hy. *The Sandman Companion*. Vertigo, 1999.

Bellot, Gabrielle. "A Young Woman Called Death." *LitHub*, Nov. 2016, lithub.com/a-young-woman-called-death.

Berlant, Lauren. *The Female Complaint*, Duke UP, 2008.

Bielby, Clare, and Anna Richards. *Women and Death 3: Women's Representations of Death in German Culture since 1500*. Camden House, 2010.

Cadle, Lanette. "The Power of the Perky: The Feminist Rhetoric of Death." *Feminism in the Worlds of Neil Gaiman: Essays on the Comics: Poetry and Prose*, edited by Tara Prescott and Aaron Drucker, McFarland, 2012, pp. 32–46.

Dae, Ashlynne. "Superhero Hype Cosplay: Death from the Sandman." *SuperHeroHype*, Nov. 2020, www.superherohype.com/cosplay/489641-superhero-hype-cosplay-death-from-the-sandman.

Donaldson, Kayleigh. "The Seduction of Death [Or, OK But What if the Grim Reaper Is, Like, Hot]." *SYFY Media*, June 2020, www.syfy.com/syfy-wire/the-seduction-of-death-or-what-if-the-grim-reaper-is-hot.

Felski, Rita. *Beyond Feminist Aesthetics: Feminist Literature and Social Change*. Harvard UP, 1989.

Felski, Rita. *The Limits of Critique*. U of Chicago P, 2015.

Felski, Rita. *The Uses of Literature*. Blackwell, 2008.

Fraser, Nancy. "Rethinking the Public Sphere: A Contribution to the Critique of Actually Exiting Democracy." *Habermas and the Public Sphere*, edited Craig Calhoun, MIT Press, 1992, pp. 109–42.

Gaiman, Neil. *The Sandman: Dream Country*. Vol. 4, DC Comics, Mar. 1998.

Gaiman, Neil. "The Sound of Her Wings." Vol. 8, Vertigo, Mar. 1997.

Guthke, Karl S. *The Gender of Death: A Cultural History in Art and Literature*. Cambridge UP, 1999.

Heath, Brad. "The Ones That Get Away." *USA Today*, 11 Mar. 2014, www.usatoday.com/story/news/nation/2014/03/11/fugitives-next-door/6262719/.

Hebdige, Dick. *Hiding in the Light: On Images and Things*. Routledge, 1989.

Holub, Christian. "Kirby Howell-Baptiste Previews Death's 'Nurturing, Caring Side' on Netflix's *The Sandman*." *Entertainment Weekly*, 19 July 2022, ew.com/tv/the-sandman-kirby-howell-baptiste-death-preview-netflix/.

Marías, Javier. "Lo que no sucede y sucede." *El País*, 11 Aug. 1995, elpais.com/diario/1995/08/12/cultura/808178408_850215.html.

Marías, Javier. *Your Face Tomorrow. 1. Fever, Spear.* Translated by Margaret Jull Costa, New Directions, 2007.

9

HORSEY-COME-LATELY

No Asian American Superhero Comics Until Little Monkey

Sheng-mei Ma

Instead of the colloquial Johnny-come-lately, how about Sheng-mei-come-lately for someone who is not only a latecomer to superhero comics but also an outsider? An international graduate student to the US and then a(n) (un) naturalized citizen-immigrant, having grown up and matured, sans comics, in the economically austere Taiwan decades ago, I claim neither birthright to, nor boyhood nostalgia for, the fantasy universe inhabited by Superman and his fellow great men and women. So as not to be guilty of exhibitionism in naming this paper after myself, I first changed it to Jimmy-come-lately. Serendipitously, "Jimmy" would pun with the stealthy act of forcing open a locked window or door, as I have managed to gain access to the pantheon of the white- and Euro-American-centric US academe—in the English department, of all places. A nonnative English-speaking English professor, an interloper fearing exposure at every turn along this long, tortuous yellow brick road, I have been a "Yellow" sojourner, whose color belongs to the dirt road to be trod on rather than the journeyman on it. There goes exhibitionism already, flaunting not the Scarlet A, but the Golden Y! A masked compromise between Sheng-mei, which is too personal, and Jimmy, which is too impersonal, lies in Horsey-come-lately, since my surname "Ma" happens to mean "horse" in Chinese. Hence, this horsing around with the Western genre of superhero comics comes straight from this immigrant horse's mouth, literally, slanting sideways like an old nag's neighing/naysaying, or, to paraphrase Emily Dickinson, tells all the immigrant truth—with a slant.

Playing with naming and self-identity is inherent in the comic conceit of Superman/Clark Kent, Batman/Bruce Wayne, Spider-Man/Peter Parker, and other white doubles. As Mircea Eliade remarks in *Shamanism* (1988), "One becomes what one displays" (179). Their clothes—masks and tights—make the men, or white "messianic superheroes," in Marco Arnaudo's words, and have since the genesis of the genre, when two Jewish comic artists, Jerry Siegel and Joe Shuster, cobbled together Superman in 1938 (54). Arnaudo sees in the masked heroes as well as in the hidden Jewish creators a "narrative reflection of the American myth of the successful immigrant," born again due to the promised land's and superhero comics' inherent "optimism," "pragmatism," and "individualism" (64–65). Arnaudo's idea strikes a chord in a creator of Asian American superheroes, Gene Luen Yang, whose *Superman Smashes the Klan* (2020) interweaves Superman coming to realize his potential with a Chinese immigrant family, the Lees, settling in Metropolis after a period in Chinatown. Both parties hail from elsewhere, and Superman is "the immigrant from Krypton" (239), as Yang's afterword "Superman and Me" puts it. As the Lees and Superman try to fit in as ordinary people, their alienness determines their different fates.[1]

Less playful than existential is my off-white, yellowish human-equestrian, Ma-Horse imposter syndrome. My personal angst over secreting and baring myself fetishistically is the Asian American neurosis writ small: the "perennial alien" moniker seems almost "justified," given the "Mongoloid" facial and physical features imposed on Asians. Yellow skin, slanted eyes, and buckteeth "stand out" as the most salient of Western stereotypes of Asian physiognomy, which allegedly veils inner differences of duplicity, deviousness, even demonology. This age-old injustice perpetrated against Asian Americans demands correction, which requires reprising the alien stereotypes in the first place. Any ethnic revision begins by relitigating the white vision; any counternarrative is sired by the narrative it aims to counter. Discursive dialectics born out of thesis versus antithesis, or us versus them, necessitates a symbiotic coexistence, as much as "we" would like to do "them" in. In terms of superhero comics, both my own and Asian American conditions originate from a socially imposed absence, a "genetic" alienation. The minority does not share the taken-for-granted white entitlement to all-American superheroes until Gene Luen Yang's *American Born Chinese* (2006) and *The Shadow Hero* (2014), albeit with their own problematics. Yang's turn to superhero comics culminates a distinguished career that centers ethnic existence in, among other works, *The Rosary Comic Book* (2003),

Loyola Chin and the San Peligran Order (2004), *Boxers and Saints* (2013), and the franchise of graphic novels *Avatar, the Last Airbender*, since 2012.

Whereas Yang evolves his early personal comics into subsequent superhero Americana, my personal "horsey" turn within the critical history of comics mirrors preceding literary movements when entrenched authorities break down. Feminists, particularly of the 1980s, have begun to "get personal," to rephrase Nancy K. Miller's 1991 book. Miller contends that the "efflorescence of personal criticism in the United States in the eighties—like the study of autobiography—has in part to do with the gradual, and perhaps inevitable waning of enthusiasm for a mode of Theory, whose authority . . . depended finally on the theoretical evacuation of the very social subjects producing it" (20). Personal criticism, maintains Miller, "blows the cover of the impersonal as a masquerade of self-effacement" and the "narcissistic fantasy . . . of [theoretical] abstraction" (24). Ethnic studies since the 1960s have advocated similar methodology of decentering white invisibility and privilege in scholarship, calling attention to minority positionality. Granted, nuances among feminists—white versus women of color, upper middle class versus working class—disturb any blanket representation of feminist approach. Likewise, differences among minorities—Black, Brown, Red, "Yellow," in addition to class and sexual orientation—defy any expedient categorization.

Emboldened by feminists' and ethnic scholars' splicing of the personal and the professional, this essay proceeds, first of all, to excavate my faint childhood memories that approximate superhero comics, one of which features classical swordsmen Silang (四郎) and Zhenping (真平). Then I move on to the collective ethnic absence of superheroes, which motivates Yang's Asian looking *The Shadow Hero*, debuting on the cover with stereotypically slanted eyes, not only masked but in the long shadow cast by white superheroes. Out of century-long comic misrepresentations of Asians, Yang fashions *The Shadow Hero*. But the seed of Yang's superhero is sowed as early as *American Born Chinese*, specifically in the character the Monkey King from the sixteenth-century Chinese classic *Journey to the West*. Yang's Monkey King opens the tripartite narrative of his graphic novel as an analogue for the protagonist Jin. Wu Cheng'en's magnum opus fictionalizes the Tang dynasty historical figure Monk Xuanzang, or Tripitaka, who undertakes the pilgrimage westward to India to obtain Buddhist sutras. The monk is escorted by three half-human, half-beast disciples headed by the Monkey King. Taking the hint from Wu's classic, Yang's comic retelling repeatedly has the Monkey King mocked affectionately as "Little Monkey" or "Silly Little Monkey" by his maker, the almighty Tze-Yo-Tzuh, which is Yang's coinage for a Chinese Jehovah (68–69). The Monkey King rather than the slant-eyed Shadow Hero occupies center stage herein.

Yang alchemizes Asian occlusion and abjection into the "Golden Age" of Asian American comics, no different from my making up a story out of the dark hole in childhood memory. Yet in this Asian/American narrative, how do I connect its Asian lower half of Silang and Zhenping, fading already, with its American upper half, purportedly in shadows but very much trending, streaming, both in print and onscreen, in university classrooms and fan cons? In this body of works, how do I graft my ashes of time, wisps of memory, from the waist down, so to speak, onto the prominent faces and torsos drawn by Yang? Am I part of the collective mud on the shadowy bottom of the Asian pond, from which Yang's lotus rises to bloom above water, into the sunny sky? We the Asian Mud; Yang the 2016 American "MacArthur Genius."

Asian Mud is neither a rhetorical hyperbole nor a Lu Xun-style Ah-Q mindset that numbs oneself by wallowing in misery.[2] Asia *is* Yang's raw materials, the launching pad to catapult into stardom. Out of the two epigraphs opening *American Born Chinese*, one is dedicated to his "Ba" (father) whose "stories of Ah-Tong, the Taiwanese village boy" inspire the book, along with "stories of the Monkey King" related by his "Ma." Ah-Tong does not appear in the graphic novel at all; his closest avatar is Wei-Chen, the Monkey King's son and emissary from heaven in the guise of an FOB (fresh-off-the-boat) from Taiwan. Be it a Chinese classic's "Little Monkey" or Taiwan's littler Monkey Son, be it the epigraphic paratext or simian subtext, Asia or the eponymous "Chinese-ness" signifies not so much a parallel universe as an immersed (outgrown?) one within Yang's American bildungsroman.

Horsey's Silang and Zhenping

Silang and Zhenping in my Taiwanese childhood brought pleasure like toy horses for a boy surnamed horse. Indeed, the two swordsmen often ride their famed steeds into battles. Instead of an American childhood gravitating to corner drugstores with racks of superhero comics, my memories of the swordsmen revolve around one particular barber shop. Taiwan's elementary school through high school required weekly haircuts in accordance with strict rules on hair length, basically a boot-camp buzz cut. That policing of young bodies has been relaxed somewhat in recent years. A barber shop called *Jiating* (家庭, "Family") was frequented by nearly all the children from our *juancun* (眷村), one of many military dependents' villages hastily thrown together to accommodate the more than one million Nationalist soldiers and refugees escaping from mainland China to Taiwan in 1949.[3] Family Barber Shop was favored for two reasons: it was cheap, and it was strewn with torn excerpts and pages of comics of the swordsmen Silang and Zhenping amid piles of clipped black hair and other dark substances. Each weekend, school children, either waiting their turn or having already had it, sat or squatted on the floor across the crammed shop, poring over fragments of the swordsmen's feats, trading half- or quarter-books, ignoring the barber's curses to vacate the premises for newcomers. In the absence of these swordsmen comics, long gone with clipped hair and childhood innocence, let me reconstruct the void that is the genesis, based on no more than fragments in the virtual space.

Before I attempt this mission impossible, I submit that this memory is not mine alone. The swordsmen are in fact so pivotal a part of the childhood memories of my peers growing up in the 1960s and '70s that they merited a line in the folk singer Luo Dayou's classic 1982 song "Childhood," from the album *Zhihuyezhe* (之乎也者): "Zhuge Silang and the Devil Gang / Who will come to possess that sword?" Silang's full name includes the compound surname "Zhuge," à la the master strategist Zhuge Liang of the fourteenth-century *Romance of the Three Kingdoms*. The Taiwanese cartoonist Ye Hongjia (1923–1990) created the characters in 1958 and continued to spin off their exploits for the next few decades. Ye's comics were adapted for films and TV series in Taiwan. The cover of *Duel with the Devil Gang* (figure 9.1) demonstrates Ye's Japanese influence, as he was educated during the Japanese colonization of Taiwan from 1895 to 1945. The representative of the Devil Gang dons a mask with bat-like ears and sharp, protruding canine teeth eerily reminiscent of the masks used in Kabuki and Noh theater to represent demons. Forever wielding a sword, the title character Silang is marked by large round eyes with twin hair buns, as opposed to Zhenping's almond-shaped eyes and a single topknot. The dress, folded scarves, cloth waistbands, and mountain peaks in the background imitate traditional Chinese paintings, not to mention the shape of galloping horses and built architecture of palaces, pagodas, arbors, and the like.

As an excerpt from the comic books available online shows, the action hinges on damsels in distress: one princess is kidnapped, another forced

Figure 9.1. *Duel with the Devil Gang*, cover, courtesy of issuu.com/345yeh/docs/__________-1

into an iron mask that not even the kingdom's best locksmiths can open. Both await rescue by the heroic duo, and Taiwanese boys project themselves onto either the lead, Silang, or the sidekick, Zhenping, as the pair liberate aristocratic women. For the life of me, I cannot recall which of the two I identified with more. I am tempted to say Zhenping for his weird-looking eyes with pinpoint pupils that seem almost blind, drunk, even prophetic. But that may well be a flashback tantamount to revisionism after a lifetime favoring such "magical disabilities" as Tiresias in *Oedipus Rex*, the blind Japanese swordsman Zatoichi since 1962, or Grasshopper's glassy-eyed Master Po in the 1972 TV series *Kung Fu*.

One giveaway that the comics' target audience is young boys is the constant use of *Zhuyin fuhao*, which comprises thirty-seven characters and five tone marks, starting with Bopomofo (ㄅㄆㄇㄈ). *Zhuyin fuhao* is Taiwan's system of notation for pronunciation, which has been all but replaced outside the island proper by the People's Republic of China's romanization in pinyin. Indeed, even the name of *Zhuyin fuhao* is rendered in pinyin rather than its natural form, the characters for which are not included in Microsoft Word's available special symbols; to include them in the manuscript for this essay, I copied "Bopomofo (ㄅㄆㄇㄈ)" from the internet. In Ye Hongjia's hand, though, *Zhuyin fuhao* is strewn across the comic book whenever onomatopoeic sounds of fighting and exclamations are required. On the one hand, the shorthand to pronunciation accommodates elementary school students who have yet to master the common literacy of about three thousand ideographs. On the other, the spontaneous cries and grunts on the battlefield, caught in crossfire, or skirting the knife edge, would find fitting expressions not in learned, acquired words once or twice removed from the action, but in actual sounds emitted by the body despite schooling, the vocalized reflexes in a state of fear, shock, glee, and a range of other raw emotions.

Consider the irony of boys indulging in and clinging to these fantasies of masculinity as their hair is being trimmed at the discretion of school authority, being paid for by their parents, and themselves in danger of being evicted by the barber. Boyhood abjection and powerlessness feed the lust for power, as they languish in the corner and on the raised threshold of the barber shop, an all-male facility with one man standing, wielding an electric clipper, and many sitting, squatting, or hiding boys. Despite the quick rinse by the barber that is de rigueur at the end of a haircut, at no additional cost, wouldn't bits of hair stick to and irritate the neck, the shoulders, and the arms exposed by the sleeveless undershirt, the after-school summer uniform of sorts, in the clammy subtropical island? Would the boy endure the itch and the sting, often on top of prickly heat rashes, so long as the ejection order is not shouted in his face?[4] Would he then turn reluctantly homeward to his family, away from Family Barber Shop? Which is his true family: the parents he comes from or the fallacies to which he dreams of going, the pathetic here and now of boyhood or the passion for the then and there of adulthood? Both are recollected herein in the fullness of time as the short black hair has grown long and white.

Unlike with such superheroes in disguise as Batman, Spider-Man, and Superman, masks are worn not by the twin swordsmen but by their antagonists. The demonic face masks dehumanize conspirators, saboteurs, and the evil forces at large. The reversal seems to stem from a fundamental difference between Western and Eastern notions of selfhood. Superheroes in US comics are formulaically born again, argues Marco Arnaudo, "after a traumatic experience that symbolically recalls a journey from death to rebirth" (18). The Judeo-Christian paradigm dictates "the persistence of thematic archetypes such as the voyage or the test," the most renowned of which being the resurrection (12). At the heart of comic narratives lies "conflict, both individual (duels) and collective (war)," climaxing in the triumph over death (12). Superheroes become Christ figures who inhabit the ambiguity of a human God, who suffers the pangs of crucifixion as the son of God in a human body. The stigmata on the body testify to, simultaneously, pain and divinity. By contrast, canonical Chinese and Confucian ideology refrains from venturing into transcendent religiosity, tarrying largely in the secular, moral realm. An ideal Confucian *junzi* or gentleman is supposed to be consistent in words, deeds, and inner thoughts. What the heart desires is shared, without guile, verbally and in action. Any masquerade of intention is beneath one's dignity, deemed duplicitous. Needless to say, both desires and intentions are of the noblest kind. Such high-flown ideology necessitates cultural repression of the deepest kind, evidenced by the tension between the doppelgangers of the Monkey King/Little Monkey in connection with the horsey. The horsey signals both the largely ignored white Dragon Horse in *Journey to the West* bearing the burden of Tripitaka and the doubleness of Ma Boshi—Dr. Ma in Mandarin or, literally, the horse doctor/vet.

The Horse and the Monkey

This horse was reared in the austerity of a postwar Taiwan, having strained against the bit to break out to the greener pasture of the promised land. My pilgrim's progress relives the classic *Journey to the West* by Wu Cheng'en. After the predestined eighty calamities in Arthur Waley's abridged translation *Monkey: A Folk-Tale of China* (1942), Wu's pilgrims Monkey, Pigsy, and Sandy escorting their master Tripitaka on horseback—the white Dragon Horse—finally reach India in the hope of bringing back to China Buddhist sutras, only to find amidst the eighty-first and last calamity that the sutras are blank—wordless, hence cryptic and mystical, heavenly books. A journeyman from Taiwan to the West for graduate studies and a career in the humanities in US higher education, I look back at this life of words, suspiciously futile like blank pages. After over a dozen scholarly monographs on Asian diaspora literature and film as well as on East-West comparative studies, I now revert to the natural form of creative nonfiction akin to my first and only collection of Chinese poems in 1989. Which English department in the US would grant me tenure if I had continued to publish in a language few, if any, of my department colleagues understand? After having swum in the hostile waters of academe over four decades, after having survived my share of low blows in higher education on both sides of the Pacific Ocean, this horse climbs back up on land for the last leg.

The immigrant truth from the horse's mouth may sound like alienating gobbledygook of an asinine "horse's ass." Authenticity issued from the mouth between the cheeks is soiled by the association with that which is voided between the posterior cheeks. Neighing runs the risk of being dismissed as naysaying since immigrants are neither here nor there, a horse whispering into a human ear, or a human into a horse's. A Chinese idiom echoes, uncannily, that Anglophone play on horsey or, simply, that horseplay: "An ass's head ill-fits a horse's mouth." It describes mismatched parts, mixed metaphors, question and answer, or search and discover, that jar. Indeed, that romantic Taiwanese boy's gaze across the Pacific, just like this (de)naturalized (un)American skeptic's sidelong glance back, is in itself so mixed-up that it appears doomed from the start.

Since we touch on that nonhuman, posthuman half: in addition to its "look-alike" ass, yet another animal—Monkey—is implicated with the Dragon Horse in *Journey to the West* and me in mine. The self-designated "Great Sage, Equal of Heaven" simian wreaks havoc in heaven before being subdued by the Buddha to serve as Tripitaka's escort. In fact, the self-aggrandizing nomenclature deliberately challenges the supremacy of the Jade Emperor in heaven, who has appeased or "played" the naïve Monkey twice before by assigning him to the minor posts of heading the celestial stables and the peach grove of longevity. Despite Monkey's power, he is consistently slighted for his petite stature, hollow cheeks, pointy mouth, and jerky movement. Friedrich Wilhelm Nietzsche agrees in *Thus Spoke Zarathustra* (1883–92): "What is the ape to man? A laughing-stock or a painful embarrassment" (13). Thus, in the promised land of Caucasian giants and white privilege, a sense of doubt, of inadequacy, invariably disturbs a new arrival's equilibrium, caught in a perpetual arriving, never quite there. Culturally speaking, *xinyuan yima* (Heart Ape Thought Horse) is a Chinese adage that likens the restless human mind to the skittish, hyperactive monkey and horse, driven by interior urges and exterior stimulations, the source of all changes or *biàn* in Mandarin.

Biàn for Change or/from Shit in *American Born Chinese*

Feeling like shit, anyone would wish to change. Among over a dozen Chinese homophones, *biàn* in the fourth tone puns with "change" (變) and "shit" (便). "Change from shit" encapsulates Gene Luen Yang's graphic novel *American Born Chinese*, that transubstantiates the rawest of materials in racial slurs and xenophobia into his MacArthur "Genius Grant" a decade later, in 2016. Textually, Yang's characters metamorphose from the caricature Chin-Kee à la the epithet "Chink" to the Monkey King of *Journey to the West*; from the Taiwanese FOB Wei-Chen in drawstring sweatpants and uncombed hair to the Monkey King's son, an envoy from heaven, albeit incognito; and from the self-loathing of the white wannabe Jin to the whiteface dream-self Danny. These three parallel instances of *biàn* sustain the plotline. As the protagonist of *American Born Chinese*, Jin, sheds his Asianness to transform into Danny, he is relentlessly pursued by his conscience in the form of Chin-Kee, who embodies the worst ethnic stereotypes that Jin himself has long internalized. Throughout the ordeal, Jin enjoys the company of Wei-Chen, who eventually rebels against heavenly edicts by assuming a gangster persona.

Of the three, the story of the firstborn of the Monkey King opens the graphic novel and runs parallel to Jin's bildungsroman, even if as a subplot. On the cover of *American Born Chinese*, despite lying crushed under the Buddha's Five Finger Mountain, sealed by the script 自有者, rendered as "Tze-Yo-Tzuh" (*Ziyouzhe* in Mandarin), the Monkey King epitomizes the quandary of the protagonist Jin in the foreground holding his toy Transformer. Both the little boy and the little monkey long for deliverance and empowerment. The last of the three metamorphoses, Jin-Danny, is the artist Gene's namesake and alter ego, reflecting the ABC condition, as the acronym of the book title for second-generation Chinese Americans goes. The "middle child" of Wei-Chen is most neglected, as his existence matters only in relation to the firstborn—his father—and the last-born—his "best friend" (40, 101). To illustrate the theme of change, study the palimpsest of the panel on Jin-Danny in figure 9.2, cropped from page 194 of the graphic novel, morphing under our very eyes:

In the process of gray-toning a graphic novel in color, the ideograph 變 (*biàn*) in the backdrop against the sound effect of "CLICK CLACK" and pointed to by the claw-like fingers is barely noticeable, losing the bright red that makes it stand out in the original. The "genetic" switch implied by the

Figure 9.2. Gene Luen Yang, *American Born Chinese*, First Second Books, March 2006. 194.

sound of turning a light on and off bifurcates into either skin-lightening and self-transcending or darkening and suicidal self-denial. As Jin clicks on the light to find himself Danny on page 195, it comes as a varied repetition of the herbalist wife's abacus clicking and clacking on pages 27, 29, and 193. Adding and subtracting on the traditional Chinese abacus, symbolic calculus in the account book of life, resonates with Jin's fate in gaining Danny while losing himself. Abacus beads moving up or down echoes the electric circuit connecting or disconnecting, not to mention the diurnal course of the sun rising or setting.

In addition, page 28 plays on the theme music of mechanical ticking when the boy Jin demonstrates how his toy robot shapeshifts, with a click-clack or two, into a truck, all the while code-switching between, on the one hand, the Chinese language explaining the mechanics to the elderly woman and, on the other, set punch lines in English from the 1980s Japan-Marvel—East-West again—collaboration franchise of the animation *The*

Transformers. These punch lines evidently lie beyond the capacity of a schoolboy to translate into Chinese. However, it is imperative to remind ourselves of Yang's "white lie" in English pretending to be in Chinese: the angle brackets asterisked as "Translated from Mandarin Chinese" parenthesize English words after all, not Chinese ideograms, just as *American Born Chinese* tells an American tale in the guise of a Chinese one (23). By law, by cultural upbringing, and by linguistic proficiency, whoever is born in the US is American, not Chinese. To say Jin—or Gene Luen Yang, for that matter—is a Chinese born in America, as the book title intimates, is tantamount to the heinous Trumpian birtherism against Barack Obama: that the ex-president is not US-born and possibly African.

Just as Jin switches, supposedly, between Mandarin and English at the herbal shop, a Chinese enclave within America, so does the theoretically Chinese-speaking woman avail herself of Americanism. Despite her lines in angle brackets, she chooses the colloquialism "let you in on a secret," and even the Faustian "become anything you wish . . . so long as you're willing to forfeit your soul," idiomatic English far beyond the majority of elderly immigrants stranded in Chinatown, especially one peddling dried herbs and animal parts (28–29). The Mephistophelian transaction with the devil would estrange any traditional Chinese psyche; the Western-educated Yang puts words, literally, into the old woman's mouth. In place of waving a magic wand, the Chinatown herbalist's wife directs her crooked digits at Jin in granting his wish to be able to whitewash himself. At the herbal medicine store, curatives for the body and the mind are both dispensed. The cinematic cross-dissolve progresses from permed hair, almond-shaped eyes, a snub nose, and theoretically "yellow" skin to, in Toni Morrison's words, "The Bluest Eye" of Danny's, plus his natural curly hair, round eyes, long nose, and white skin. The nameless Chinese old crone is cast in the West's imagery of a witch with missing teeth and talon-like fingernails. Though she is supposedly a good witch helping Jin bleach himself, her physical traits associate her, nonetheless, with evil counterparts from Disney, such as Maleficent in *Sleeping Beauty* (1959). The mystical Orient makes Jin's dream come true in unintelligible Chinese, indicated by angle brackets, suggesting the dark power of the unknown. The sublime and beautiful, as Edmund Burke maintained in *A Philosophical Enquiry* (1757), border on awe and terror.

As such, the aesthetic and the abominable Orient have formulaically polarized Orientalism in Western imaginary, at once loving and hating its doppelganger. Beyond these holographic stereotypical features, one, in particular, impugns Yang for self-Orientalization. In a Chinese matron's tight bun, the otherworldly healer, like a blind seer in Greek tragedy, keeps her eyes tightly shut not just here but throughout her cameo appearance at the San Francisco Chinatown shop—as does Chin-Kee since his debut in a frog-buttoned tunic, high water pants, platform shoes, a long hair queue, a skull cap, and, of course, buckteeth (48). Likewise, Chinese Canadian filmmaker Domee Shi has deployed the same style of two thin, choppy lines for the proverbial "slitty" eyes in her animations *Bao* (2018) and *Turning Red* (2022), mercifully without the buckteeth. Both Yang and Shi resort to Western typecast of Oriental slanted eyes and other features to initiate their fantastical Eastern tales, features Sean Metzger describes in *Chinese Looks* (2014) as "yellowface performance" (61). The "hairpiece" of a queue, such as Chin-Kee's, is identified by Metzger as "the key signifier of Chinese particularity" (28). Are Asian North American artists changing from crappy stock images fashioned by whites or is this change itself crap still? The clichéd argument that Asian North American art reprises stereotypes in order to debunk them eerily reprises the double entendre of *biàn*: change from shit when it is what it is all along.

Fraught with the ambiguity of *biàn*, Yang's sleight of hand flipping between the Anglophone and the Sinophone extends to the toy Transformer itself. What Jin treasures in the Japanese-US robotic Transformer doubling as a truck becomes Wei-Chen's "heirloom" of a robot that reverts into "a robot monkey," "a good-bye present" from his father the Monkey King (39). Ironically, contrary to the three frames on page 28 that incrementally alter Jin's automaton into a truck, page 39 fails to sync words and graphics: while the speech balloon says "a robot monkey," the illustration remains a robot transformer. The monkey self, similar to the racist caricature of Chin-Kee who haunts Danny, embodies Wei-Chen's and Jin's repressed self in hope of becoming either human or white. Yet Wei-Chen's true form does not manifest itself, foreshadowing his abandonment of the heavenly edict.

Wei-Chen's monkey-ness, akin to Jin-Danny's Chinese-ness, only comes through toward the end when Jin "sees through" Wei-Chen's bombastic rebel front in aviator sunshades, with a cigarette dangling from the mouth, flashy earrings, and Boyz-n-the-Hood necklace. Having been rudely awakened by the Monkey King-cum-Chin-Kee, the dream-self Danny is beaten to a pulp and, figuratively, beaten. The restored Jin comes to acquire a privileged perspective, the bird's-eye view of a "has-been," that penetrates what Wei-Chen subconsciously conceals in his transformation. From Jin's eyes, a pale, X-ray image of the scrawny, miniature monkey barely above the steering wheel materializes behind Wei-Chen's scowl and hostility worthy of gangsta rappers. Despite the revving of engine and loud music, Wei-Chen's souped-up, flamboyant sports car with a dramatic tailfin sports a 孫 ("Sun") in large print across the driver's door (229). Revolting against the Monkey King, known as Sun Wukong, the son announces himself, nonetheless, as Sun—Sun's son, as it were. Even the same tuft of stuck-up, straggly hair graces the heads of all three avatars: the FOB's, the rebel's, and, in Jin's panopticon gaze, the little monkey's. Once posing as an uncouth, farcical FOB, Wei-Chen swings to the other end of the pendulum and adopts the stance of an antiestablishment outsider, an outcast who betrays, unwittingly, his monkey heritage through the emblem brandished on his steed of a car and through his "inborn" hairstyle.

To rub it in, the discordant montage of words and deeds, speech balloons and graphics, concludes the book with yet another contradictory message. During the finale of a reunion with Jin, the rebel Wei-Chen dismisses the pearl milk tea as having "an oily taste, like they were stir-frying something nearby . . . the boba reminds me of rabbit crap," despite the fact that he has helped himself to most of it while Jin has barely touched his (232). The greasy smell and taste come, alas, with fine Chinese cuisine utilizing stir-fry woks. The pearl milk tea is a global phenomenon originating from the Pacific Rim, regrettably with the misogynistic association of round tapioca boba pearls likened to female breasts. The "crap" is the bodily discharge of the timid prey rabbit that Wei-Chen, the born-again "predator," renounces. The posture of repudiation of the bad tea is gainsaid by his drinking it to the lees. The proverbial "my bad"—undesirable grease, sexism, and body waste—is mine, like pain, which may or may not secrete "my good." The past impregnates the present, whether one is in denial or not.

Not just the boba tea but the venue itself carries significance. As the Monkey King rides his cloud to take leave of Jin, a business card advertising "490 餐廳餅家 BAKERY CAFE" falls from the sky like biblical manna, where Jin stakes out Wei-Chen for "over a month" until Sun's son arrives in his fancy car (226–27). The café lies, possibly, in a metropolitan Chinatown, serving primarily Chinese-speaking customers in such a way that the menu is in Chinese, which Jin cannot read and makes a fool of himself by randomly pointing to an item that says, "Cash Only." The server takes the order in Chinese and switches to English to accommodate Jin. The store name cries out the Taiwanese-ness that is otherwise missing in Yang's "Chinese" fictional universe, evidenced by the marginalization of Wei-Chen supposedly from the island and the utter disappearance of "Ah-Tong" post-epigraph. 餐廳餅家 (*canting bingjia*), in the traditional characters used in Taiwan and Hong Kong, would be rendered 餐厅饼家 in the simplified characters of China, with the strokes of the second and third ideograms drastically reduced.

These four Chinese ideographs come after the universal Arabic number "490" and before the translation of "Bakery & Restau . . . ," the last word covered by Jin's finger (224), which shifts into "BAKERY CAFÉ" on the store front, the last letter's diacritic—the acute accent (ˊ)—covered by tree branches (226). The palimpsest of multiple translations, which at once explain and veil, illustrates the paradox inherent in the four Chinese words that name the store while remaining ornamental, Oriental. To Chinese customers, the four words not only identify the establishment but also its Taiwanese rather than mainland Chinese aura. To non-Sinophone readers, they tease with a touch of unknowable exoticism. Even the universal Arabic number of "490" rings of specific Sinitic connotation that eludes non-Chinese. Traditionally in China, the mourning period for a loved one is forty-nine days, seven multiplied by seven. The upcoming reunion at the café celebrates their undying friendship over the dead bodies of the FOB and Danny, the double demise of their incarnations.

The number forty-nine's association with the dead harkens back from the recent to the remote selves. Born and raised in San Francisco's Chinatown, Jin relocates to the suburban Mayflower Elementary School as part of any immigrant parents' American dream. The severance from Chinatown resembles a childhood trauma, the first incision of the wound made by Mayflower's third-grade teacher Mrs. Greeder, who blithely mispronounces his "foreign" name on top of introducing him as an alien "all the way from China," while "the scent of our old [San Francisco] home still [lingers] in my clothes" (30). To Mrs. Greeder and those like her, Chinatown and China are alike. That old home receives one snapshot when Jin the toddler in snap-crotch pants looks out the apartment window at Chinatown store signs, including one reading 楊 (Yang), feet away from the toddler's head. Across the frame on the right side is exhibited a McDonald's sign in Chinese, with the recognizable "M" (25). The switch from the old Chinatown signs of his own surname "Yang" to the all-American "McDonald" and, eventually, to what is likely to be the new Chinatown's "490" marks the metamorphosis or *biàn*, the rise and fall, of selves.[5]

Notwithstanding the critical accolade and the commercial success of *American Born Chinese*, "my bad" of smell and self may not lead to "my good" because of the duality of *biàn*. Change to/from shit remains indeterminate, as glamorously shiny and golden as Yang makes it out to be. The ethnic pride in reverting back to Jin's Chinese-ness amounts to "faking it," since it unfolds entirely in English within the genre of a graphic bildungsroman for American readers. More glaringly, such nominal sinologizing is perpetuated, even perpetrated, by way of the post-human species pride of Wei-Chen's monkey-ness and by Yang's authorial faith in Christianity. Contrary to the feel-good self-confirmation, Wei-Chen appears largely as a humanoid, while Yang cloaks Christianity so that *American Born Chinese* reads like a crypto-Christian text. Ethnic undermining of white privilege comes at the cost of the Monkey King's subordination and Yang's mainstreaming.[6]

In *Journey to the West*, the Monkey King's meteoric rise in the first thirteen chapters is shattered once he is tempted into wearing the gold fillet around his forehead. With the magic ring in place, whenever the Monkey King disobeys, his master Tripitaka recites the fillet-tightening sutra handed down from the Buddha via Guanyin, the Goddess of Mercy. The hubris of the self-described "Great Sage, Equal to Heaven" crumbles into a pathetic primate rolling around in agony, regressing to his animal instincts in a flattened fetal position. The turning point occurs at the end of chapter 14 when the Monkey King plays along while secretly raising his cudgel to beat Tripitaka to a pulp, only to wind up "stand[ing] upside down, turn[ing] somersaults, ears and face both bloodshot, eyes swollen, body going numb" as Tripitaka, in self-defense, redoubles his chanting of the sutra at the point of crushing his disciple's skull (*Xiyouji* 146, translation mine). The Monkey King would have smashed his father figure and savior, had his instinct of self-preservation prevailed over the history and the system of patriarchy whereby the nativist, Confucian Jade Emperor joins hands with the Buddha from the West of China—India. Between quasi-patricides against Tripitaka and the Big Daddies behind him, on one side, and, on the other, quasi-suicide against the lone monkey self, the conservative Chinese hegemony unequivocally chooses self-abnegation. Wu Cheng'en's style smacks of "sci-fi" future perfect in that Buddhism is already a fait accompli, as predestined as the law of nature, not only in chapter 14 but also from the very outset, although it is yet to be imported by Tripitaka upon completion of the journey to the West.

Yet another West, the Christian West, courses through the vein-like plot of *American Born Chinese* to the extent that the graphic novel could be facetiously christened *American Born Christian*. By the end of the journey, instead of the wordless, mystical scriptures initially bestowed on Tripitaka, the Buddhist heaven in the West has to settle with their pale imitations in words in order for humans to understand. To convert Chinese heathens, Indian Buddhism has to be indigenized, sinologized. In the name of sinologizing *American Born Chinese*, Yang functionally Christianizes it. In modern lingo, the Buddha had to dumb down His scriptures for dummies, and Yang evangelizes the Monkey King as much for comics fans as to be in keeping with his personal faith.

In Wu Cheng'en's classic, the nativist Jade Emperor solicits "foreign" help from the Buddha to subdue the Monkey King. The fantastical duel consists of the Monkey King turning his magical somersaults persistently to reach what he believes to be the end of the universe with five soaring peaks. Animal instinct leads the Monkey King to mark the territory by urinating and inscribing "The Great Sage, Equal to Heaven," only to realize the peaks are the Buddha's fingers, which summarily crush him for five hundred years under the Five Finger Mountain to await the coming of Tripitaka to release the spell. The Monkey King has not been able to escape from the Buddha's palm, a common Chinese expression similar to "under one's thumb" in English. The reprise of "five" (五, or wǔ in the third tone) puns with "awakening" (悟, wù in the fourth tone) and "emptiness" (無, wú in the second tone). Awakening to emptiness happens to be the Monkey King's "school name" Wukong (悟空), as it were, given by his master Puti at the end of chapter 1. Kong (空) and wu (無) are so interchangeable that they constitute a compound word for "void." The Buddha imprisons the Monkey King to ready him for the journey.

By comparison, the "foreign" help in Yang comes from, not to mince words, Jehovah, or Moses at the very least. Shocked to find the smell and trace of his pee on the ball of Tze-Yo-Tzuh's hand, the Monkey King awakens to the might of this tall man in a long, slender face, long white hair and beard, holding a long shepherd's crook, attributes signaling not so much a Chinese likeness as Charlton Heston's in the 1956 epic *The Ten Commandments* (78–82).[7] Although no such phrasing exists in Taiwanese or Chinese, the foreign-sounding name Tze-Yo-Tzuh is coined solely by Gene Luen Yang, just like the name's meaning. The name is translated as "He Who Is," resonating with the voice from the burning bush that answers Moses, "I am that I am," or a name that is not a name (67). When the Monkey King continues to defy Tze-Yo-Tzuh, the stone bridge on which they travel collapses, drowning the Monkey King in a sea of rocks, reminiscent of the Red Sea that swallows up Pharoah's army as it pursues Moses and the Jews.

The Christian top dog rebranded as Tze-Yo-Tzuh commands Sinitic lieutenants whose Old and New Testament bloodline is readily apparent. The journey to the West of Tripitaka's three disciples Monkey, Pigsy, and Sandy turns out to follow the star leading them to the Nativity of Joseph, Mary, and the newborn Christ (215). The three Magi pay homage to the son of God. Tripitaka's comic version, Wong Lai-Tsao, is earlier entrusted by "the lion, the ox, the human, and the eagle, emissaries of Tze-Yo-Tzuh" to embark on the west-bound pilgrimage (67, 138). The four deities spring straight from Ezekiel 1:10: "As for the likeness of their faces, they four had the face of a man, and the face of a lion, on the right side: and they four had the face of an ox on the left side; they four also had the face of an eagle." Yang revises the Chinese classic as much as the Judeo-Christian one. The collective morphing of, for lack of a better term, the Fantastic Four to the three beasts and one human is constantly in flux. What the King James Version visualizes approximates CGI holographs flipping schizophrenically among each "likeness" of the four figures, epitomizing the very definition of *biàn*—not only changes envisioned by the mad prophet Ezekiel in a moment of ecstasy but also changes that may well be symptomatic of madness in itself. Yang elects to compartmentalize and stabilize each of them, forgoing the fluidity inherent in the images shared by the plural "they." After all, Ezekiel goes on to describe that the four "had one likeness; and their appearance and their work was as it were a wheel in the middle of a wheel" (1:16). The metaphor of turning axle spokes (faces) and wheels (universe in rotation), along with kaleidoscopic manifestations, are ripped asunder by Yang into four fixed cartoon figures. One biblical magic lantern show, or even motion picture, seizes in Yang.

Beyond biblical extractions, even the loaded Christian figure of speech "signpost" slips out, anachronistically, from the Monkey King's self-identification as Jin's "conscience . . . a signpost to your soul" (221). In an unconscionable bait and switch from human psychology to superhuman religion, from literary conceits to articles of faith, Yang first dissembles the minority—Chinese American—consciousness as the Chinese conscience, which then segues into the Christian soul in line with, among other allusions, Jeremiah's exhortation: "Set up markers for yourselves. Erect signposts for yourselves" (ISV Jer 31:21). Such embedded Christianity grows out of Yang's early comics expressly, unabashedly devoted to the faith. *The Rosary*

Comic Book comes across as Christian catechism on the life of Jesus Christ. Likewise, *Loyola Chin and the San Peligran Order* imagines a futuristic scenario for a Christian order. Even a decade later, *Boxers & Saints* transports Joan of Arc into the Qing dynasty's Boxer Rebellion.

Biàn or change from shit never quite sheds the homonymic sound-alike that is what it is. Superheroes embody little American boys' fantasies at the corner drugstore. Toy Transformers realize little Jin/Gene's yearning for assimilation. The Great Sage, Equal to Heaven is Little Monkey in denial. The Monkey King, at least in the opening thirteen chapters as an id-driven Boy-God, becomes as domesticated and indentured as Tripitaka's white Dragon Horse, a beast of burden. This horse doctor rears up like a horse, in fact, from the hirsute floor of Family Barber Shop. The drive to change dictates the horse, the monkey, and the human to become more than themselves, bigger than life. One's being puts under erasure what one had been, no matter how much one indulges in bittersweet nostalgia. Whichever word I type next, like uttering a sound, like breathing into this being of mine, stirs up the blank page and space. Which is more desirable, the word or the blank, the sound or the silence? Would the former be a mere blot on the latter, merely some dust gathered on the Zen mirror of nothingness?[8] This line of rhetorical questions *biàn* to the dragon mere into which the Nordic "superhero" Beowulf plunges.[9] Between the infinitesimal of a mere speck of Buddhist dust and the infinitude of the subterranean mere of water, this horsey ponders by the mirror pond flowing from East to West and back again.

Notes

1. In the superhero genre, *Superman Smashes the Klan* may be the most substantive work Gene Luen Yang has authored. He has also collaborated on *Batman Superman: The Archive of Worlds* (2021) and *New Super-Man and the Justice League of China* (2019). Taking on the superhero comics does not mean that Yang has forgotten the early exposure to the Chinese equivalent of the Monkey King. Yang writes in the foreword to the 2021 translation of *Monkey King* by Julia Lovell, "I realized that American superheroes hadn't replaced Sun Wukong in my heart after all. Superman, Spider-Man, Captain America were simply Western expressions of everything I loved about the monkey king" (x).

2. See Lu Xun's "The True Story of Ah Q."

3. For *Juancun* literature and film, see Sheng-mei Ma's "Get Out of the Village" and "Forgotten Taiwanese Veteran's Memory of Compulsory Service."

4. Endurance training since early childhood, such as persevering despite heat rashes, physical discomfort, and psychological pressure in Taiwan, must have given me the thick skin to survive academic onslaughts later in life.

5. See Sheng-mei Ma's "Gene Luen Yang's Graphic Bi-Bye to China/town" in *Sinophone-Anglophone Cultural Duet* (2017).

6. For a detailed analysis of such childlike rebels as the Monkey King and Nezha subjugated by Chinese authorities, see Sheng-mei Ma's "Mazu's Touch, Taiwan Nezha and Crying" in *The Last Isle* (2015).

7. The Monkey King's animal instinct for marking territory is so strong that his avatar Chin-Kee plays a prank on his schoolmate Steve by peeing in his Coke bottle (75).

8. In seventh-century China, a duel showcasing Chan/Zen one-upmanship pits Shen-hsiu's poem against the Sixth Patriarch Hui-neng's. It goes without saying that Hui-neng triumphs by virtue of a poetic kinship to Buddhist nothingness. Shen-hsiu writes of due diligence and gradual awakening:

> The body is the bodhi tree,
> The mind is like a clear mirror.
> At all times we must strive to polish it,
> And must not let the dust collect.

This is trumped by Hui-neng's poem advocating sudden illumination to emptiness more consonant with Zen Buddhism:

> Bodhi originally has no tree,
> The mirror has no stand.
> Buddha-nature is always clean and pure;
> Where is there room for dust to alight?

9. Readying himself to dive into the pool to fight Grendel's dragon mother, Beowulf equips himself:

> To guard his head he had a glittering helmet
> That was due to be muddied on the mere bottom
> And blurred in the upswirl. (ll. 1448–1450)

Here and elsewhere, the Nobel laureate Seamus Heaney's translation of "mere" for the pool of water is taken directly from Old English, such as "mere-grundas" for "sea bottom" in line 1449.

Works Cited

Arnaudo, Marco. *The Myth of the Superhero*. Translated by Jamie Richards, Johns Hopkins UP, 2013.

Beowulf. Translated by Seamus Heaney, illustrated by John D. Niles, Norton, 2008.

Burke, Edmund. *A Philosophical Enquiry into the Origin of Our Ideas of the Sublime and Beautiful*. 1757. Routledge, 2008.

Eliade, Mircea. *Shamanism: Archaic Techniques of Ecstasy*. Penguin Arkana, 1988.

Lu Xun. "The True Story of Ah Q." *Selected Stories of Lu Hsun*, translated by Yang Hsien-yi and Gladys Yang, Foreign Language Press, 1978, pp. 65–112. (Orig. pub. 1918)

Luo Dayou. "Childhood." From the album *Zhihuyezhe* (之乎也者), 1982. www.youtube.com/watch?v=mRKTOZmX2cE.

Ma, Sheng-mei. "Forgotten Taiwanese Veteran's Memory of Compulsory Service." *Journal of Veteran Studies*, vol. 6, no. 3, 2020, pp. 23–29.

Ma, Sheng-mei. "Get Out of the Village: Watching *The Prisoner* with Chinese Subtitles in *Juancun*." *Taiwan Lit*, vol. 2, no. 1, Spring 2021, taiwanlit.org/essays/get-out-of-the-village-watching-the-prisoner-with-chinese-subtitles-in-juancun-1.

Ma, Sheng-mei. *The Last Isle: Contemporary Film, Culture and Trauma in Global Taiwan*. Rowman & Littlefield, 2015.

Ma, Sheng-mei. *Sinophone-Anglophone Cultural Duet*. Palgrave Macmillan, 2017.

Metzger, Sean. *Chinese Looks: Fashion, Performance, Race*. Indiana UP, 2014.

Miller, Nancy K. *Getting Personal: Feminist Occasions and Other Autobiographical Acts*. Routledge, 1991.

Nietzsche, Friedrich Wilhelm. *Thus Spoke Zarathustra*. Edited by Bill Chapko, 2010, nationalvanguard.org/books/Thus-Spoke-Zarathustra-by-F.-Nietzsche.pdf. Accessed 21 July 21 2022.

Wu Cheng'en. *Monkey: A Folk-Tale of China* (*Xiyouji*). Translated by Arthur Waley, Grove, 1943.

Wu Cheng'en. *Xiyouji*. Diyi (First) Bookstore, n.d.

Yang, Gene Luen. *American Born Chinese*. First Second, 2006.

Yang, Gene Luen. *Batman Superman: The Archive of Worlds*. DC Comics, 2021.

Yang, Gene Luen. *Boxers and Saints*. First Second, 2013.

Yang, Gene Luen. "Foreword." *Monkey King: Journey to the West* by Wu Cheng'en, translated by Julia Lovell, Penguin, 2021, pp. ix–xi.

Yang, Gene Luen. *Loyola Chin and the San Peligran Order*. AmazeInk, 2004.

Yang, Gene Luen. *New Super-Man and the Justice League of China*, nos. 20–23, DC Comics, 2019.

Yang, Gene Luen. *The Rosary Comic Book*. Pauline, 2003.

Yang, Gene Luen. *The Shadow Hero*. First Second, 2014.

Yang, Gene Luen. *Superman Smashes the Klan*. DC Comics, 2020.

Ye Hongjia. *Duel with the Devil Gang*. issuu.com/345yeh/docs/__________-1. Accessed 14 July 2022.

10

"The Black Girl You Cannot Kill"

Autoethnographic Reflections on Black Girlhood, Power, and Superheroes

Sika Dagbovie-Mullins

If Paris could have a superpower, it would be to make herself visible.
—**Nafissa Thompson-Spires,** "Heads of the Colored People: Four Fancy Sketches, Two Chalk Outlines, and No Apology"

I

When I was invited to write an essay about my personal relationship to superheroes, I immediately thought of dressing up as Wonder Woman for Halloween as a child. If you were a kid in the eighties, you remember those paper-thin plastic masks with the weak elastic band that went around the back of your head, depicting whatever cartoon or television character was popular. I was Wonder Woman. I remember the spandex suit and plastic wrist cuffs but especially the white "skin" of my plastic face mask, the space around my eyes betraying my true identity. I called my mom to see if she could find a photo. "Remember when I was Wonder Woman for Halloween? Can you find that picture of me in the album with the black photo sleeves?" My mom sounded surprised: "You were never Wonder Woman!" I insisted, of course I was. "Can you please look for the photo? I need it for an essay," I said.

My mom got back to me in a few days; she'd found the photo (figure 10.1). I was not, in fact, Wonder Woman. I was correct about where to find the photo and accurate about my age, but I was a witch that year (long black wig, flimsy plastic mask, kitchen broom). The only thing my memory had right was that I was white.

Figure 10.1. Author's personal archive.

I am the squatting
Goddess
Supergirl
Not a white girl in tights [. . .]

—**Kelly Norman Ellis,** "Superhero"

II

A few years ago, my daughter was obsessed with superheroes. Some of her favorite movies were the classic *The Adventures of Sharkboy and Lavagirl* (2005) and the more recent *We Can Be Heroes* (2020). She had Bumblebee and Supergirl dolls and furiously read through my *Moon Girl and Devil Dinosaur* comics during online learning Zoom breaks throughout the beginning of the COVID-19 pandemic. Her favorite superhero texts/shows (*DC Superhero Girls, Ultra Squad, Miraculous: Tales of Ladybug and Cat Noir, Moon Girl and Devil Dinosaur*) all feature a Black girl superhero, a powerful affirmation of her Black girlhood. Still, my daughter also loved

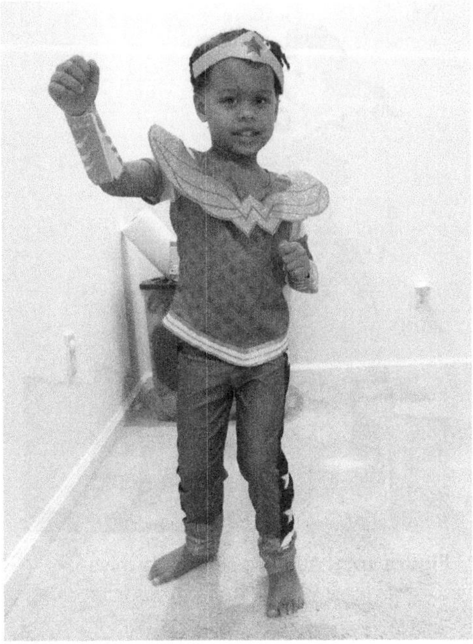

Figure 10.2. Author's personal archive.

Wonder Woman. When she was three years old, she chose a Wonder Woman costume for Halloween. (Did I merge my memory of her with a memory of myself? Ironically, she dressed up as a witch the following year.) The year before, she'd been Elsa from *Frozen* (primarily because she wanted to swing that long, blonde braid. I compromised and bought her a blue and white yarn braid off Etsy). So I was secretly thrilled when she chose a cool spandex one-piece Wonder Woman costume. That year in her preschool class there was a Rapunzel, an Elsa, a Skype (*Paw Patrol*), a skeleton, a witch, a Gekko and two Owlettes (*PJ Masks*), a Batman, and a Spider-Man. My daughter and the only other Black girl in the class were both Wonder Woman.

That October my daughter was all about the Wonder Woman pose, her arms up in a fighting stance or crossed in front of her chest, taking a cue from images of Gal Gadot from *Wonder Woman* (2017) and related media. This continued throughout the year; I have several photos of her mirroring Wonder Woman's iconic stance. Her costume came with Wonder Woman's infamous boomerang tiara, which she wore proudly. Although she had delighted before in wearing princess tiaras with make-believe,

Figure 10.3. Author's personal archive.

T-shirt-on-her-head long hair, she now seemed uninterested in Wonder Woman's hair. I've noticed that my daughter had previously chosen her Halloween costume based on the hair; that is, whether or not she'd be able to rock a long wig. But when she chose Wonder Woman, she did not ask for a black wig. I think what she wanted to be—powerful, not her conception of "pretty"—was enough. To return to my (incorrect) memory, why did I recall being Wonder Woman? Did I inadvertently substitute white for powerful?

In her article in *The Atlantic*, "Imagining a Black Wonder Woman," Maya Rupert remembers asking her mother if Wonder Woman was Black, hoping to dress up as her for Halloween when she was eight years old. Rupert shares the connection she felt with Wonder Woman, whose story and background felt "familiar," particularly Wonder Woman's otherness as Amazonian and more-than-human. Such an identification highlights Ramzi Fawaz's consideration of the counterpublic this collection takes up. Discussing the Fantastic Four's counterpublic, Fawaz writes, "The sensibility of this counterpublic linked a shared pleasure in superheroic fantasy with a value for the status of the outsider or socially maladjusted, a figure, that the superhero, and its fans, had clearly become both" (98). Rupert discusses the difficulties she has navigating a world that sees her Blackness and Black femaleness as threatening and aberrant: "As a girl, I most commiserated with Wonder Woman when she sought to reconcile her inner strength and ferocity with the need of others to see her as peaceful and feminine. I had learned early on that it wouldn't take a lot for me to be viewed as angry and deemed unlikeable." As I have watched my daughter consume images of smart, powerful, and strong Black girl superheroes, I think how Black girls and women are frequently positioned as always already both angry and tough in the media and popular culture, where the Angry Black Woman and Strong Black Woman archetypes compete for dominance. Rupert explains, "Wonder Woman's fate was one I had tried to avoid for years with a painful balancing act. Black women have long had to navigate stereotypes that create a similar sort of bind: Our reputed preternatural strength is used as a weapon to force us to withstand greater physical, emotional, and spiritual burdens." In Melissa Harris-Perry's *Sister Citizen: Shame, Stereotypes, and Black Women in America* (2011), she identifies the Strong Black Woman archetype as a "complicated cultural myth": "Even though the strong black woman is a more positive image than Jezebel, Mammy, or Sapphire, she is still inadequate to allow black women to enjoy the benefits of recognition and therefore opt into an experience of full citizenship. Still masked behind a façade of impervious strength, black women remain unable to reveal their fragile humanity" (217). Perry's description of Black women "masked behind a façade" fittingly nods to the dual identity trope of the superhero. Barbara Brownie and Danny M. Graydon remind us that "the superhero identity does not exist independently of the costume. In many ways, the costume is the superhero" (29). According to popular culture (and as sometimes internalized by Black women), our identities can be inextricably connected to our "costumes" or how we are perceived by white dominant culture. This essay is an attempt to lift off the metaphoric mask Black girls are forced to wear while reflecting on the significance of Black girl superheroes in a culture that denies Black girls their full humanity. I place various narratives side-by-side (including brief moments my daughter, my mother, and I have been linked to Wonder Woman) in an effort to think about Black women's perceived superheroic toughness (emotional, mental, physical), the adultification of Black girls, and the double-edged sword of Black girl strength, superheroic and otherwise.

For I am
the Black girl
you cannot kill,

what a thought
—**Jasmine Mans,** "I Got Gold Mines"

III

Five days before Halloween 2015 (and the year before my daughter dressed as Wonder Woman), a sixteen-year-old Black girl was savagely handled for refusing to get off her cell phone in the classroom by a school resource officer in Columbia, South Carolina. The high school sophomore, Shakara, was in math class when her teacher and vice principal asked her to leave for not complying. "When she continued to silently refuse, [Officer Ben] Fields flipped Shakara out of her chair and physically dragged her out of the classroom. In an ironic twist, the incident was captured on the also prohibited cell phones of the other students in class" (Bailey 58). Both Shakara and eighteen-year-old Niya Kenny, who videotaped the incident, were arrested for disturbing school. (Shakara, a minor, was released to her foster mother, while Niya spent the night in jail).[1]

Niya's recollection of the incident lays repeated emphasis on Shakara's age and positionality: "I'd never seen nothing like that in my life. Like, a man use that much force on a little girl. A big man, like 300 pounds of full muscle. . . . Like, you can't do that to no little girl" (*On These Grounds*). Her repeated use of the phrase "little girl" reminds us that, while Shakara was a teenager, she was still a minor. It is worth noting that some students nicknamed Fields, a competitive body builder, "The Incredible Hulk" (Hensley), a fitting descriptor for an officer who is represented in starkly contrary ways. That superhero/antihero was first introduced by Stan Lee and Jack Kirby in the comics as an uncontrollable monster (the first cover reads, "Is he Man or Monster or . . . is he both"). Still, in *The Incredible Hulk* (1962), Hulk saves a school bus of children when the bus gets stuck on railroad tracks: "Deep within the monster's brain; a tiny spark of Bruce Banner comes to life! And then, without conscious thought, moving like a gigantic, living battering ram, the Hulk takes over, performing a feat which no other living human could have accomplished" (Lee and Kirby 6). The documentary *On These Grounds* presents Fields as the uncontrolled behemoth, clearly not the

Hulk who instinctively saves the schoolchildren in the 1962 issue. However, supporters of Fields interviewed in the documentary, such as his ex-girlfriend (who is Black), states, "It's shocking to see someone that you know plastered all over TV and being talked about in a way that you know isn't true, so my heart went out to him because I know that Ben is not what he was portrayed as." Still, his actions on the video are clear. It seems the video was even too much for Fields to handle. In the documentary he admits to never watching it. In "From Comicbook to Road Narrative: The Incredible Hulk (1977–1982) as Serialized Drama," Fernando Pagnoni Berns writes that in the television series, "Banner/Hulk finds pockets of moral decay he must resolve wherever he goes. America is full of geographies affected by economic inequalities, social prejudices, moral decay and poverty" (Berns 20). In contrast, Fields/Hulk resists admitting any "moral decay" related to systematic racism and school policing.

When Fields was terminated, the sheriff clarified it was due to his not using "proper technique." The school and administration had "no problem with the physical part" of the video. In fact, though he was let go from the Richland County Sheriff's Department, they found no grounds to charge him. In an interview with the press, the sheriff stated, "We must not lose sight that this whole incident was started by this student. She is responsible for initiating this action. . . . She was very disruptive, she was very disrespectful—she started this whole incident." He added that she must be "held accountable" (Sorkin). The sheriff's language reflects the racist adultification of Black girls, what Ashley Smith describes in *The Black Girlhood Studies Collection* as "the process of viewing, associating, and treating children as adults, including expecting them to behave or respond in an adult-like manner and making children responsible for every action or behavior they engage in while depriving them of childhood innocence" (38). The sheriff claimed Shakara suffered no injuries "except possibly 'rug burns'; [and when] asked why there were . . . reports that she had multiple injuries, he suggested that they had emerged only 'now that she has an attorney'" (Sorkin). The sheriff's comments not only ignore the very real injuries Shakara suffered but also suggest she was somehow invulnerable to being hurt, symbolically both superhuman and not human. I am reminded of the nine-year-old in Rochester, New York, who was having a mental health episode and was subsequently pepper sprayed by a police officer after her mother called 911 in January 2021. Officers attempted to restrain the girl and place her in a patrol car while she screamed for her father. Before pepper spraying her, one of the officers told her, "You're acting like a child" to which she responded, "I am a child" (Hong).

In my own state of Florida, there have been multiple publicized incidents involving police officers and Black girls at school.[2] As Christina Sharpe writes in reference to a twelve-year-old Black girl who faced a felony charge after writing on school walls, "These stories, too, accumulate; the ditto ditto in the archives of the present" (82). In Tampa in 2015, seventeen-year-old Brittany Overstreet received a broken jaw and concussion after an altercation with a police officer who falsely accused her of having mace in her backpack. In 2021, sixteen-year-old Taylor Bracey was body-slammed onto a concrete walkway by a police officer who was called to break up her verbal fight with another student in a Kissimmee, Florida, high school. In 2019, six-year-old Kaia Rolle was arrested for having a temper tantrum at a school in Orlando. The school had been notified that she was experiencing side effects from sleep apnea. However, the first grader was zip-tied and put in a patrol car; they took her to a juvenile detention center, took her mugshot, and charged her with misdemeanor battery for hitting three staff people (at the time there was no minimum age for arrest in Florida). This egregious example of reading Black girls as immune to or more tolerant of pain merges with our nation's tendency to view them as nonhuman: "Black girls having temper tantrums that result in arrests are not solely tied to them being viewed as loud, angry, Black women, but instead exacerbates [*sic*] the ways in which they maintain a non/child position in schools and society due to their blackness" (Smith 34). The arresting officer (who was Black) was fired, but the damage had been done; Kaia was later diagnosed with posttraumatic stress syndrome and separation anxiety. In 2021, two years after the incident, Senator Randolph Bracy was instrumental in passing a bill mandating a minimum age of arrest. The Kaia Rolle Act prohibits children under the age of seven (!) from being arrested unless they've committed a felony. Kaia, now eight years old, and her grandmother attended a ceremony to celebrate the bill. When asked by the press how she felt, Kaia responded, "It makes me feel like a superhero!" (Boey).

i understand the cape,
the leggings, [. . .]
there is no planet stranger
than the one i'm from.
—Lucille Clifton, "note, passed to superman"

IV

In the 1970s when my mother, who is white, was working on her MA in Urban Elementary Education, she was sent to teach at an all-Black junior high school in Pontiac, Michigan. She remembers the time as quite depressing. It was the kind of school where the social studies teacher would set up a projector for the class to watch a film and then leave for the entire class period while he smoked. The administration, she recalls, was "not worth a darn," and her mentor was kind but too rigid. One bright spot was her students, who seemed to like her too. The girls would walk into class expressing their love for Michael Jackson and the Jackson 5, and she remembers students constantly saying she looked like Wonder Woman—Lynda Carter as Wonder Woman from the television show. And she did look like Carter's character, Diana Prince, Wonder Woman's nonsuperhero identity: long black hair pulled into a bun, blue eyes framed by oversized round glasses, and what my mom would call her "chubby" face (figure 10.4). Around this time, Wonder Woman had a Black twin sister, Nubia, who was introduced in a 1973 comic. It strikes me that Nubia could also be considered mixed-race, having been created by a white mother. In *Wonder Woman* #206, Wonder Woman learns that another child was created by her mother, Queen Hippolyta. Hippolyta formed two babies from clay who were brought to life by Aphrodite. While Wonder Woman is made from light clay, Nubia is made from dark clay. Mars, the god of war, abducts Nubia, raises her, and brainwashes her to fight the Amazons.

Nubia was supposed to appear in the television show *Wonder Woman* but was dropped when the network changed from ABC to CBS. Still, the Mego corporation made Nubia into a doll in 1976 to promote the show. The box she came in did not introduce her as Wonder Woman's sister or even her ally. Instead, she is "Wonder Woman's super foe" and "the heartless arch-mistress of evil." *In Black Women in Sequence: Re-Inking Comics, Graphic Novels and Anime*, Deborah Whaley explains how mythologies of African primitivism frame Nubia: "Diana Prince and Nubia are sisters,

Figure 10.4. Author's personal archive.

brought to life by the same white mother and made from the same brand of 'clay,' but it is Nubia's imagined Africanness and symbolic blackness that apparently makes her susceptible to violent behavior, and perhaps most erroneous, masculinist and supremacist ideology" (100). It is unsurprising that Nubia is marketed as evil and destructive, repeating a familiar narrative about Black women's supposed inherent hostility and antagonism. Still, this portrayal of Nubia has not dominated contemporary popular culture representations of her. Darieck Scott writes that Nubia is now "a template figure for a range of fantasies of black power and beauty proliferating in a fan counterpublic. Typing 'Nubia Wonder Woman' into an internet image-search engine nets you pages of digital fan-artist-created images of the character, as well as references to the webpage for 'Nubia, The Illustrated Index'" (56). One of the most recent representations imagines Nubia as a Black girl, Nubia L'Shea Johnson, a teenager with two Black moms who has been taught to keep her powers a secret in L. L. McKinney and Robyn Smith's YA graphic novel, *Nubia: Real One* (2021). Such texts offer an alternative fantasy space where Black girls can be both vulnerable and strong, human and magic, enraged and peaceful, all the while remaining girls. Here Aimee Cox's theory of shapeshifting (discussed in her ethnography on young Black women living in a Detroit shelter) is helpful in thinking about Nubia. Cox asserts, "Black women are, out of necessity, inherently shapeshifters" (25).

She proposes that shapeshifting offers "opportunities to interrogate the texture of citizenship for Black girls." In her study, shapeshifting speaks to the ways Black girls reveal the "destructive nature of normative ways of life that valorize white supremacy, patriarchy, and modes of production that render Black women at best superfluous and at worst valueless" (9). Nubia's superheroic transformations, where she no longer hides her strength and power, approximate a kind of shapeshifting while her resistance and challenge to misogynoir underscore Cox's understanding of shapeshifting.

In *Nubia: Real One*, Nubia deals with typical teenager issues and problems but must also contend with a host of more serious issues: the racial bias of police officers, racial profiling, misogynoir, and violence directed at her best friend. Throughout the text, she is viewed as a threat by whites and has two run-ins with white male police officers. First, she is misidentified as an armed robber by a store clerk and shortly after handcuffed by a police officer who says she looks like a suspect in the robbery; he places her in his police car (figure 10.5) while falsely calling her "uncooperative" (McKinney 28). She has an additional confrontation with the police when she and her friends attend a Black Lives Matter protest in response to police shooting a Black boy in the back (he had gotten scared and run when questioned about an incident in which he was not involved). After her best friend's white assailant and stalker, Wayland, throws a brick at police to falsely pin violence on the protestors, Nubia is asked to put her hands up and police read the metal bracelets Wonder Woman has given her as a weapon and shoot at her. Nubia's interactions with police officers reflect the misrecognition at play when white officers confront Black girls. I'd like to spend a moment examining the more subtle ways the text comments on the erasure of Black girls' humanity during confrontations with police, when they are either misread or interpreted as nonhuman. Each time Nubia is confronted by police, accused of wrongdoing, or erroneously imagined as a threat, she appears in a panel that zooms in on just her in a light pink wash, what I will call "pinkglazing." The background in these panels is a neutral cream or pale-yellow blank space, and Nubia is colored all pink (with the exception of her black hair). Of note in these panels is her expressivity; while she is, of course, frightened and anxious in these moments, her eyes are drawn in a more cartoonish fashion, often resembling anime eyes.[3] In Brie Henderson's coloring of the comic, pinks and purples dominate (along with yellows and blues). Illustrator Robyn Smith notes that the "colour palette was chosen with warmth in mind. Colours that can both reflect the brightness of youth

Figure 10.5. Elle McKinney and Robyn Smith, *Nubia: Real One*, DC Comics, February 2021, 28.

and can be muted to match the seriousness of the emotional tone throughout" (Hyman). The pinkglazing in these panels emphasizes Nubia's youth and innocence while simultaneously de-racing and racializing her. The term "pinkglazing" most obviously refers the monochromatic pink that covers Nubia in various panels, but it also gestures at the ways her innocence and goodness are emphasized. To glaze something is to give it a smooth and glossy cover or surface. Of course, another meaning of glaze is to stare. Thus the term is also intended to draw attention to how Nubia must resist

Figure 10.6. Elle McKinney and Robyn Smith, *Nubia: Real One*, DC Comics, February 2021, 25.

the dehumanizing white gaze. The first instance of pinkglazing happens after Nubia has just run from the convenience store where she threw an ATM machine at the armed robber and is mistaken as the thief by the convenience store worker. As she sits on the sidewalk, regretting that she's exposed her superpower to the public, she hears a police siren. Two panels, zoomed in on Nubia from the waist up, show her (figure 10.6) in fear; she thinks, "Nononono, NO!" She is wide-eyed, thus looking more like a child-like than a teenager (McKinney 25). This kind of pinkglazing happens again in part III, when Nubia is shot by police and uses the bracelets Wonder Woman gives her to deflect the bullets. On the bottom right-hand side of the page, a small panel zooms in on Nubia's expression after the bullet hits her ("AHH!!!"). Her eyes are preternaturally large, looking especially like anime eyes. On the next page she realizes her crush, Oscar, has been shot.

I'm suggesting these panels are critiquing a system that refuses to see Black girls as children (and the characteristics and associations that come with that: innocence, softness, trustfulness, tenderness) by using a solid color wash or glaze inextricably connected with girls and femininity. In reference to her use of pink, Smith notes, "Pink is capable of conveying so much, both strength and tenderness, and I thought that would be fitting for the story" (Hyman). The cartoonish eyes, in contrast, freeze Nubia as an unrealistic and nonhuman figure, reflecting how Black girls are perceived under the white gaze. Of note is the fact that Nubia is on the verge of tears in both instances, fearfully aware of the predicament she is in. Her teary eyes capture her momentary vulnerability ignored by dominant society. As Rebecca Epstein writes, "Black girls are often not viewed as fundamentally human and not afforded the leniency given to White girls. Black girls' tears are not valued the way we value White girls' tears because we associate White girls with an innocence that engenders compassion and sympathy by adults" (Diaz 101).

I should say here that there are other times where Nubia or other characters appear in pink (or another color) with a blank, single-color background. However, my focus is how pinkglazing, coupled with a focus on Nubia's expression, invites readers to recognize the predicament of Black girls. It is fitting that such pinkglazing also occurs before Nubia has violent interactions with Wayland Copeland: both times she is coming to the rescue of her best friend Quisha. When Nubia and her friends sneak out to attend a party, she loses track of Quisha. In one panel, Nubia resembles a deer-in-the-headlights when she worries Quisha must be outside where she knows Wayland is hanging out with his friends (McKinney 94). Indeed, Nubia finds Quisha being forcibly kissed by Wayland. They begin fighting, and after Wayland hits her, Nubia knocks him out. Nubia comes to the rescue of her friend again at the end of the novel, when Wayland brings a gun to school, targeting Quisha. It should be noted that Wayland's outfit resembles the costuming of the alt-right group the Proud Boys. He wears a black and yellow polo shirt, the de facto uniform of the racist group.[4] When Nubia runs into the library to find Quisha, a small rectangular panel at the top of the page uses pinkglazing again: we see a side profile of Nubia with wide eyes presumably looking at Wayland. In the next panel Wayland tells Quisha, "You don't get to say no to me. NOT you!" (185). This happens right before Nubia throws what is presumably a bell hooks (!) book at him, knocking the gun out of his hand.

Although he is a teenager and obviously not a police officer, Wayland exercises and exploits his power as an upper-class white male. He is from a wealthy family and uses his family's status in the community to intimidate others and protect himself. Ironically, Wayland is the name of "a heroic smith of Germanic legend."[5] Wayland is far from heroic, but he thinks of himself as such when he presents his racism, resentment, and hatred as heroism in a high school message board: "Someone should do something about these dangerous thugs [from the protest] before they hurt innocent people. I'll do it if no one else will" (McKinney 169). Quisha tells Nubia that Wayland previously broke the neck of another classmate, though that student claimed it was an accident: "He probably promised to do worse if she said anything. With his family's money and connections, that's no empty threat" (51). Wayland confirms this later when he tells Nubia, "Maria didn't know her place. None of you bitches do" (189). Given Wayland's powerful position and the violence he has gotten away with, it is easy to see a connection between Nubia's interactions with him and her interactions with police.

Nubia's second to last altercation with Wayland is at the Black Lives Matter protest that Quisha has helped to organize in support of Quentin, a Black boy who has been murdered by police. As previously mentioned, Wayland frames Nubia and her friends by making it seem as if they are attacking the police. When the police point their guns at protesters, Nubia does not resist the officers, but they still shoot when her friend/crush, Oscar, steps in front of her to protect her. Nubia, in tears with her hands up, begs for the police to help her bleeding friend while she recalls a litany of past insults and grievances: "One misstep and they crucify you. People don't really see Black and brown kids as kids" (163). She then angrily grabs the officer and throws him away from her friend, emphatically thinking, "So they see us" (164). It is important to note Nubia's emphasis here on being seen. Her comment bemoans how Black and brown kids are simultaneously read as adults and dehumanized. Nubia's reflections on being acknowledged and viewed accurately when Black speak back to the epigraph of this essay from Nafissa Thompson-Spires' short story "Heads of the Colored People: Four Fancy Sketches, Two Chalk Outlines, and No Apology," which tells the story of Riley, a Black cosplayer, who is shot by police along with Brother

Man, a Black avocational comics writer, after they get into an altercation outside a comics convention: "And you should fill in for yourself the details of that shooting as long as the constants (unarmed men, excessive force, another dead body, another dead body) are included in those details" (12). That Paris, Riley's girlfriend, would choose visibility as her superpower ironically calls attention to the fact that Riley and Brother Man are paradoxically both highly visible and invisible when they are killed by police. People attending "Comic-Love" watch and record the fight, making them highly visible. Yet the disturbing murder of the unarmed men renders them symbolically invisible. As a Black cosplayer, Riley finds visibility both affirming and burdensome: "With Riley she could be seen, since they got a decent amount of attention when they were together and especially when they were dressed up. Certain cosplayer purists (read: racists) did not always approve of Paris's or Riley's respective costume choices or the idea of black people dressed as nonblack characters" (10). This returns me to Nubia, who understands that visibility is only helpful when images are truthful and free from racist stereotypes. When her punching Wayland at the party goes viral, the headlines are telling: "Local Boy Attacked at Party" and "Tall, Dark, and . . . Dangerous?" (McKinney 125). Wayland remains a "boy" while Nubia becomes a threatening (Black) monster.

At the end of the graphic novel, Nubia emerges as a hero. She rescues Quisha, exposing Wayland and her superhero powers. Once Wayland threatens, "I got video of you attacking those cops at the protest," Nubia immediately takes out her phone and records him as he talks, positioning herself as the viewer rather than the one being viewed (190). In Nubia's first interaction with a police officer at the beginning of the novel, the police officer tells her, "I'm watching you" as he places her in his vehicle and lies about her being "uncooperative" (28). This final scene restores Nubia as a Black girl, not the "dark . . . dangerous" threat (125). The news report later describes her as "a young woman possessing superhuman abilities who stepped into to neutralize the shooter . . . making her a hero" (194). She is finally seen.

> Like her Amazon sisters she revels in the health and power of her body claiming, "there is no greater exhilaration than the sheer joy of flying . . . the incomparable sensation of pure unbridled freedom!"
>
> **—Joan Ormrod**

V

The cover of *Wonder Woman*, vol. 2, #62 (1992) proclaims, "An Era Ends for Wonder Woman," and pictures (figure 10.7) Wonder Woman in mid-flight, leaving her homeland of Themyscira for America. She carries a brown duffle bag and looks ahead, her facial expression embodying the serious business of international travel, the traversing of geographic borders and boundaries. The war of the gods has ended, leaving the capital city destroyed. The location of Themyscira has been revealed to the world, leading Wonder Woman to think, "It all feels so bizarre. So many times I have traveled from Themyscira to the world outside but never like this" (Pérez, Thompson, and Tanghal). Themyscira's location has been revealed to the world, and thus things will no longer be the same. One thing that immediately strikes me is how Jill Thompson has drawn Wonder Woman on the cover: something about her excessively curly hair, nose, and full lips hint at a nonwhite racial identity. (Wonder Woman is often portrayed with curly hair and has curly hair in the comic; however, this cover is distinctive in how it features her curls as uniquely curly/kinky with their own mind). In "Reading Wonder Woman's Body: Mythologies of Gender and Nation," Mitra C. Emads notes that on the cover "her face and body convey a specific 'ethnic' identity rather than a general superhero identity" (974–75). Something about how she looks reads to me as Black. On the cover, Wonder Woman also embodies the freedom of mobility. She looks ahead with anticipative eyes, one arm in back, advancing her forward, while the other firmly holds her duffle strap. Her legs are in an active flying stance with one knee bent and the other leg extended behind her body. She is determined and flying free, leaving her homeland behind as she travels abroad.

In 1992 my brother and I traveled without our parents for the first time to Togo, West Africa, my father's homeland. I was in high school; my brother was in college. At the end of our long trip back to the US, we went through customs in New York City, a tedious process. Returning to the US and going through customs was always anxiety-inducing for me, especially as a young child. (Would they throw away the homemade

Figure 10.7. George Perez, Jill Thompson, and Romeo Tanghal, *Wonder Woman*, vol. 2, #62, DC Comics, February 1992, cover.

achamo cookies my aunt had given me? Would they mistake the garri, a light-colored flour, for something illegal? Were any of the roasted or sugar-coated peanuts packaged in old water bottles prohibited?) Even with my white mother as the "safe" face, my family felt under the microscope. In what seemed like an unspoken agreement, we would instinctively look for the agent who was Black or who had a kindly face or who looked as if they were ready to go home.

On this trip I don't remember which line we stood in, but I imagine we might have lucked out and found a Black woman. I had freshly done microbraids down to my waist and was wearing one of the many colorful African print skirts I had gotten tailored. My brother had thick dreadlocks at the time and was wearing jeans and a well-worn Black History T-shirt (or was it an African batik daishiki-style shirt with threaded embroidery?). We may have looked like members of the hip-hop group Arrested Development who had just released their album *3 Years, 5 Months and 2 Days in the life of . . .* —mixing styles and wearing our consciousness on our bodies.

I walked up and placed my suitcase on the table and then turned around to see my brother being taken away by two men (were they airport officials? police officers? customs agents?). I panicked and was immediately in tears. During an era of missing children on milk cartons and child kidnapping reenactments on *America's Most Wanted*, I sincerely thought my brother was being abducted. A white female officer approached me and took me away to a room where she said she needed to ask me a few questions. The rest is blurry—how much of this is what I remember vs. what my mind has filled in? When I call my brother for the specifics I cannot recall, his memory is equally unclear; we both remember the incident but not the details. A call to my mother is the same: Pause. "Ohhhhh, yeessss. I remember something like that."

This was my first direct interaction with a police officer. I was patted down and questioned, though I was a teenager and had no parent or guardian present. No one called my parents or asked my older brother to be with me. (Did I have to remove any articles of clothing? I cannot remember). In my memory I see a small windowless room with chairs. Given my age, this seems wrong at best and illegal at worst. In addition to being racially profiled, I was treated like an adult suspect and not the young teenager I was. When I was reunited with my brother, he was furious. Somehow it never occurred to me that they thought we were smuggling drugs or that I was perceived as already criminal. That this took place in an airport, a transitional and liminal space, spoke to my own liminality as a (mixed-race) Black girl traveling between homeland and home, Black and white, childhood and adulthood, safety and danger, flying free and being restrained. This in-betweenness recalls Corinne T. Field and Lakisha Michelle Simmons's assertion that "the in-between space of not white girls and not yet Black women provides a standpoint for imagining few futures, demanding justice, living wholeness and loving in new ways." What might be imagined from spaces where Black girls' strength and potential is in between superheroic and vulnerable? Perhaps models of shapeshifting offer a possibility. As Aimee Cox explains, "*Shapeshifting* describes how young Black women living in the US engage with, confront, challenge, invert, unsettle, and expose the material impact of systematic oppression. Shapeshifting is an act, a theory, and in this sense, a form of praxis that—although uniquely definitive of and defined by Black girls—reveals our collective vulnerabilities" (7). Like Nubia's shapeshifting (both superheroic and everyday), there is power in confronting, challenging, and unsettling. Writer and poet Morgan Parker writes of Black women, "Contradictions, colors, varieties, inventions. We are growth embodied. We are shape-shifting" (Parker).

This essay's title is from Jasmine Mans's poem "Like I Got Gold Mines," which signifies on Maya Angelou's famous 1978 poem "Still I Rise." Mans's speaker exists in a liminal space: she is both a werewolf with "bare fangs," who can violently, attack and "the Black girl / you cannot kill" (Mans 189). She is seemingly immortal and invulnerable, a shapeshifter and superhero of sorts. The Black girl werewolf/shapeshifter is graceful and terrifying and will "leave a blood trail," reminding us that she can be fierce and fearless. As Mans concludes her poem, "what a thought."

Notes

1. "Disrupting school is a crime in South Carolina, a misdemeanor carrying a possible penalty of ninety days' imprisonment or a thousand-dollar fine, and Sheriff Lott had no qualms about pronouncing the girl's guilt, even though what he meant by "disrupting" sounded singularly vague; there is no allegation, for example, that she was screaming or throwing things in the class, but, rather, as the Sheriff haltingly put it, 'she wasn't doing what the other students were doing. . . . He was trying to teach . . . she was preventing that from happening by not paying attention'" (Sorkin).

2. A 2021 study, "The Thin Blue Line in Schools: New Evidence on School-Based Policing Across the U.S.," affirms that "School police . . . increase suspensions, expulsions, police referrals and arrests." For Black students, the rate of punishment was unsurprisingly two times higher than their white peers.

3. Stevie Suan defines anime eyes as "eyes that are overtly large, filled with bulbous reflections of light, sometimes appearing like shimmering water . . . conventionally made to glimmer to express overflowing emotion."

4. Wayland's outfits reveal his racist leanings at other moments in the narrative. At the party, he wears a long-sleeved T-shirt with a snake whose tongue is sticking out of its mouth right above the shirt front pocket. This symbolism recalls the "Don't tread on me" Gadsden flag imagery often used as a far-right hate symbol.

5. See www.merriam-webster.com/dictionary/Wayland.

Works Cited

Bailey, Moya. *Misogynoir Transformed: Black Women's Digital Resistance.* NYU Press, 2021.

Battle, Nishawun T. *Black Girlhood, Punishment, and Resistance: Reimagining Justice for Black Girls in Virginia.* Taylor & Francis, 2020.

Berns, Fernando Pagnoni. "From Comicbook to Road Narrative: The Incredible Hulk (1977–1982) as Serialized Drama." *Polyptych: Adaptation, Television, and Comics*, edited by Reginal Wiebe, Vernon Books, 2021, pp. 1–22.

Boey, Valerie. "Girl, 8, Honored for Helping to Change Florida Law Dictating Arrest of Children." Fox 35 Orlando, 28 July 2021, www.fox35orlando.com/news/8-year-old-kaia-rolle-honored-by-senator-bracy-in-ceremony. Accessed 19 Oct. 2022.

Brownie, Barbara, and Danny M. Graydon. *The Superhero Costume: Identity and Disguise in Fact and Fiction.* Bloomsbury Academic, 2015.

Clifton, Lucille, "note, passed to superman." *Poems About Love, Death, Religion, Art, Politics, Sex, and Everything Else*, edited by Barbara Hamby and David Kirby, U of Georgia P, 2010, p. 6.

Cox, Aimee Meredith. *Shapeshifters: Black Girls and the Choreography of Citizenship.* Duke UP, 2015.

Diaz, Angela, Rebecca Epstein, Bob Filbin, Amanda Sheffield Morris, and Martin Teicher. "Addressing Trauma and Building Resilience in Children: Science and Practice." *Community Resilience: Equitable Practices for an Uncertain Future*, edited by Alonzo L. Pough, Oxford UP, 2021, pp. 92–105.

Ellis, Kelly Norman. "Superhero." *Of Poetry & Protest: From Emmett Till to Trayvon Martin*, edited by Philip Cushway and Michael Warr, W.W. Norton, 2015, pp. 64–65.

Emads, Mitra E. "Reading Wonder Woman's Body: Mythologies of Gender and Nation." *The Journal of Popular Culture*, vol. 39, no. 6, 2006, pp. 954–84.

Fawaz, Ramzi. *The New Mutants: Superheroes and the Radical Imagination of American Comics.* NYU Press, 2016.

Field, Corinne T., and LaKisha Michelle Simmons. "Introduction: Looking for Black Girls in History." *The Global History of Black Girlhood*, edited by Corinne T. Field and LaKisha Michelle Simmons, U of Illinois P, 2022, pp. 1–27.

Harris-Perry, Melissa. *Sister Citizen: Shame, Stereotypes, and Black Women in America.* Yale UP, 2011.

Hensley, Nicole. "Spring Valley High School's 'Incredible Hulk' – Deputy Ben Fields – Has History of Alleged Misconduct and Racial Bias." *NYDailyNews.com*, 27 Oct. 2015, www.nydailynews.com/news/national/spring-valley-incredible-hulk-history-misconduct-article-1.2412435. Accessed 19 Oct. 2022.

Hong, Nicole. "Rochester Officers Suspended After Pepper-Spraying of 9-Year-Old Girl." *The New York Times*, 11 Apr. 2021, www.nytimes.com/2021/01/31/nyregion/rochester-police-pepper-spray-child.html. Accessed 22 Oct. 2022.

Hyman, Paula Chase. "Spotlight on Elle McKinney & Robyn Smith's Nubia: Real One." The Brown Bookshelf, 1 Mar. 2001, thebrownbookshelf.com/2021/03/01/spotlight-on-elle-mckinney-robyn-smiths-nubia-real-one/. Accessed 12 Nov. 2022.

Lee, Stan. *Mighty Marvel Masterworks: The Incredible Hulk Vol. 1—The Green Goliath.* Marvel Entertainment, 2021.

Mans, Jasmine. "Like I Got Gold Mines." *Black Girl, Call Home: Poems*, Berkley, 2021, p. 189.

McKinney, L. L. *Nubia: Real One.* DC Comics, 2021.

Ormrod, Joan. *Wonder Woman: The Female Body and Popular Culture.* Bloomsbury, 2020,

On These Grounds. Directed by Garrett Zevgetis, Gravitas Ventures, 2021.

Parker, Morgan. "A Love Letter to Poetry; A Love Letter to Black Women." *Buzzfeed News*, 14 Feb. 2017, www.buzzfeednews.com/article/poetmorganparker/four-love-poems-for-black-women-by-black-women. Accessed 1 Aug. 2024.

Pérez, George (writer), Jill Thompson (penciller), and Romeo Tanghal (inker). "Pages Turned." *Wonder Woman*, vol. 2, no. 62, DC Comics, Feb. 1992.

Rupert, Maya. "Imagining a Black Wonder Woman." *The Atlantic*, 29 May 2017, www.theatlantic.com/entertainment/archive/2017/05/imagining-a-black-wonder-woman/528375/. Accessed 19 Oct. 2022.

Scott, Darieck. *Keeping It Unreal: Black Queer Fantasy and Superhero Comics.* NYU Press, 2022.

Sharpe, Christina. *In the Wake: On Blackness and Being.* Duke UP, 2016.

Smith, Ashley, "Theorizing Black Girlhood." *The Black Girlhood Studies Collection*, edited by Aria S. Halliday, Canadian Scholars, 2019, pp. 21–44

Sorkin, Amy Davidson. "What Niya Kenny Saw." *The New Yorker*, 30 Oct. 2015, www.newyorker.com/news/amy-davidson/what-niya-kenny-saw. Accessed 22 Oct. 2022.

Suan, Stevie. *Anime's Identity: Performativity and Form Beyond Japan.* U of Minnesota P, 2021.

Sorensen, Lucy C., Montserrat Avila-Acosta, John B. Engberg, and Shawn D. Bushway. "The Thin Blue Line in Schools: New Evidence on School-Based Policing Across the U.S." *Journal of Policy Analysis and Management*, vol. 42, no. 4, 2023, pp. 941–70.

Thompson-Spires, Nafissa. "Heads of the Colored People: Four Fancy Sketches, Two Chalk Outlines, and No Apology." *Heads of the Colored People: Stories.* Atria, 2018.

Whaley, Deborah. *Black Women in Sequence: Re-Inking Comics, Graphic Novels and Anime.* U of Washington P, 2015.

Yan, Holly, Kevin Conlon, and John Newsome. "S.C. School Officer Ben Fields' Career Marked with Lawsuits, Praise." *CNN*, 27 Oct. 2015, www.cnn.com/2015/10/27/us/south-carolina-who-is-ben-fields/index.html. Accessed 22 Oct. 2022.

ABOUT THE CONTRIBUTORS

José Alaniz, professor in the Department of Slavic Languages and Literatures and the Department of Cinema and Media Studies (adjunct) at the University of Washington, Seattle, has published the monographs *Komiks: Comic Art in Russia* (University Press of Mississippi, 2010); *Death, Disability and the Superhero: The Silver Age and Beyond* (UPM, 2014); *Resurrection: Comics in Post-Soviet Russia* (OSU Press, 2022); and *Comics of the Anthropocene: Graphic Narrative at the End of Nature* (UPM, 2025). He has also coedited two essay collections, *Comics of the New Europe: Reflections and Intersections* (with Martha Kuhlman, Leuven University Press, 2020) and *Uncanny Bodies: Disability and Superhero Comics* (with Scott T. Smith, Penn State University Press, 2019). He formerly chaired the executive committee of the International Comic Arts Forum (ICAF) and was a founding board member of the Comics Studies Society. He has published three comics/prose collections: *The Phantom Zone and Other Stories* (Amatl Comix, 2020), *The Compleat Moscow Calling* (Amatl, 2023) and *Puro Pinche True Fictions: Prose and Comics* (FlowerSong Press, 2023). His current scholarly book projects include a monograph on the representation of historical trauma in Czech graphic narrative.

Michelle Bumatay is an assistant professor of French at Florida State University. She specializes in African Francophone and diasporic cultural production focusing primarily on *bandes dessinées*. She is the 2015 recipient of the annual Lawrence R. Schehr Memorial Award for her conference paper "*Madame Livingstone* and *Notre Histoire*: Travels in Time," which was subsequently published as an article in *Contemporary French Civilization*. Interested in questions of representation, migration, transcolonial power, and historiography, she has contributed to several anthologies (*Postcolonial Comics: Texts, Events, Identities; Immigrants and Comics: Graphic Spheres of Remembrance, Transaction, and Mimesis*; and *Intermediality in French-Language Comics and Graphic Novels*) and has articles in *European Comic Art, Research in African Literatures, Francosphères*, and *Alternative Francophone*. Her book *On Black* Bandes Dessinées *and Transcolonial Power* (Ohio State University Press) explores the diversity of Black Francophone cartoonists' artistic, narrative, and material practices since the 1960s and illustrates the reparative dimensions of their work.

Sika Dagbovie-Mullins is a professor of English at Florida Atlantic University, where she specializes in twentieth and twenty-first century African American literature. She is author of *Crossing B(l)ack: Mixed Race Identity in Modern American Fiction and Culture* (2013) and coeditor of *Mixed-Race Superheroes* (2021), which examines representations of racial mixedness and the idea of the superhero.

Michael Kobre is Dana Professor of English at Queens University of Charlotte. His essays and stories have appeared in *Michigan Quarterly Review, Inks: The Journal of the Comics Studies Society, South Atlantic Review, Tin House, TriQuarterly, The International Journal of Comic Art, West Branch*, and other journals. He's the author of *Walker Percy's Voices*. His writing has also been featured in the collections *Reading the Boss: Interdisciplinary Approaches to the Works of Bruce Springsteen, Walker Percy's The Moviegoer at Fifty*, and *Superhero Bodies: Identity, Materiality, Transformation*.

Samantha Langsdale (she/her) is the Assistant Director of Academic Success at Menlo College. Her research focuses on the cultural politics around representations of gender, sexuality, and race in visual culture. Her comics scholarship has been published in peer-reviewed journals such as *Signs: Journal of Women in Culture and Society* and in award-winning volumes like *Supersex: Sexuality, Fantasy, and the Superhero* (University of Texas Press). She is also the proud coeditor of *Monstrous Women in Comics*, published by University Press of Mississippi. Her monograph *Searching for Feminist Superheroes: Gender, Sexuality, and Race in Marvel Comics* (University of Texas Press) is now available. You can read more about her work at www.samlangsdale.com/

Sheng-mei Ma (馬聖美) is professor of English at Michigan State University, specializing in Asian diaspora culture and East-West comparative studies. He is the author of over a dozen books, including *Cultural Bifocals* (2025), *China Pop!* (2024), *The Tao of S* (2022), *Off-White* (2020), *Sinophone-Anglophone Cultural Duet* (2017), *The Last Isle* (2015), *Alienglish* (2014), *Asian Diaspora and East-West Modernity* (2012), *Diaspora Literature and Visual Culture* (2011), *East-West Montage* (2007), *The Deathly Embrace* (2000), and *Immigrant Subjectivities in Asian American and Asian Diaspora Literatures* (1998). He has coedited five books and special issues, among them *Transnational Narratives* (2018) and *Doing English in Asia* (2016), and published a collection of poetry in Chinese, *Thirty Left and Right* (三十左右).

John Edward Martin is the Director of Scholarly Communication and Comics Studies Librarian at the University of North Texas Libraries. He is a scholar of gothic and horror literature, comics, and film, whose work has appeared in *DH+BH: An Interdisciplinary Collection on Digital Humanities and Book History* (Windsor & Downs/Illinois Open Publishing Network, 2024), *Poe and Women: Recognition and Revision* (Lehigh University Press, 2023), *Fear and Learning: Essays on the Pedagogy of Horror* (McFarland, 2013), and *Deciphering Poe: Subtexts, Contexts, Subversive Meanings* (Lehigh University Press, 2013). He is currently working on a book on comics adaptations of the work of Edgar Allan Poe. He holds a PhD in American literature from Northwestern University and a MS in Library Science from the University of North Texas. He occasionally still attempts to climb sheer surfaces and spin webs, just in case.

Anna F. Peppard is an award-winning researcher and public scholar. Her work on representations of gender and sexuality in comics and pop culture is widely published in academic books and journals and on websites such as Shelfdust, Women Write About Comics, and ComicsXF. She is the coproject lead of the social media research project Sequential Scholars, cohost of the *Oh Gosh, Oh Golly, Oh Wow! Podcast*, and editor of the anthology *Supersex: Sexuality, Fantasy, and the Superhero*, which won the Comics Studies Society Prize for Best Edited Book.

Peter Nagy is an associate professor of English at Cedar Crest College in Allentown, Pennsylvania. His work on genderqueer masculinity and trans representation in comics and in US literature has appeared in *Modern Fiction Studies*, *College Literature*, and *The Journal of Men's Studies*. His work on gender and sexuality in comics has also been featured in *The Atlantic*, *Ms.*, and *Bitch Magazine*.

Alison Wellford is an associate professor and director of the Pan-European MFA in Creative Writing at Cedar Crest College. She has published a novel, *Indolence*, and her short fiction has appeared in the *Gettysburg Review*, *Barcelona Review*, and *Fence*. Her articles on antidiscrimination law and environmental justice have appeared in *The Nation* and *Modern Farmer*. She has received fellowships from the Virginia Center for the Creative Arts, the MacDowell Colony, and the Barbara Deming Memorial Fund.

INDEX

Printed and bound by CPI Group (UK) Ltd, Croydon, CR0 4YY
22/10/2026
14987998-0004